D1264146

Caribbean Series, 1

SIDNEY W. MINTZ, *Editor*

FREE JAMAICA

1838-1865

An Economic History

BY DOUGLAS HALL

University College of the West Indies

New Haven

YALE UNIVERSITY PRESS, 1959

To **PATRICIA**

Preface

THERE are many published accounts of Jamaica in the nineteenth century. Most of them were written by contemporary observers who came to see how the island fared after the emancipation of the slaves in 1838. They tell of the religious condition of the ex-slaves, the economic state of the peasantry, the decline of the estates, and so on. Many of these writings contain much useful information and are quoted or referred to in this volume, but none of them deals fully with the period between the emancipation and the notorious riot in Morant Bay in 1865. In consequence, this quarter century has been described as the dark age of Jamaican history; yet, comprising what might be called the first generation of freedom in the island, it is obviously a period of great importance.

During the past few years, however, a number of scholars, mostly West Indians or Americans, have been doing research in the history of this period, and one published work in particular must be mentioned: Philip Curtin's *Two Jamaicas*, Harvard University Press, 1955. This well-written and highly readable book deals with Jamaica during 1830–1865. Curtin, a sociologist, emphasizes the growing separation between the European-orientated planter oligarchy and the mass of the emancipated people, who gave their chief attention to the development of peasant agriculture rather than to estate production. He makes the point that the Morant Bay rising of 1865 followed inescapably from the failure of the planting class to meet the social and economic problems arising out of this separation. Curtin's work is important and his arguments are persuasive, but in the pages of the present book, and especially in the final chapter, it will become clear that I do not wholly accept them. The concept of inescapability or inevitability in human affairs I find impossible to admit.

I have, in the final assessment, posed questions rather than

offered definite opinions. This is because I think that the time
is not yet ripe for firm opinion. There is still much factual
data to be discovered, and much exchange of ideas to be
undertaken, before that time of conviction arrives.

For those readers who are unfamiliar with the outline of
Jamaican history before the emancipation, the following brief
summary may be useful.

The English took the island in 1655 from the Spaniards, who
put up a long, spasmodic, and quite ineffectual defence. At
that time it was sparsely populated and almost entirely undeveloped, the original population of Arawak Indians having
died or been killed off during the Spanish occupation of about
150 years. This fact is important to the argument of Chapter 8.

Settlement by the English really began after the Stuart
Restoration in 1660, when the civil government of the island
by a governor, nominated Council, and elected Assembly was
introduced. This administrative organization persisted until
the end of our period, and is described in Chapter 1.

From the late seventeenth century onwards the island
rapidly grew in importance as the largest British colonial
producer of cane-sugar, and by the mid-eighteenth century it
was the most prized possession of the British Crown, far exceeding in importance and value any of the other British
Caribbean or American mainland colonies.

The sugar estates and other properties were worked by
slaves imported from Africa and their local-born descendants.
Although other crops, such as coffee, cotton, and pimento,
were exported, the economy of the island was founded on
slave-labour, sugar, and the protection given to colonial producers in the British home market. Within the compass of the
British acts regulating colonial trade an important commerce
was carried on with the American mainland colonies, whence
the Jamaica planters imported foodstuffs, lumber, and certain
other estate supplies.

Soon after the mid-eighteenth century, however, the fortunes
of the island began to decline. The declaration and winning
of American independence reduced the direct American trade
(since the United States was barred from direct British colo-

nial trade) and increased the cost of American supplies. Increasing sugar production in the French and Spanish islands
(especially French San Domingo before 1791 and Spanish
Cuba afterwards) by planters in North and South America
(chiefly Louisiana and Brazil) and by other British producers
(in Mauritius and the Far East) tended to depress sugar
prices, while the costs of production tended to increase. The
expenses of planting were affected by much more than the new
scarcity and dearness of American supplies. Planters were
faced with soil deterioration on their estates; rising prices for
slaves, as sugar producers throughout the Caribbean increased
their production; and increasing costs of shipping and marketing their sugar in Britain.

The long period of almost unbroken war between England
and France between 1793 and 1815 temporarily arrested the
decline, but even so, new problems were introduced by such
events as the ending of the British slave trade in 1807 and the
beginning in France of the manufacture of sugar from beetroot
(though the full effects of this new source of competition were
not felt before the 1870's and 1880's).

After 1815 the sugar industry and trade suffered by the long
post-war depression of the 1820's and 1830's, during which the
reformed British Parliament voted the emancipation of the
slaves.

Between 1834 and 1838 labour in nearly all the British
Caribbean territories was organised on an "apprenticeship
system" by which the slaves (now called "apprentices") were
required to give about forty hours of unpaid labour a week to
their owners but were allowed to demand wages for any time
worked in excess of this maximum. For many reasons apprenticeship did not succeed: it was a misconceived attempt at
compromise that pleased neither planters nor apprentices, and
it was therefore terminated before the appointed date.

The scene in Chapter 1 is set against a background of con-
flicting interests and opinions, in which the Island Assembly is
in violent disagreement with the metropolitan Government
over the emancipation and with successive governors who
show greater concern for the welfare of the ex-slaves than for

the state of the large plantations. The planters, suffering the effects of depression, are dismayed by increasing competition from foreign producers who still employ slave-labour, by declining profits, and by their increasing indebtedness to the merchant houses in Britain to whom they consign their sugar and through whose agency they obtain their supplies from across the Atlantic. Within the Island itself they are alarmed by the fact that the ex-slaves, instead of continuing to work the estates for wages, are busying themselves with the acquisition and cultivation of small landholdings. Also, they fear that one effect of emancipation and economic depression will be a lessening of their political power.

The map at the end of the book shows most of the places mentioned in the text and indicates the boundaries of the several parishes of the island. The three "county" divisions of Cornwall, Middlesex, and Surrey have no political significance whatsoever, but the parishes were and still are the areas of local government. At the time of the emancipation each parish was administered by its parochial vestry, of which the custos, appointed by the governor subject to the approval of the Crown, was chairman.

This book is very largely based on my thesis presented at the London School of Economics in 1954 for the degree of Doctor of Philosophy. Subsequent research (which has necessarily been limited) has revealed nothing to alter my main arguments, but I have done much editing, revising, and rewriting.

In all of this I have been helped and encouraged by many people. Above all, I am grateful to F. J. Fisher of the London School of Economics, who supervised my postgraduate studies. I thank him for his patient guidance, and for showing me a skill which I have tried to learn. Since my return home to the West Indies a number of friends and colleagues have been very kind. I mention, in particular, P. M. Sherlock, Vice Principal of the University College of the West Indies; Michael Smith, Shirley Gordon, and Lloyd Braithwaite of the University College; and Sidney Mintz of Yale University. Librarians and archivists have, in my experience, always shown a special regard for the needs of the student, and, in particular, I thank George Miller of the West India Committee in London for the great freedom he allowed me in the use of the excellent library in his care. Finally, I express my gratitude to the Institute of Social and Economic Studies in the University College of the West Indies for their help towards publication.

D.G.H.

University College of the West Indies
April 1959

Contents

There are three charts, on pages 43, 117, and
186, and a map of Jamaica follows the index.

CHAPTER 1

Jamaica, 1838–1846

THERE are three dates of outstanding significance in Jamaican nineteenth-century history: August 1838, when slavery was finally and completely abolished; July 1846, when a British Act of Parliament introduced a new scale of duties on sugars entering Britain; and October 1865, when there occurred a civil disturbance which was to result in constitutional change abolishing the old Jamaica Assembly.

Of these three dates, it is upon the second that this story is focused. As we shall see, the passing of the Sugar Duties Act brought enormous consequences for the economic, political, and social affairs of people living in Jamaica and of people abroad who owned property in the island.

The immediate effects in Jamaica of this act emphasized the island's economic rather than its political connection with Britain, but to appreciate the full significance of the passing of the act some review of conditions in the island between the emancipation and 1846 is necessary.

As a business man, the sugar planter was primarily concerned with the price obtainable for his produce and with the costs of production. But the planter was also, sometimes, a local politician, and policy in Jamaica might be designed to promote the welfare of the sugar industry, even by limiting the freedom of the newly emancipated workers to choose their employers and employments. Political strategy of this nature was, however, affected by the ultimate power of the Sovereign to disallow acts of the Island Legislature, and by the fact that emancipation seemed likely to threaten the political supremacy of the planter class.

1

The emancipation had not been accompanied by any statutory change in the political constitution of the island.[1] But even without such change it was apparent that freedom and small freehold settlement would exert political pressures, for attempts to raise the franchise had been disallowed the royal assent [2] and the number of the electorate was likely to increase.[3]

Another development, less obvious at the time, was affecting the constituency of the Legislature rather than the size of the electorate. This was the decline of the great estates and the growing importance of the local mercantile body and the class of small farmers. In future, candidature for seats in the Assembly was to be less confined to those involved in large-scale sugar production.

The Island Legislature consisted of two bodies, the Assembly and the Legislative Council. The Assembly had forty-seven members, all of whom were elected, two from each parish and an additional one each from the urban area of Kingston, Spanish Town, and the town of Port Royal. The ordinary life of each Assembly was seven years. The qualification for candidature was the possession of a freehold of £300 value in any part of the island, or other property worth £3,000, or the payment of not less than £10 a year in direct taxes. The franchise, though narrow before 1838, when the majority of the population had been slaves, was potentially wide in the subsequent years of freedom. The right to vote was open to every sane adult male who owned and had paid taxes on a freehold of £6 value, or paid an annual rent of £30, or paid direct taxes to the amount of £3 a year. In all cases the individual was required to register his name on the local voters'

1. An attempt in 1839 to suspend the Assembly for five years was defeated in the House of Commons. See H. Wrong, *Government of the West Indies* (Oxford, 1923), pp. 57–8.

2. W. L. Burn, *Emancipation and Apprenticeship in the British West Indies* (London, 1937), p. 323.

3. Colonial Office Document (C.O.) 137/251, Metcalfe to Russell, No. 84, 9 June 1840. The number of freeholds acquired, with electoral rights, since 1 Aug. 1838, was 934.

list.[4] When numerous freeholds were being acquired and the price of land averaged about £6 an acre, these conditions would at first glance appear to have imposed no significant limitations on the attainment of the vote by ex-slaves. It is clear from the occasional contemporary comment, however, that the general policy of the Legislature during the whole of our period was to restrict rather than to encourage the growth of the electorate.[5]

The Assembly boasted a violent history in which defiance to governors and to the Colonial Office was common. It played a more important role than that of the Legislative Council. Since the mid-eighteenth century the Assembly had been the sole originator of bills, and even before then the Council had failed to establish its power to amend money bills. In addition to its legislative function the Assembly had assumed much executive authority. Not only did it impose taxes and appropriate the revenues to various uses, but it also, through a system of boards or committees, collected the revenues, spent the money voted, and audited the accounts. These boards, moreover, sat permanently, refusing to be disturbed by prorogation of the Assembly or even by a dissolution, until after the elections a new Assembly actually held its first meeting and new boards were set up. On some of these boards (but not the Board of Accounts) members of the Council sat with assemblymen,[6] but their presence can hardly have been more than a formality.

The Council consisted of seven to twelve members, none of whom was elected. The governor, the chief justice, the Bishop,

4. For details see J. M. Phillippo, *Jamaica: Its Past and Present State* (London, 1843), ch. 7, on "Government"; and C.O. 137/343, Darling to Bulwer Lytton, No. 31, 10 Feb. 1859, with enclosures.

5. See Phillippo, p. 112; and C.O. 137/331, Barkly to Labouchere, confidential, 9 April 1856, in which he comments on a recent refusal by the Legislature to extend the franchise and simplify the vote qualifications, "which almost require a man to keep a lawyer to look after his vote."

6. C.O. 137/255, Metcalfe to Russell, No. 189, 12 Feb. 1841; and C.O. 137/319, October 1853, Newcastle's instructions to Sir Henry Barkly.

and occasionally other officers such as the attorney-general
were members ex-officio. Others, up to the conventional maximum of six, were appointed by the governor subject to royal
approval through the Colonial Office. Duration of office was
at the pleasure of the Crown. The functions of the Council
were limited, but on occasion it could be useful.

> As a means of imposing a negative upon the Assembly, the
> Council was of use, although there were obvious disad-
> vantages in the way of so using it. As an advisory body,
> with its members old, ailing, or living in remote places,
> it was of very little use indeed. Yet whatever the com-
> position and however limited the usefulness of the Council
> the Governor was obliged to be highly circumspect in his
> relations with it. The members might be moribund, distant
> or recalcitrant, but they were the first line of defence
> against the pretensions of the Assembly.[7]

By exercising care in his recommendations for filling Council
vacancies, a governor might be able to command a majority
sufficient to reject or amend ordinary bills sent up from the
Assembly.

When a bill had been passed by both houses of the Island
Legislature the governor could, at his discretion, allow it,
disallow it, or allow it with a suspending clause which made
it inoperative until the decision of the Sovereign-in-Council
was known. Finally, the Sovereign-in-Council exercised the
ultimate power of disallowance of Jamaica acts, even if they
had received the assent of the governor.

Between the Assembly and the Colonial Office a long-drawn-
out controversy existed as to the degree of autonomy rightfully
to be enjoyed by the former. For our purpose it is sufficient
to show that the British Government, through the Colonial
Office, could check the obstreperousness of the Island Assembly
in three ways. The first and gentlest method was to intensify
the scrutiny of Jamaica acts submitted for the royal assent; the
next step would be to get Parliament to enact legislation re-

7. Burn, pp. 150–1. Besides its legislative function the Council also
fulfilled the role of Privy Council.

lating to or regulating colonial domestic affairs; the third and ultimate step would be to press the British Government to amend the colonial constitution in order to remove the Assembly altogether or to reduce its power.[8] Of these courses the first was generally practised throughout our period; the second was also used when, especially at the time of emancipation, the colonial Legislature would not introduce measures which the British Government considered to be urgent and essential; the third was never actually employed. Constitutional changes which came in 1854 and 1865 were introduced by the Jamaica Assembly itself, though under the pressure of extraordinary circumstances.

The position of the governor was, clearly enough, difficult. He stood between the Colonial Office and the Island Legislature without a firm foot in either, and without any dependable expectation of continued support from either side. If he tried to introduce measures which the Colonial Office desired, he was likely to incur the hostility of the Assembly; if he leaned backwards to support measures proposed in the Assembly he was liable to receive a rebuke from the secretary of state for the colonies. He was, nominally, the executive branch of the island government, but even his constitutional position was not comparable with that of the executive in Britain.

> It is a mistake to consider the constitution of a West India colony as similar to that of Britain. The only mode of communication with a Legislature open to a Governor is either personal or by message. He has no ministry and no available patronage. In addition to a general dislike on the part of the Local Legislature to measures emanating from home, his recommendations to the Council and Assembly are liable to be dealt with capriciously, as one or other Colonial Party happens to obtain a momentary ascendancy. His best means of overcoming these difficulties consists in the acquirement of personal influence among the members of the Council and Assembly.[9]

8. Ibid., p. 330.

9. Sir Murray McGregor to Stanley, 5 May 1834, quoted by Burn, p. 146.

Nor was it only with the Colonial Office and the Island
Assembly that the governor had to contend. There were also
the twenty-two parish vestries, each presided over by a custos
rotolorum who was appointed by the governor subject to
confirmation by the Crown. The parish vestry was responsible
for local administration. It levied taxes, appropriated local
revenues, appointed parochial officers such as the waywardens
(to superintend road maintenance), the coroner, the clerk of
the peace, the pound-keeper, and the clerks and keepers of
markets. The vestry was also responsible for the distribution of
poor relief and the maintenance of poorhouses, public "hospitals," and dispensaries. Vestry-men included the parish rector,
the churchwarden, the local justices, and a number of elected
members to bring the total strength up to ten, exclusive of the
custos.[10] The franchise for parochial elections was the same as
that for the Island Assembly.

At the beginning of our period of Jamaica history the Colonial Office suspected the motives of an Island Legislature that
was mainly representative of planter interests; the Jamaica
Assembly, concerned primarily with ensuring the survival of
the sugar industry, protested violently against all indications of
Colonial Office solicitude for the welfare of the ex-slaves. In the
parishes, the custodes and local justices of the peace resented,
and often actively opposed, the stipendiary magistrats [11] who
were appointed and paid by the Colonial Office.

Early in 1841 the governor, Sir Charles Metcalfe, received
suggestions from the secretary of state for the colonies about
ways in which the executive authority might be strengthened

10. Phillippo, p. 110; and Burn, p. 165 n. Occasionally, however, a
large number of justices and other ex-officio members would result in a
large vestry.

11. The stipendiary magistrates (SM's) were a body of paid magistrates appointed to Jamaica and other colonies after the passing of the
Emancipation Act. They were to be the local administrators of the
provisions of the act and had right of jurisdiction in all questions relating
to dispute between ex-masters and ex-slaves. The standard survey of
their work is Burn's *Emancipation and Apprenticeship in the British
West Indies*. See also my "The Apprenticeship Period in Jamaica, 1834–
1838," *Caribbean Quarterly*, 3, No. 3, 1935.

to meet the hostility of the Assembly. The formation of a nominated Executive Council of "Governor's Men" was proposed. To this, Metcalfe replied in a brilliant dispatch. He said that outright opposition would serve no useful purpose, and that authority would best be derived "from conciliation and mutual cordiality and co-operation." As the size of the electorate increased, the governor anticipated a considerable change in the constituency of the Assembly by the emergence of an opposition to the sugar planters. Almost prophetically, as 1854 and 1865 were to show, he continued:

> The time when the Government might expect to possess the greatest influence in the Assembly would probably be during its state of transition from representing the Proprietory of the Island to representing the Mass of the People. When the Proprietory before being actually reduced to a Minority in the Assembly see nevertheless that such a fate is inevitable, they may naturally become more disposed to add strength to the Government and to reduce the power of the popular branch of the Constitution within the bounds beyond which it has extended itself.

In such circumstances the government would be most likely to obtain, with the assent of the Assembly "that degree of Executive Authority which Your Lordship deems to be essential for the due administration of the government." [12]
But things did not turn out quite as Metcalfe had anticipated. An "opposition" party did slowly develop in the Assembly. It was composed, for the most part, of coloured and Jewish merchants and newspaper editors,[13] and was known as the Town party, as opposed to the Country party, which represented the planter interest. The Town party, however, often provided a working majority in the Assembly, because the legislative session, held in British fashion during the winter months, clashed with the harvest season on the sugar estates,

12. C.O. 137/255 (see n. 6, above).
13. C.O. 137/324, Barkly to Sir George Grey, No. 107, 19 Oct. 1854; and C.O. 137/380, Eyre to Newcastle, confidential, 9 March 1864.

when planters found it most inconvenient to remain in Spanish Town.[14]

The important thing about the Town party is that it did not develop as a group representative of the mass of the people. It, or individual members of it, opposed immigration and declared for Jamaica as an island of small independent farmers, but it produced no constructive proposals to facilitate the growth and establishment of such a class. Although it often enjoyed a working majority, it introduced no bills to promote road-building, to establish a secure system of land tenure, or to provide credit or marketing facilities for the producers of minor export and domestic consumption crops. Indeed, the activities of the Town party appear to have been almost entirely devoted to political ends, such as the championship of the rights and privileges of the Assembly. In a way, this was perhaps to be expected. It might be argued that until the party had established itself as a political force and gained general acceptance as such it would have little time to engage in constructive economic legislation. Its emergence as the guardian of the rights of the Assembly was in accord with Metcalfe's theory. As a new group, with control of the Assembly in sight, it would seek to conserve all that power to which it might one day succeed. The Country party, on the other hand, might be willing to surrender power to the executive rather than see it fall to the opposing faction in the Legislature.

But this is to anticipate later events. During the early 1840's the Assembly was still essentially a planter stronghold, and the Town party opposition had not yet hardened into distinctive size and shape. On matters of policy, and in the voting on individual measures, there was much "crossing the floor."

Some thirteen miles from Spanish Town, the Island capital and seat of government, was Kingston, the city of commerce, the main port of entry, and site of the Island's largest slum.

> The city forms an irregular quadrangle, and covers an area of nearly two square miles. The streets run north and south and are crossed by others at right angles; all are

14. C.O. 137/380, Eyre to Newcastle, No. 109, 23 March 1864, points to the weakness of the Country party despite its numerical superiority.

tolerably wide, and, in the upper part, generally open to the sea-breeze. A large square in the centre of the town, called the Parade, contains the large barracks, a handsome Wesleyan chapel, a theatre, and some tolerable dwelling-houses. The chief public buildings are, a Court House, and Church of England, Wesleyan, Presbyterian, Baptist, Independent, Roman Catholic, and Jewish places of worship. . . . Some of the private houses are well constructed and abundantly provided with verandahs, windows, and jealousies [*sic*], for the free admission of the refreshing sea-breeze, by which the extreme heat of the city is materially mitigated; but the merchants' stores are mostly dark and ill-ventilated; and the shops in the main street resemble those of an inferior English town; not a decent inn or hotel exists; there is no paving or macadamizing, no drainage, no gas-lights (as in most of our colonial cities), and scarcely any side-way.

During the heavy rains in May and October, the water finds its way, by broken and irregular channels, into the gullies on the east and west sides of the town, but much of it pours down the steep streets, forcing along a broad muddy stream a foot or more in depth. As none, even of the leading thoroughfares are paved, nor provided with any artificial channels for the water, and the soil is generally loose and sandy, their surface has become ploughed up with deep ruts and broken hollows; while, from the quantity of gravel, stones, and bricks strewn about, they present more the appearance of river courses than of streets in an inhabited city. The amount of vegetable refuse and other rubbish brought down and lodged at the bottom of the harbour is usually considerable; and as there is no sewerage, the poorer classes avail themselves of the current caused by the periodic rains to cast the accumulated filth of their dwellings and yards into the streets; all this noxious matter accumulates and sinks into the porous ground of the lower part of the town, where there is no declivity. The cross streets are, in some respects, still worse, being often flanked by delapidated buildings, and littered

over with rubbish, which renders driving by day perilous
to carriage springs; while walking by night through these
unlit pitfalls, is manifestly to hazard broken limbs. Nor is
it only by inanimate objects that the senses of sight and
smell are offended: lean, mangy hogs are to be seen at all
times rolling about in the noisome puddles, while others
are wandering here and there, grubbing up the rubbish for
food, bestrewing the surface with their ordure. Besides
the swine and goats, constantly moving about, Kingston
has always been noted for its number of half-starved dogs.
It is no uncommon thing to see the carcass of one of these
unfortunate brutes lying in the middle of a street, with a
troop of the vulture crows, which are ever wheeling about
the city, tearing it to pieces, while the air all around is
tainted with the most baneful effluvia.[15]

According to the census of 1844 this two square miles of
commercial slum and the four square miles of outskirts which
went to make up the Parish of Kingston contained 3,831 inhabited houses and 52 "pens with residences" (see below), the
names of many of which, such as Admiral's Pen, Slipe Pen, and
Rollington Pen, are still familiar to Kingstonians. Here lived
32,943 people, slightly more than half of whom were women,
employed in a variety of non-agricultural labours, in skilled
jobs, and in trade and commerce. The well-to-do tried to escape the pitfalls and "baneful effluvia" of the city itself by
living in the lower districts of the neighbouring Parish of St.
Andrew, indulging in a side-line agriculture or merely inhabit-
ing one of the more congenial "pens with residences" which
were so numerous in that area. (In the country parishes "pens"
were properties on which cattle were raised, but in the plains
above Kingston the word usually signified a large, residential
holding on which there might be economically important trees
and perhaps some livestock.) The cooler and sweeter at-
mosphere of parts above the Clocktower at Half-Way-Tree
in Lower St. Andrew has long been appreciated.

15. R. M. Martin, *The British Colonies* (13 vols. London), Vol. 4,
Africa and the West Indies (1853), 76, 77.

Most of the island's port towns developed in this way as rather dirty commercial centres on the coast, from which the houses of the wealthy radiated outwards and upwards into the surrounding foothills. But Kingston, with its dingy stores, bepuddled streets, and blackened ruins from a great fire which swept the eastern half of the city in 1843, was not the best place to look for evidence of Jamaica's condition in the early 1840's. Two important series of developments had been at work to undermine Kingston's importance as a thriving centre of commerce. One of these was the decline in the volume of sugar exported from the island since the emancipation; the other was the loss of the quite important middleman service Kingston had given to trade between Spanish America and Great Britain. The recognition by the British Government in 1825 of the independence of the Spanish-American republics and the gradual freeing from political control of the trade with these foreign parts had operated to lessen the importance of Kingston.

On the other hand, one favourable development acted to bolster the sagging consequence of the city, namely the great increase in the import trade which followed the introduction of wage labour, and the increase in the volume of those articles of export which the new class of peasants could profitably produce.[16] There are two factors to be borne in mind when looking at the figures of imports in Table 1. The first is that whereas during slavery estate owners had usually ordered their estate supplies direct from Britain, in freedom the demand of the working population for consumer goods was met by the local merchants and storekeepers, who thus came into a large import trade which had previously by-passed them. Secondly, as freehold settlement and provisions growing increased in the Island, the demand for goods such as flour and cornmeal would have tended to diminish in favour of such locally cultivated crops as corn, yams, plantains, and cassava. It is also relevant that 1850 to 1851 was a period of severe cholera epidemic in the island, which would have seriously affected commerce.

16. W. J. Gardner, *A History of Jamaica* (London, 1873), p. 420.

The exports listed were generally the produce of small farmers and peasants, although, on a few estates land had been planted in ginger. Along with beeswax, cassava, fruit, and certain other minor crops, none of them had been important

TABLE 1. *Selected Imports into—and Exports of Island Produce from—Jamaica, various years, 1834–50*

Imports	1834	1838	1846	1850	1851	
Flour (barrels)	53,998	69,111	107,330	77,469	66,106	
Meal (barrels)	13,152	11,569	19,333	18,705	9,497	
Fish (casks)	7,563	9,633	—	—	—	
(boxes)	7,848	9,387	—	3,571	2,401	
(Various)						
(tierces)	194	896	1,558	—	—	
(barrels)	69,122	41,557	40,669	44,865	50,632	
(kits)	642	1,034	—	—	—	
Soap (cwts.)	18,866	11,350	39,076	37,936	46,308	
Exports	1841	1842	1843	1844	1845	1846
Ginger (lbs.)	382,326	503,706	444,958	579,624	750,616	613,579
Arrowroot (lbs.)	149,618	92,338	172,528	158,891	145,447	62,567
Coconuts (no.)	103,452	138,637	192,020	134,901	242,936	245,450
Honey (lbs.)	13,340	6,284	13,027	19,343	1,203	3,191
					(galls)	(galls)

Sources: Imports—R. M. Martin, *The British Colonies* (London, 1853), Vol. 4. These are the only early period figures I have been able to find.
Exports—Jamaica Blue Books.

before the emancipation; only the estates' production of sugar, rum, coffee, pimento, and various dye-woods and other woods gathered on estate lands had been significant.

From Kingston the post roads spread out through the Island. They were not good roads and were often impassable during wet weather, but they were the main highways of the Island. The numerous tracks and paths which supplemented them were in even worse condition, the majority being narrow bridle tracks, with some cart or wain roads serving inland estates whose produce had to be sent down to the coast.[17] In such

17. C.O. 137/266, James Anderson, F.R.S.E., to Lord Stanley, 1 July 1842: "The Roads in Several districts of the Island are so specially bad that it requires no fewer than Sixteen Oxen or Steers in a Wain with four wheels to convey one Hogshead of Sugar to the Wharf for Shipment."

circumstances the sea provided a well-used alternative for travellers and for the carriage of goods. Coastal craft of all sizes plied between estate "barquadiers" or shipping points and the official export centres, and between local market areas near the sea.

Jamaica is a small island about 145 miles long with a maximum width of about 50 miles, its coastline indented by innumerable bays and inlets. In the interior, the land rises rapidly from sea-level and is broken up by mountains; the backbone range runs east and west and reaches a height of about 7,500 feet in the eastern part of the island. There are no expanses of flat country except some coastal areas on the south side, and from the mountains numerous rivers and streams run down, most of them small and capricious, a few of them larger and well defined and, in some cases, navigable by very small craft for a few miles. The prevailing north-east winds bring the heaviest rainfall to the areas which lie in the eastern sector of the island and on the north side of the Blue Mountain range.

These general observations alone are sufficient to suggest that competition between the various uses to which land might be put was significantly affected by local features of soil and climate. Thus it was that the sugar-cane, under the stress of increasing costs and falling prices, had, since the last quarter of the eighteenth century,[18] slowly retreated down the mountain slopes into the valleys, coastal plains, and river basins and deltas which were most suitable for its growth. In the opposite direction, coffee cultivation had tended always to move upwards, so that coffee estates filled the mountains of Manchester, Clarendon, St. Andrew, and Port Royal. Finally, as the cane-fields retreated and as the coffee planters moved from one eroded mountain slope to begin their ruin of another, the emancipated negroes and coloured people swarmed in search of freeholds, buying up the ruined acres of abandoned estates and the less accessible runs of still virgin estate land which were suitable for market-gardening.

In 1844 sugar was being cultivated in every parish of the

18. Except for a brief period of sharp revival during the French war at the end of the eighteenth century.

island with only two exceptions: small, urban Kingston and
Manchester, which specialized in coffee. Nonetheless—and this
was widely recognized at the time—there were some areas
which had considerable advantages for cane cultivation.[19]
There were the fertile interior valleys, for example, such as the
entire parish of St. Thomas in the Vale, the neighbouring
Luidas Vale in St. John, the Queen of Spain's Valley on the St.
James-Trelawny boundary, and the Upper Clarendon Valley.
These inland depressions constantly benefited from the deposits
of top soil brought down by rains and rivers from the slopes of
the surrounding mountains. But against their great fertility
two drawbacks had to be measured: the difficulty of transportation to the coast, and the fact that the surrounding mountains tempted the labourers away from the estates to establish
freeholds on whatever land might be available above the level
of sugar cultivation.

Another type of locality favourable to sugar was land along
the lower basins and deltas of larger rivers such as the Plantain
Garden in St. Thomas in the East, and the Cabaritta in Westmoreland. In St. Elizabeth, the lower reaches of the Black River
were generally too swampy for cultivation, but farther up-
stream, towards Lacovia and beyond, there were, and still are,
sugar estates. Not only did the rivers sometimes provide facilities for transport, irrigation, and water power for the mills, but
they also brought down deposits of silt from their highland
sources.

Thirdly, there were the coastal areas which were dependent
on adequate local rainfall or costly irrigation works for their
successful cultivation. Such were the parishes of Vere, St.
Dorothy, and parts of St. Catherine; and on the north-west,
St. James and Trelawny. Many of the estates in these districts
had advantages of easy shipment from some small cove or
harbour, and, in some parts, their distance from the mountains
gave them greater security of retaining labourers. It was also
in the favour of these and other "dry-weather" estates on the
south side and north-western districts that they could

19. Lord Olivier, *Jamaica, the Blessed Isle* (London, 1936), ch. 3.

"ratoon" [20] their canes successfully. In the wet districts prolonged ratooning was not possible, and the additional cost of
constant replanting had to be borne. On the other hand, the
dry-weather estates could be ruined or at least severely in-
convenienced by drought.

Then, as now, the planter was above all dependent on a
continuous supply of labour and on favourable seasons, meaning by the latter a sufficiency of rainfall in May and October.
No matter how much capital he invested in agricultural machinery and labour-saving devices which might reduce his
demand for labour, the fact still remained that whatever labour
was needed had to be dependable in supply, both quantita-
tively and qualitatively. Well-managed estates were run to a
routine which had to be followed if favourable seasons were
in fact to be favourable; for if the May and October rains
caught the estates unprepared for them great loss could result:

> Cane plants require fifteen months before they arrive at
> maturity, and are the most productive; and Ratoons re-
> quire *Eleven* months; but on most of the Estates I have
> visited *Sixteen* months will elapse this year ere half of
> these *latter* canes can be got off the ground for want of
> field labourers, and the consequences will be that if they
> are not completely destroyed by the rains, they will be
> so deteriorated as not to yield half the quantity they
> would otherwise do, and even that of bad quality. Besides,
> the canes being allowed to remain so long uncut, injures
> the crop for the following year.[21]

20. To "ratoon" is to leave the cane roots in the ground after harvesting the crop and to allow these roots to produce new shoots for the
following year. With certain conditions of soil and rainfall it was possible
to ratoon canes for many successive crops, though the crop from each
successive ratooning would be smaller. See H. C. Cahusac, "Practical
Aspects of Agricultural Problems," in *The West Indian Review* (Kingston,
Jamaica), 17 May 1952, for a present-day assessment of the value of
ratooning as a cost-reducing factor.

21. C.O. 137/266 (n. 17, above).

Of course there was also the contrary danger that even if an estate had no labour problem and the routine of cultivation was successfully followed, damage and loss could result from the too early or too late arrival of the seasons. Worse still, the seasons might not arrive at all. Thus in the middle of the long drought which lasted from late 1843 to late 1844 Stipendiary Magistrate Bell reported from St. Dorothy,[22] as others did from other parishes and districts of the island, that the long lack of rain had ruined crops, affected livestock, and made any returns on capital investment impossible. Moreover, locally grown food provisions were scarce and dear, a greater reliance had to be placed on imports of flour, corn, rice, and salt provisions, and there was "no labour at times for the peasantry."

Prolonged drought was feared by the entire population. The planters might not only lose their standing crops but also find their agricultural programme for the following year upset. The same consequences faced the small proprietors who grew minor export crops. The labourers were hit on both sides, for their provision grounds became unproductive, the demand of estate-owners for labour diminished, and wage rates tended to fall. The merchants and retailers suffered least immediately. The first weeks of dry weather brought the exhaustion of local stocks of provisions and an increasing demand for imports, but if the drought continued long they suffered from a reduction in local trading and a smaller volume of export produce; and eventually, as savings were used up and wages kept low, the demand for imports lost its effectiveness.

The mountain parishes, Manchester and Port Royal, were coffee producers. St. Andrew, too, produced a large share of the Island's coffee, and deserves more particular attention. Upper St. Andrew is entirely mountainous; Lower St. Andrew lies in the Liguanea Plain. The coffee was grown on the high ground, and on the plain sugar estates and residential pens lay side by side with the settlements of those producing food crops for the Kingston market. The parish was partly rural, partly urban, for already its lower fringe was being settled as a "dormitory" suburb of Kingston. The great cattle pens were

22. C.O. 137/279, reports of the S.M.'s.

to be found chiefly in the central and western parishes: St. Catherine, St. Ann, Clarendon, and St. Elizabeth. Parts of these large parishes were unsuitable for sugar or coffee, and best suited for pen-keeping of a general kind. On the pens the production of dye-woods, lime, bricks, and a variety of other commodities was as much a part of the business as the rearing of cattle.

Of the remaining parishes, Portland, St. George, and St. Mary lay in the north-east rain belt, and estate cultivation was handicapped by the heavy rainfall, which not only made field work more difficult and sometimes damaged the crops, but also played havoc with transportation. In this part of the island there is a sizable area of heavily forested and almost inaccessible mountain land which still remains uncultivated. Metcalfe, a new parish carved out of St. Mary and St. George in 1841, contained some good sugar land, which is still in production. On the south side, St. David included both sugar estates and small settlements along the Yallahs valley, but on the coast, towards St. Andrew and beyond, drought could be severe.

Before discussing the locality of peasants' and labourers' freeholds a few remarks about landownership are necessary. In Jamaica the general practice, ever since the mid-seventeenth century when the Island was taken from the Spaniards, had been to plant on a large scale; and as the method was extensive rather than intensive, an estate usually contained an acreage far greater than the quantity actually planted in canes at any given time. The large estate, containing some pasture and woodland as well as cultivated fields, made the planter less dependent on extra-estate sources for building materials, livestock, and food for his slaves. Moreover, the cane-fields were commonly planted in rotation, so that at any given time a certain amount of cane-land would be lying fallow. The point is that large land grants combined with inadequate surveying and overestimation of the size of the Island [23] led to a mistaken idea

23. Even today the exact area remains uncertain. See *An Economic Survey of the Colonial Territories, 1951* (London, H.M.S.O., 1953), *4*, 116: "The area of the island is often given as 4,404 square miles, but the figure now accepted is 4,411 square miles." In the 1840's it was thought to be no less than 6,400 square miles.

that large reserves of Crown land remained unalienated.[24] In fact such areas were small in extent and difficult to place exactly.

Areas of peasant cultivation that developed after the emancipation were therefore built not out of idle Crown lands newly alienated but out of the existing estate acreages. We find freehold settlements growing most rapidly in those districts where abandoned estates are being put up for sale and where estate owners are selling idle acres in order to raise money to invest in a more intensified agriculture based on machinery and fertilizers and less on labour.

The exact location of a small settlement was also influenced by nearness to a good local market, to a much frequented highway, or to the coast, and (apparently to less extent) by the quality of the land itself. It must be made clear, however, that convenience of location was not generally within the discretion of the intending small settler; many of the abandoned estates were badly served by roads, many were on poor land, and any estate-owner who decided to sell a part of his property would have disposed of that part of it which was the least suitable for cultivation. The choice of the small holder was almost invariably limited.

In addition to this very general and summary description of Jamaica in the mid-1840's, one other aspect of the Island must be reviewed to complete the background against which the later economic development took place. With the possible exception of the present period since the ending of World War II, Jamaicans have never been so alert and enterprising as they were during the first few years of the post-emancipation era, between the ending of slavery and the first decisive step of the British Government in 1846 towards free trade in sugar.

It would not have been humanly possible for all classes of Jamaican society to step smoothly and easily from the state of slavery into a condition of freedom. The four years of the "apprenticeship," the sort of semi-slavery which lasted from August 1834 to August 1838, had been intended as a transition

24. C.O. 137/240, report of the Jamaica Crown Lands Commission, 10 Oct. 1839.

period during which both masters and slaves would readjust their relationships in preparation for full freedom. In fact the time had been put to no such fundamental purpose. It had been a period in which masters in general had tried to squeeze the last juice out of compulsory labour before the expected ruin of freedom set in; and both masters and apprentices learned only one lesson, namely that when labour had to be bargained for, the labourers would be able to name their price.

The strong position of the labourers was based on the fact that as an alternative to wages for labour on the estates they were able to grow food crops, not only for their own use but for sale in local markets. This was no new discovery. During slavery the Jamaica slave laws had required that slave owners who had available land should provide "grounds" on which the slaves might grow food. The regulation had been observed because in Jamaica, where estates were large, it was cheaper to allow the slaves land from which they could feed themselves than to import foodstuffs for them. The practice also had developed of allowing the slaves to sell any surpluses in the local markets,[25] and Sundays, being the only completely free day at their disposal, had become the established "market days" throughout the island.

When freedom came, the estate-owner had to face a double-edged problem. He was well aware that freedom would bring a great diminution in the number of ex-slaves who would continue to work his estate. The young children and the old people would very likely cease work, and many of the women would withdraw from wage labour and give their time to domestic matters. Furthermore, if he allowed his ex-slaves to continue to cultivate their "grounds," which were estate property, they would continue to raise surpluses which they could sell locally. Also, being free men, they would now be able to devote as much time as they chose to the growing and marketing of pro-

25. The exact conditions under which this practice had become traditional have yet to be discovered. See Sidney W. Mintz, "The Jamaican Internal Marketing Pattern," *Social and Economic Studies* (U.C.W.I.), 4, No. 1, March 1955.

visions, and might well leave the estate in dire need of labour.

The first reaction of the planter was intended to secure two results: first, that the labourers would still find it necessary to earn money wages; and secondly, that they would earn that money working on his estate and not for some neighbouring proprietor. The answer seemed to lie in charging them high rents for the use of huts and "grounds" which they had formerly occupied as slaves. But this sudden demand proved offensive to the labourers, who had never thought of these places as being anybody else's property, and they complained, often with very good reason, that the rents demanded were exorbitant, and that if they paid rent they were free men and should be allowed to work for whom they chose.

These disputes became general throughout the island; and as long as they continued, a stalemate was encouraged in which both estate labour and the cultivation of provision grounds suffered. The situation was broken by the exodus of labourers from the estates. In some cases they were ejected by estate owners who thought that by doing so they would divorce them from their provision grounds and force them into the market for estate labour. The policy would have worked but for two factors which together completely nullified its effect. This was a time of great stress for many estate owners, and on many properties the cultivation of export staples was being either abandoned or reduced, hence there were people with land they were prepared to sell in order to ease their financial problems; secondly, many labourers had enough money saved from sales of provisions and from their paid labour as apprentices to buy land at prices from about £2 to £10 an acre. The ejected labourers, therefore, instead of becoming a body of dispossessed, wage-hunting, agricultural labourers, rapidly established themselves as small freeholders, and their dependence on estate wages was not one whit increased. Since the numbers moving away from the estates also included many who, without having been served ejection notices, were voluntarily moving out in search of land and an indisputable independence of landlord-employers, the planters found it necessary to retreat from their aggressive policies, which had so obviously backfired.

The change of policy followed also from the failure of immediate post-emancipation schemes for European immigration. The theory had been quite straightforward. During the apprenticeship period it had been noticed that many of the apprentices were buying plots of land to which they might retire, when complete freedom came, as independent small cultivators. The planters had been greatly concerned. As one of them put it: "If the lands in the Interior get into the possession of the Negro, goodbye to lowland cultivation, and to any cultivation. You are aware, I dare say that very many of the Apprentices are purchasing their Apprenticeship and buying 5, 10, 15, 50, and even 100 acres." [26] In order to deny land to the negroes, it was decided to encourage the importation of whites who would fill the cooler interior mountain districts.[27] The Europeans began coming in towards the end of 1834. The first lots were brought in by individual planters under a bounty system, but others were to be introduced on a government scheme to settle in a number of inland towns built specially to receive them. Those imported by individual employers were expected to work as labourers on interior estates, those brought in by Government were to be established as small settlers in the planned townships. The combined effect would be to deny both land and employment in the cooler interior to the ex-slaves and so make it necessary for them to move to the sugar areas in the lowlands. The Assembly, in 1835, appointed an agent to proceed to Europe to recruit settlers.

But these schemes failed to produce the desired results. The few thousands [28] who did arrive in the island generally failed to settle or to remain as labourers. In part, the Jamaica Legislature was to blame, for very often the proposed settlers had arrived to find no accommodation prepared for them. This had been the case in the later 1830's with Seaford Town. In the

26. C.O. 137/217, C. S. Salmon to W. Burge, 4 Oct. 1836.

27. C.O. 137/198, "The Memorial of Proprietors, Planters, and others . . . in the Parish of Trelawny," May 1834; C.O. 137/207, the proposals of A. A. Lindo to Lord Aberdeen; and C.O. 137/217, the prospectus of the proposed Jamaica Immigration Company.

28. About 2,685 from Britain and 1,033 from Germany came in during 1834–42. See C.O. 137/273, Elgin to Stanley, No. 108, 15 April 1843 (enclosures).

early 1840's four other proposed townships—Barrettville and
New England in St. Ann, Ashentully in Manchester, and Mul-
grave in St. Elizabeth—were in the same state of unprepared-
ness. Those brought in on bounty as labourers also found conditions disagreeable. They had been recruited in European
town and port areas and found agricultural labour distasteful.
They joined the police, wandered off into the coastal towns,
left the island, and, in many cases, departed this life altogether
under the stress of too much alcohol in the tropics.

In 1842 a new Immigration Act prohibited the continuance
at government expense of the importation of Europeans, and
ended the services of the agent in Europe. Private importations could continue, however, and if the immigrants remained
in service for a full year a small bounty would be paid to the
importer. The provision enabled planters and others to bring in
various skilled workers whose services were thought to be essential in a period of industrial reorganization.

The failure to organize a large-scale settlement of whites
resulted in the elevation of the Jamaican negro from the status
of labourer to that of "potential yeoman." Henceforth, immigration plans were concerned with the importation of indentured
estate labour. This was not an entirely new idea. The immigration figures for 1834 to 1842 show the entry of a number of
Africans as well as Europeans. Some were from the Bahamas,
Canada, and the United States, but the majority were from
Sierra Leone [29] and included both local residents recruited
there by a Jamaica agent appointed in 1841 and a number of
people liberated by British warships from vessels engaged in
the foreign slave trade.[30] Liberated Africans, in much smaller
numbers, also came to Jamaica from St. Helena and Havana.
Until 1843 these people were brought in by individual importers on a bounty system, and it was from the general satisfaction with their work as estate labourers that the planters

29. The numbers were: from the Bahamas, Canada, and the U.S.A.
a total of 778 (some of whom may have been whites); and from Africa
(Sierra Leone) 1,270. See record in C.O. 137/273, Elgin to Stanley,
No. 108.

30. G. W. Roberts, "Immigration of Africans into the British Caribbean," *Population Studies*, 7, No. 3, March 1954.

moved towards plans for large-scale importations of indentured labour. By early 1842 three other important changes had been introduced. The various systems of exorbitant rent charges had been replaced by a rather uniform practice of charging one day's wage as the weekly rent for a cottage, and one day's wage as the weekly rent for the use of provision grounds; the payments of rents and wages had been separated, so that the confusion and argument arising out of the dual roles of landlord-employer and tenant-employee were largely eradicated; and the freedom of the labourer to choose his employer, irrespective of his landlord, was established and estate-owners were competing for the services of labourers in general, rather than attempting to force their own tenants to work for them.[31]

In this happier condition of social and economic relationships, the way for economic advance was made easier, and from the early 1840's until 1846 there was a spate of energy and enterprise among all classes. A general attitude of optimism and a noticeable pride in new accomplishment became evident, where previously pessimistic groans and unswerving attachment to traditional method had been the rule. The various reports and documents which reached the Colonial Office during this period illustrate that in spite of some old guard opposition from those who would always continue to mourn the passing of slavery, Jamaicans were now willing to face their problems and to act to overcome them.

The most rapid change was taking place among the labourers who were establishing their freeholds. In September 1840 the Reverend J. Picton wrote to Stipendiary Magistrate Finlayson in St. James about several of these new peasant establishments. He mentioned particularly the free village of Maldon in the interior of the parish, about sixteen miles south-east of Montego Bay. It had been established soon after emancipation by the Reverend Walter Dendy, a Baptist Missionary.

A particular enquiry was made in August, 1840, into the condition and employment of the 52 on the land sold by

31. C.O. 137/237 to 262, governor's Dispatches and S.M.'s reports during 1839–42.

Mr. Dendy and Mr. Clark. Of these, 27 were constantly
jobbing out, a considerable part of them being either
carpenters or masons; 12 were growing provisions for
sale, splitting shingles, sawing boards, &c., off their own
land for sale; 11 are still working on the pens or estates
where they were slaves; one is a schoolmaster employed
by Mr. Dendy; and one is employed in the barracks at
Maroon Town as a servant. Of the 12 who turn their attention to the growth of provisions for sale, four are old,
disabled, people, and two have large runs of land elsewhere. One of the jobbers, a former slave of Spring Mount
Estate, named John Gray, is now (September) at work
on Williamsfield estate where he has taken a job of about
36 acres of very foul pasture; and he brings about 10 or 12
able hands with him from Maldon to this work, which he
is doing to the entire satisfaction of the overseer and attorney. Of course a very large portion of the time of the
labourers in this district has been taken up in clearing the
land and building their houses, and this will continue until the necessary work is done. But as soon as an able man
has completed this, he immediately turns his hand to some
job or other. There is no single instance in the whole
Maldon district of an unemployed man, or of one who can
justly be termed idle.[32]

In St. Ann, two years after the final emancipation, it was
estimated that upwards of 3,000 acres had been bought and
partly resold at prices varying from £4 to £20 an acre.[33] In
Lower Clarendon, in 1840, Stipendiary Magistrate Carnaby
claimed that

> Perhaps few parishes have made such rapid progress in the
> establishment of small settlements and townships since
> freedom as Clarendon, but particularly in the lower por-
> tions of it. . . . Indeed all along the great leeward road
> from Kingston, which runs through Clarendon about 20

32. C.O. 137/250, statement from the Reverend Picton to S. M.
Finlayson, Sept. 1840.
33. C.O. 137/250, report of S.M. Dillon, 20 Sept. 1840.

miles, new settlements may be perceived rearing into existence every two or three miles. This may be said to be the condition of the parish generally. These small lots, with the dwellings erected, do not in my estimation generally afford a freehold qualification, the owners appearing simply to wish for an independent residence to enable them to devote their time and labour to the best advantage, and upon the most favourable localities.[34]

In St. Thomas in the East new settlements were growing up at Spring Mount, Unity Valley, Elmwood, Pigeon Hill, Batchelor's Hall, Stoake's Hall, Belle Castle, Happy Grove, and elsewhere.[35] After a year's absence in England Stipendiary Magistrate Chamberlaine, a coloured Jamaican, wrote to the governor:

I trust I may be pardoned for adverting to the alterations which so forcibly struck me on a visit to the Parish of St. Thomas in the East, where I had been stationed previous to my departure. In travelling through the Parish [in August 1840] I was astonished and delighted, to perceive the number of Settlements and Cottages that had sprung up right and left, in places before overgrown in Bush and jungle, the improved construction in the Cottages, the enlargement of the different Villages, the number of new Shops and houses that had arisen in the Rural Towns, and general improved appearance and comfort of the labouring population, all afforded satisfactory evidence of the rapid but sure blessings which followed the establishment of general Freedom.[36]

Mr. Chamberlaine went on to describe similar happenings in Hanover, where he had recently been posted.

In St. Dorothy, as in some other parishes, old villages had blossomed into new towns.

34. C.O. 137/250, report of S.M. Carnaby, Sept. 1840.
35. C.O. 137/255, report of S.M. Pryce, March 1841.
36. C.O. 137/257, report of S.M. Chamberlaine, Nov. 1841.

Old Harbour Market, which consisted formerly of two
taverns, one or two houses, the post-office and pound,
a slave blacksmith's and a jail or house of correction, now
consists of a neat court-house, many good houses, and
more buildings, ten or twelve small shops, three blacksmith's shops, one tin-smith's, two taverns as usual, the
post-office, the pound, a police station, and *no* Jail or
House of Correction, a well attended Market on Saturday
for Breadkind, Pork, Poultry, Corn, common Crockery
wares, fruit & Salt provisions, but very inconvenient, from
the want of Stalls and other Buildings, Water, &c., chiefly
owing to the state of the parish funds.[37]

In every parish of the island the formation of these small
freeholds was going on in some degree, and Lord Elgin's comment after his return from a tour through the western districts
early in 1843 can be given a more general application:
"wherever I had an opportunity of questioning the peasantry
as to their condition they bore a cheerful and willing testimony
to the comforts they enjoy, and the satisfactory understanding
established between them and their employers." [38]

A mere few years previously these people had been slaves,
giving slow and unwilling labour on the estates of their owners.
Freedom, giving them the will to work, had unleashed energy
the whip had never been able to bring forth. As one of the
Stipendiary Magistrates put it: "It would appear wonderful
to those whose knowledge of the physical power of the negro
is only confined to his unremunerated specimens of labour during Slavery and Apprenticeship, how so much could have been
accomplished on the small lot lands in Building, planting,
digging Ponds and making Fences, as has been done without
entailing an entire cessation of labour on the Plantations of
the larger Proprietors." [39]

But of course, as he implied, there had been a considerable
withdrawal of labour from the estates, and it is in the reactions

37. C.O. 137/255, report of S.M. Bell, Jan. 1841.
38. C.O. 137/273, Elgin to Stanley, No. 112, 20 April 1843.
39. C.O. 137/257, report of S.M. Grant, 30 June 1841.

of the big planters that the most remarkable behaviour is to be found. The enthusiasm of the peasantry was only to be expected of a people newly freed from slavery. That the ex-slave owners should have met crisis with enthusiasm is more significant. The answer to a reduction in an agricultural labour force is to attempt to maintain the volume of production by substituting animal and mechanical power for human effort, and to increase the average productivity of the remaining labourers. The planters continued to stress their need for labourers, and to complain that the shortage of labour made wages high, but at the same time they took up the challenge inherent in the new situation.

The plough and the harrow, both great savers of labour, were for the first time brought into general use throughout the island. Two conditions were prerequisite: first, capital resources; secondly, the will to experiment. It was suggested by many contemporary observers that the former proved the greater handicap. Those who could afford the new methods were generally willing to try them. The planters, it was said,

> have evinced neither lukewarmness nor a lack of ingenuity, and no little of the latter has been required, in the adaption of European Agricultural Implements, to the cultivation of tropical products, and in the invention of others. . . . The prejudice against research and experiment has vanished, and all the exertion of the mind is being employed in extracting the wealth of the soil. The planter is now only earning for himself the character of an agriculturalist.[40]

Specific inventions included a new type of vacuum pan and other machinery for sugar factories, designed and built by Mr. Noyes, an English engineer who had long been living in St. Thomas in the East; [41] a new machine for peeling the thin skin (not the pulp) from coffee beans, introduced by Mr.

40. C.O. 137/284, report of S.M. Hall Pringle, 1 June 1845. Other similar comments in C.O. 137/275, S.M. Fyffe, 20 Dec. 1843; and C.O. 137/273, Elgin to Stanley, No. 112, 20 April 1843.
41. C.O. 137/284, S.M. Ewart, 3 June 1845.

Humble of St. Ann; [42] and an improved type of cattle pen which was shown at an agricultural exhibition by Mr. George Might, attorney for Belvedere in St. Thomas in the East.[43]

More generally, the number of agricultural societies increased, and they began to show an enlightened interest in agriculture. According to Hall Pringle and many of the stipendiary magistrates, the governor, and other commentators, these societies—and particularly the Royal Agricultural Society, which had been established in February 1844—provided a great stimulus. The planters discovered interests in subjects such as soil chemistry,[44] and the pen-keepers ordered quality live stock from Britain to improve the local strain.[45]

For the first time, in 1844, there are general reports of experiments with the use of guano and various other kinds of fertilizers.[46] A particular demonstration of this was on Molynes Estate in St. Andrew, where the overseer, by applying liberal quantities of manure to a small part of the estate, obtained 5 hogsheads of sugar per acre at a labour cost very little above that on an acre of untreated land giving only 2 hogsheads.[47]

Nor were these efforts purely local and individual in their effects: the new interest in scientific agriculture [48] carried with it both a general willingness for discussion and a general spirit of rivalry in which individual planters or districts or parishes sought to show that their methods were superior to those of others. The reports of agricultural shows and competitions were numerous: "On the 8th of this month [December 1843]

42. C.O. 137/250, S.M. Grant, 20 Oct. 1840.
43. C.O. 137/279, S.M. Ewart, 28 May 1844.
44. C.O. 137/284, S.M. Hall Pringle, 1 June 1845.
45. C.O. 137/275, S.M. Grant, 29 Nov. 1843.
46. C.O. 137/279, reports of the stipendiary magistrates.
47. C.O. 137/282, W. Smith of Manchester to Lord Stanley, 15 July 1844, enclosing his brother's letter from Jamaica.
48. In this the West Indies were not far behind Britain, where the "scientific" approach commenced at about the same time (ca. 1840), with the publication of works by Liebig and others on soil chemistry and the first imports of natural guano from South America. In England, however, an improved agriculture, based on better methods of crop rotation, had been notably developing since the early eighteenth century.

the largest exhibition in this Island of Stock, and the greatest competition in Agricultural labour by the plough and by the application of the hoe harrow as a substitute for the former expensive expedient of hand hoeing took place in this parish. The Assemblage of persons comprised many of the most eminent and extensive planters of the Colony." [49]

From St. Ann, in the same year, came the shorter but perhaps more important note that a livestock fair at River Head Pen on August 8 had been well attended by "Gentlemen from almost all parts of the Island" but that little buying had been done because money was scarce.[50] In other words, planters and pen-keepers had travelled over the wretched roads of the island to attend a fair at which they would probably be unable to buy anything. They must have been interested.

In the *Morning Journal* of 27 May 1843, two challenging notices appeared:

> the three Caymanas Estates shall manufacture for crop 1844 sugar and rum of better quality; at a less expense per ton, and puncheon, and more of it than the whole parish of St. Andrew put together.

> As the frequent exhibition of Stock (say Horse-kind Cattle and Sheep) is allowed by general consent to aid much in developing the resources of this Splendid Island, the parish of St. Catherine will show stock against the whole County of Surrey.[51]

A year later Lord Elgin sent to the Colonial Office newspaper cuttings which listed prizes recently offered by various agricultural societies and by himself for a wide range of competitions, including an essay on the cane-borer and how to destroy it; an essay on a system of industrial education suited to the wants of Jamaica; the best improvement in the cultiva-

49. C.O. 137/275, report, dated 19 Dec. 1843, of S.M. Ramsay, who was also the custos of the parish of St. Catherine.

50. C.O. 137/275, report of S.M. Woolfrys, St. Ann, 1 Nov. 1843.

51. C.O. 137/274, report of Custos Ramsay, St. Catherine, 6 June 1843.

tion of guinea grass; mechanical inventions or innovations; initiative shown in estate management; the most efficient methods of sugar manufacture, coffee-planting, and pen-keeping; and the best rearing of live stock of all kinds. These, it might be said, were for the proprietors and the managers, although they would indirectly benefit the workers. But the latter were not left out, for prizes were also offered for the best examples of ploughing and harrowing; for the best domestic servants and estate labourers; and for proficiency in many other jobs.[52]

Competitions and fairs were valuable in the encouragement they gave to employers and employees alike, and in the opportunities they gave for new methods and techniques to be demonstrated; but if the resources of the island were to be put to their fullest use, something more was needed. The need was realized. Lord Elgin made the important point that the use of greater skill and intelligence on the part of the labourer not only served the planter, but also gave a dignity and credit to "the pursuits of the husbandman" which had not been possible in times of slavery.[53] There was a growing interest in industrial training. The labourer must be given a job to do, he must learn that there are several ways of doing it, and he must be taught to take pride in doing it the best way.

In 1843 a society was formed in St. James and Trelawny for the promotion of "industrial education." The purpose was to help remove the prejudices against agricultural labour by showing the labourer that his work demanded a degree of skill and knowledge of good farming practice.[54] In 1845 schoolmasters were advised that financial assistance would be granted by the Island Board of Education to those who undertook the education of the industrial classes. At the same time notice was given of a series of eighteen to twenty-four lectures on agriculture to be given at Mico College in Kingston. Schoolmasters were invited to bring their best students. The need for textbooks was realized, and Lord Elgin offered a prize of £100

52. C.O. 137/279, Elgin to Stanley, No. 63, 17 April 1844.
53. C.O. 137/284, Elgin to Stanley, confidential, 5 Aug. 1845.
54. C.O. 137/275, report of S. M. Laidlaw, St. James, 28 Nov. 1843.

for the best such book on agriculture for use in the schools, the Royal Agricultural Society offering second and third prizes.[55]

The results of these endeavours were almost immediately noticeable. Mr. Ramsay had written from Spanish Town in December 1843: "the expence of cultivation has been considerably reduced from what it was in the first year of the emancipation, and . . . a judicious and enlightened system of cultivation now substitutes the old inefficient and expensive mode which prevailed in a State of slavery, and . . . there has been prodigious improvement in scientific agriculture." [56] His opinion was generally supported by others. Lord Elgin stressed the fact that these great improvements were all the more significant because they had come about during a period in which Jamaica had suffered from prolonged droughts, and in which the fiscal policy of the British Government, as it affected or threatened the preferential duties on colonial produce, was causing serious apprehensions on the part of the colonists.[57]

The droughts and the doubts nonetheless had their effects. The economic history of Jamaica can be seen as a continuous series of alternating tendencies towards sugar monoculture and diversity of production. This is not to say that the making of sugar has ever been entirely abandoned in favour of other things. The amount of capital invested in the sugar industry has prevented that, even when the prospects have been dimmest. In slave days, when the capital outlay had largely been in the form of slaves, the sugar planter had enjoyed a greater mobility between alternative uses for his capital. When the slaves became free and, almost at the same time, nineteenth-century industrialization began to introduce the modern factory with its large permanent buildings and expensive heavy machinery, conditions were radically changed. Labour was no longer a capital investment, and the factory now represented a large outlay which had to be maintained, with the additional qualification that unlike labour it could serve only that purpose

55. C.O. 137/284, Elgin to Stanley, confidential, 5 Aug. 1845.
56. C.O. 137/275, report of Custos Ramsay, 19 Dec. 1843.
57. C.O. 137/284, Elgin to Stanley, confidential, 5 Aug. 1845.

for which it was originally designed, namely the manufacture of sugar.

In the 1840's the sugar industry was not expanding. The period was one of reorganization and consolidation to meet the new conditions of production by free labourers. For some people the sugar industry offered no further attraction; either they lacked the will or the ability to carry through the fundamental readjustments which were necessary, or they lacked the capital resources with which to meet the new system of paid labour and mechanical innovation. These people were abandoning production, and many of them were selling land. In company with them in the search for new fields for investment were others who were reluctant to invest in sugar at a time when everything seemed so uncertain. Simultaneously, therefore, with the activities of the labourers settling their freeholds and the determined planters reorganizing their estates in the light of science, we find a sudden outbreak of other undertakings, some entirely new to the island, others revived after long neglect. The most important of these endeavours were mentioned by Lord Metcalfe in his speech opening the Legislature on 26 October 1841:

> The prospect is now, in some respects, more cheering; for, by the blessing of Almighty Providence, the late rains have produced abundant crops; and it is expected that, in the approaching season, our staple exports will considerably exceed those of late years. Agricultural societies are being extended over the whole island—the silk company, and the copper-mine company, are proceeding, I understand, with favourable prospects. Cotton has been produced sufficiently to show, that if it were not excluded by devotion to more valuable articles, or by insufficiency of labour, it might become an additional source of prosperity. The cultivation of tobacco on a large scale, I hear, is about to commence; and the discovery of a method by which the supply of one of our staple exports may be greatly augmented [Mr. Humble's coffee-peeler], promises a large increase to the wealth of the agricultural community.[58]

58. C.O. 137/256, Metcalfe to Stanley, No. 2, 27 Oct. 1841.

Of these new enterprises it must suffice here to say that they were being launched in a spirit of almost unqualified hopefulness, encouraged in most cases by good reports on the quality of samples of the new products. In May 1842 Mr. Whitmarsh, the manager of the Jamaica Silk Company situated at Metcalfeville, in the parish of St. Ann, took a twelve-pound sample to England, where it was shown to an eminent silk broker.

> In the presence of a gentleman having large possessions in this Island the case containing the silk was first opened and Mr. Durant without being informed from whence procured was required to state his opinion of it. He immediately exclaimed "Ah, that is beautiful silk, it appears from its nature to be Spanish, which is the best in the world, but the Spanish is badly reeled, and this is perfect." He then valued it at 22/– per pound, and in better times he thought the same quality might be worth 30/– to 36/–.[59]

In December 1840 samples of copper ore raised by the Mount Vernon Mining Company in the parish of Port Royal were sent to Britain to be analysed. Early in the following year Mr. R. Phillips of the Museum of Economic Geology notified the Colonial Office that two boxes had been received. The contents of the smaller box were unlabelled and quite small and therefore had not been submitted to any tests, although some had "very favourable appearances." The contents of the larger box had been analysed, and their copper content had been found to vary between 20 per cent and 34.8 per cent. The report continued: "As the Copper ore of Cornwall averages only about 8 per cent it is evident that the Jamaica ores are extremely productive & must be very valuable, provided they can be raised in sufficient quantity and not at too great expense." [60]

Only a month previously a letter from Mr. Shaw Lefevre, president of the Board of Trade, to the secretary of state for the colonies, had enclosed a report of a committee of Liverpool brokers on samples of Jamaica cotton which had been

59. C.O. 137/275, letter from B. Walker, Esq., solicitor in Kingston, to Lord Elgin, enclosed in Elgin to Stanley, No. 162, 4 Oct. 1843.

60. C.O. 137/265, Phillips to the Colonial Office, 5 March 1842.

submitted for their opinion: "Clean & well got up, but rather speckled with brown and dead bits. Staple rather uneven, but on the whole long and strong; worth today 8d. to 8½d per lb. If any quantity could be had as good & clean as the sample would be freely used at the above price." [61]

Of course it was not always a success story, but every effort was a welcome sign of enterprise. John Candler, the Baptist missionary who toured Jamaica in 1839–40, visited the home of Stephen Bourne, a stipendiary magistrate who lived with his family at Strawberry Hill, in the mountains north-east of Kingston. Mr. Bourne had ten acres of land which were planted in vegetable and root crops. To help in the cultivation he had seven boys, to whom in return he gave lodging, food, clothing, and instruction. The boys, in fact, formed a small industrial school in which Mr. Bourne and his two sons and daughter were the teachers.[62] This in itself was a praiseworthy enterprise, but Mr. Bourne tried to do even more. In March 1841 Lord Metcalfe sent samples of hemp to England for examination. One was from the penguine plant, and had been produced by Mr. Dubuisson, "a meritorious Assistant in the Office of my Secretary." Another sample had been made from another wild plant, the spanish dagger. A third had been produced from the stalks of plantain and banana trees "by Mr. Bourne a Stipendiary Magistrate who has under his care at his own residence a School of Industry, which he superintends and supplies accommodation for with very laudable zeal generosity and public spirit." Unhappily, these specimens were given unfavourable reports by the master rope maker at Deptford, to whom they had been submitted by the Colonial Office for testing; and although Lord Metcalfe saw a report in an English newspaper that Mr. Bourne's fibre had been mixed with cotton and other materials and worked into cloths, there was no further news of it and the experiment must have failed.[63]

61. C.O. 137/265, Shaw Lefevre to Colonial Office, 17 Jan. 1842.
62. J. Candler, *Extracts from the Journal of . . . whilst Travelling in Jamaica* (London, 1840), p. 40.
63. C.O. 137/255, Metcalfe to Russell, Nos. 202, 208, 10, 28 March 1841, and drafted replies.

The evidence shows, however, that the initial successes outweighed and outnumbered the failures, and the most obvious and perhaps most significant success of all was the Kingston to Spanish Town Railway. Early in 1844 Lord Elgin had sent the secretary of state for the colonies an abstract of the Jamaica Act authorizing the railway. He remarked that the proposal was good because of the heavy traffic and bad carriage road between the two centres. The undertaking was to be a private one, and the capital had been subscribed in England.[64] Six months later the governor followed up with a strongly worded dispatch:

> I should consider any delay in its confirmation by the Queen much to be regretted. It is one of the few instances in which British Capitalists have come forward to promote a work of Public Utility in the British West Indian Colonies. The same reluctance has not been exhibited in respect to undertakings which have had for their object the development of the resources of Foreign Colonies in this quarter, for Cuba possesses a line of Railway of considerable length executed, I am informed, entirely by British Capital.[65]

The single-line railway was opened in November 1845. It was thirteen miles long and cost £222,250. The original plan had been more optimistic, for it had been estimated that the original capital, amounting to £150,000 in 30,000 £5 shares would have been sufficient to construct three lines. The promoters of the Jamaica Railway Company, which had been incorporated in 1843 and issued its prospectus in 1844, were William Smith of Manchester and his brother David Smith in Jamaica.[66] The optimistic spirit in which they had set about their task and the great benefits they expected would come from it may be judged from the following extract of a letter written by David Smith to his brother in June 1844. The British Government had just reduced the preference given to British

64. C.O. 137/278, Elgin to Stanley, No. 9, 9 Jan. 1844.
65. C.O. 137/279, Elgin to Stanley, No. 69, 20 July 1844.
66. A. E. Aspinall, *The British West Indies* (London, 1912), p. 328.

colonial over foreign free-grown sugars, but the Smiths were not alarmed:

> I feel assured you will agree with me in my view of the matter as to the alteration in the duties having any effect on our Railway, I do not fear it in the most remote degree. St. Thomas in the Vale and Luidas Vale in St. John's whence we shall get the bulk of our produce are the most seasonable & most thickly populated districts in the Island and the facilities which will be afforded them by the establishment of the Railway will enable them to keep up their cultivation when other less favored Districts may perhaps fail. I this morning had a long conversation with 2 of the most experienced planters in that quarter and their opinions coincided with my own. They say that if I give them the Railway and carry manure at a low price they can double their Crops.[67]

About six months after the line had been opened, Lord Elgin referred to its great success, which "is said to have fully realised the expectations of its promoters," and remarked that other lines had been proposed and that work on them only awaited the sanction of Her Majesty. Apart from the saving of labour and expense to the planters, he thought that they might perhaps lead in the near future to the establishment of central factories in the sugar industry.[68]

I have quoted an extract from an address by Lord Metcalfe on the opening of the Legislature in October 1841, to illustrate the beginning of new hope and the vitality which so rapidly followed the social and economic upheavals of the emancipation. In October 1845 Lord Elgin told the secretary of state for the colonies about the reply he had received from the Assembly to his opening address of that session of the Legislature.

> The hearty tone of that document, and the sentiments expressed in it with respect to the reviving prosperity of

67. C.O. 137/282, D. Smith, enclosed in W. Smith to Stanley, 15 July 1844.
68. C.O. 137/288, Elgin to Gladstone, No. 52, May 1846.

the Colony—the effect of the improvements which have taken place in our agriculture and manufacturing processes —the necessity of general education—and the advantages of a well-ordered system of prison discipline, are in the highest degree gratifying, and can hardly fail to be productive of good both here and among persons interested in the Colony at Home.[69]

Early in 1846 Lord Elgin left Jamaica. His successor, Sir Charles Grey, was long delayed in arrival and in the interim the government was administered by Lieutenant General Berkeley. In Britain on July 16 of the same year, a new government led by Lord John Russell succeeded that of Sir Robert Peel, who had been defeated on an Irish bill. This new government passed an act declaring that the duties charged on sugar entering Britain were gradually to be equated, so that by 1852 all sugars coming into the country, whether foreign or colonial, whether grown by slave-labour or by free men, would pay the same rates of duty based entirely on the quality of the article.

Late in November, in Jamaica, the acting governor decided that he could no longer postpone the summoning of the Legislature in the expectation of Sir Charles Grey's immediate arrival. In his opening speech he referred to the delicacy of his position and refrained from any important comment. The Assembly's reply acknowledged the good intent of his behaviour and the difficulty of his situation:

> We are aware that under the circumstances in which Your Excellency is placed you could not allude to the momentous affairs which claim and must engage our attention. We cannot anticipate the probability of accomplishing the business of the Session during the few weeks remaining of this year however anxious to devote ourselves to it with every diligence. The critical position to which the recent policy of the Imperial Parliament has reduced the Colony leaves us no alternative but to announce to Your Excellency our utter inability to continue to maintain our institutions upon their present scale.

69. C.O. 137/285, Elgin to Stanley, private, 23 Oct. 1845.

We cordially join Your Excellency in expressions of gratitude to the Almighty for the propitious seasons with
which we have been recently blessed. This favourable
change would under other circumstances have cheered
our hopes and stimulated our Agricultural exertions. Abandoned, however as we now are to a hopeless competition
with Slave cultivating and Slave trafficking countries we
fear that even this Merciful interposition of Providence
cannot avert the ruin which threatens to overwhelm us.[70]

It is a condition of local administration by colonial authorities that their plans and deliberations are subject to acts of the
Imperial Power which may come as suddenly and as effectively
as acts of God. Although this is not a history of British commercial and tariff policies, it is in part a history of the repercus-
sions of those policies on Jamaican affairs. The address of the
Assembly in November 1846, a sad document, shows that the
policy of the new Government in Britain had completely de-
flated their spirit.

Since the majority of the Jamaica Assembly at this time were
planters or planting attorneys who managed the estates of absentee proprietors, most of whom lived in Britain, it was only
to be expected that their reaction to the news of diminishing
protection for their produce would be pessimistic. But we
shall see, in subsequent chapters, that the Sugar Duties Act of
1846 exerted strong influences, directly or indirectly, on every
aspect of post-emancipation economic development in Jamaica.
It affected the introduction of immigrant labour and improvements in the cultivation and manufacture of sugar; it affected
the growth of other industrial or agricultural ventures; it
brought indirect pressures to bear on both urban and rural
development beyond the estates; and it brought political discord.

In part, these wide consequences followed from the fact that
the sugar interest did have a majority in the Assembly; but
they also followed inevitably from the fact that despite all
changes the sugar industry had always been, and continued to

70. C.O. 137/289, Berkeley to Earl Grey, No. 42, 21 Nov. 1846.

be, the most important feature of the Island economy. Exports of sugar, and its by-product rum, far outvalued those of any other product (see Table 2).

TABLE 2. *Estimated Values, in £ Sterling, of Major Exports (Jamaica Produce)*

Year	Sugar	Rum	Coffee	Pimento
1841	1,100,568	282,198	211,427	29,569
1845	1,304,836	193,480	131,857	33,785
1850	585,096	175,996	118,603	53,644
1855	364,688	312,387	96,191	131,165
1860	646,385	297,278	113,343	53,061
1865	430,285	162,751	159,999	30,527

Source: Jamaica Blue Books.

NOTE. The duties on foreign and colonial coffee entering the United Kingdom had been equalized in 1844. The reaction in Jamaica had been comparatively negligible.

By its direct contributions through the land tax and taxes on live stock, and fixed capital assets (hereditaments), and by indirect yieldings through tonnage duties on shipping, the sugar industry was a major source of government revenues. As the largest single employer of local labour it provided the wages of labourers and skilled workers and so contributed to the growth of the local and import trades. Quite clearly, any event which threatened to make sugar production in Jamaica unprofitable could have serious and widespread effects.

Directly, and immediately, the consequences would fall upon the sugar industry. The success, or failure, of the planters to meet their problems, and the measures which they adopted, would, indirectly, bear heavily upon the welfare of the people as a whole.

CHAPTER 2

The Re-Organization of Sugar Production, 1838–1846

EMANCIPATION in Jamaica, through its influence on the
estate-labour supply, had introduced problems of production
which the planters set about to overcome. Generally speaking,
by 1846 these difficulties had been defined and remedial measures formulated. In these years the essential emphasis was on
measures designed to meet the labour shortage. The Sugar
Duties Act of 1846, by severely affecting the prices obtainable
for sugar in Britain, sapped the confidence of the planters and
their creditors and thus handicapped, and in some instances
completely stalled, the reforms suggested or actually being
undertaken in production methods. For these reasons, it is
convenient to take the sugar industry in two periods: the first
up to 1846, the second from 1847 to 1865. In the first period,
dealt with in this chapter, we meet the problems and the
initiated or proposed solutions. In the second period, Chapter
3, there is only one new important problem. The ways to
cheaper production had already been seen, and the new
difficulty was concerned only with means. When sugar sold at
not much over 30/– a hundredweight, excluding duty, the
planter was aware of the need to reduce costs and could still
command the credit which enabled him to buy more efficient
and labour-saving implements and machinery. But at 25/– a
hundredweight, though the need was even greater, the credit
was less readily forthcoming.

In 1842, Mr. S. G. Barrett,[1] a planter and attorney of sugar
estates in the western parishes of Jamaica, told a Select Com-

1. He was a member of the Wimpole Street family.

mittee of the House of Commons how sugar was made in the Island.[2] First, the land was prepared for planting by burning and clearing grass and shrubbery; then the labourers marked it off in lines for cane holes, which were dug about six inches deep and about 2,700 to the acre. When this was done two or more cane tops were placed parallel at the bottom of each hole and lightly covered with earth. As the canes grew, more and more earth was put around them until eventually the holes were entirely filled.

During the time when the canes were maturing, gangs of workers were employed in weeding the rows and removing any dry trash from the stalks. This would be done three or four times, according to need, during the twelve to fifteen months before the canes were ready for grinding. When the crop was ready the canes were cut by labourers using machetes, bound together in bundles, loaded on to cattle-wains, and taken to the mill.

As the canes were passed through the mill, the juice was conveyed by gutters into the first receptacles, called the siphons, while the trash ("bagasse") was collected and taken off to special storage for use as fuel for the various boilers. Exclusive of the siphons, in which the juice was clarified by heating with the addition of a small quantity of lime, there were at least three other boilers, or "coppers." In the process of clarification the impurities in the cane-juice were brought to the surface and skimmed off into a receiver in the still-house, where later they would be used with molasses in the manufacture of rum. The clear liquid was then "skipped" or ladled into the grand copper, the largest of the three, and heated. After a certain amount of evaporation had taken place, the hot juice was skipped into the second and smaller copper which was hung over an even hotter fire. More evaporation occurred, and finally the reduced volume of liquor was skipped into the smallest and hottest copper of the three, called the "teache," where it was heated until it became thick and tacky,

2. Minutes of Evidence, 5278–79. Some details are taken from other sources. See, for example, J. Biggs, *Observations on the Manufacture of Sugar and Rum in Jamaica,* London, 1843.

so that a drop of it would stretch between the fingers. When it reached this stage the boiling was over.

The sticky mass next was run into large shallow coolers, usually made of wood, where it remained until it was nearly cold. Then it was potted into hogsheads, in the curing-house. The process of curing was simply to leave the sugar in the hogsheads, which had perforated bottoms, for about three weeks. During this time the molasses would drip out leaving the crystallized sugar in the hogsheads, which were then sealed up and dispatched for shipment. But not all the contents reached the market in Britain. Crude manufacture and inefficient curing meant that the sugar still contained a large proportion of molasses, some of which leaked from the hogsheads during the voyage across the Atlantic.[3]

The planter's main concern was to realize a profit, and as prices declined between 1840 and 1845 it was necessary for him to attempt to reduce his costs of production. But the largest item of cost was the wages of labour, which during these years remained firm at rates the planters found excessive, especially after the price fall of 1841. As a result, there was no assurance that the planter's highest possible offer, in view of falling sugar prices, would secure all the labour he required. The situation is well illustrated in a reported conversation between a British Guiana planter and one of his employees in 1842:

> "You see, David, if the sugar I make sells for no more than twenty thousand dollars, and if I pay more than that in expenses, I won't continue to make it."
> "Certain."
> "Well, sugar will not rise—the price is higher now than it was before the great first of August, so we must not look to that, then the only thing left to us is to reduce expenses."
> "Certain; but wages no all."

3. In 1845 this loss was calculated at about 3 cwts. from a hogshead of 20 cwts. See A. G. Fyfe, *Suggestions for Separating the Culture of Sugar from the Process of Manufacture; with a Plan for Establishing a Central Sugar Factory at Annotto Bay, Jamaica* (London, 1846), pp. 10–15.

"The other expenses of an estate are all as much reduced as possible, even the salaries of the whites, many of them depend on the cost of articles in Europe, such as coals and staves."

"All true, Massa."

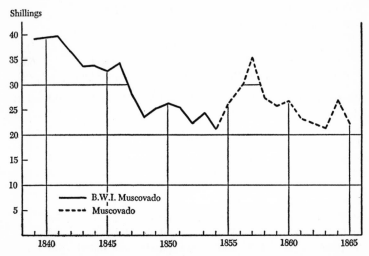

Chart 1. Average price per hundredweight in London (excluding duty) of muscovado and of B.W.I. muscovado, 1839–65. *See also below, Appendix 2.*

"Then you see that we cannot help this reduction—it is forced on us by absolute necessity."

"Massa remember I told him before time, if white people don't gib good money, Negro won't work?"

"I remember it quite well."

"Da so he stand." [4]

This conversation might well have taken place in Jamaica. The myth still exists today of a wicked plantocracy under which the ex-slaves were bullied and browbeaten into submission and the acceptance of starvation wages. In freedom, as in slavery, there were employers who were ignorant and dictatorial, and who attempted to oppress their workers. In

4. Barton Premium, *Eight Years in British Guiana (1840–48)* (London, 1850), p. 96.

slavery they had held the whip, but in freedom they had to bargain, and as Table 3 clearly illustrates, it was the labourers who held the upper hand in wage negotiations.

According to the old slave system, estate labourers were still divided into gangs according to physical strength. In the

TABLE 3. *Daily Wages (in Sterling) of Estate Labourers in Jamaica*

Parishes	(a) 1838 (Oct–Dec)	(b) 1840 (Oct–Dec)	(c) 1854 (Jan–Mar)	(d) 1865 (April)
Westmoreland	9d. – 1/6	1/– – 1/6	1/– – 1/6	9d. – 1/3
Hanover	9d. – 1/6	1/– – 1/6	not stated	9d. – 1/3
St. James	9d. – 1/–	1/– – 1/6	9d. – 1/6	9d. – 1/3
Trelawny	9d. – 1/–	1/– – 1/6	9d. – 1/–	6d. – 9d.
St. Elizabeth	9d. – 1/–	9d. – 1/–	9d. – 1/–	9d. – 1/–
Manchester	9d. – 1/6	1/– – 1/6	9d. – 1/–	9d. – 1/–
Clarendon	not stated	1/3 – 1/6	not stated	9d. – 1/3
Vere	9d. – 1/–	1/6 – 2/–	not stated	9d. – 1/–
St. Dorothy	not stated	not stated	9d. – 1/–	9d. – 1/–
St. Catherine	9d. – 1/–	not stated	9d. – 1/–	6d. – 1/–
St. John	1/3 – 1/6	not stated	not stated	9d. – 1/–
St. Thomas in the Vale	6d. – 1/–	not stated	9d. – 1/–	9d. – 1/–
St. Ann	9d. – 1/–	1/– – 1/6	9d. – 1/6	9d. – 1/–
St. Mary	9d. – 1/6	1/– – 1/6	not stated	9d. – 1/–
Metcalfe	(Founded in 1841)		not stated	9d. – 1/–
St. George	not stated	not stated	not stated	not stated
Portland	6d. – 1/6	not stated	9d. – 1/–	9d. – 1/–
St. Thomas in the East	9d. – 1/–	1/3 – 1/6	not stated	9d. – 1/–
St. David	9d. – 1/–	9d. – 1/–	9d. – 1/–	9d. – 1/–
Port Royal	6d. – 1/–	9d. – 1/–	9d. – 1/–	not stated
St. Andrew	9d. – 1/–	1/– – 1/6	9d. – 1/–	9d. – 1/3

Sources: (*a*) C.O. 137/230, stipendiary magistrates' reports; *Colonial Magazine*, 3 (London, Sept.–Dec. 1840), 50–60; (*b*) C.O. 137/250, stipendiary magistrates' reports; (*c*) C.O. 137/322, stipendiary magistrates' reports; (*d*) C.O. 137/390, reports of the clergy and custodes.

NOTE. Wages paid before 1841 in Jamaica currency have been translated into sterling by multiplying by three-fifths.

first gang were the best workers, chiefly strong young people; the second gang contained older men and women and adolescents; the third gang was composed of young children, old people of both sexes, and the physically handicapped. These were the usual divisions, but the system varied slightly on different estates. As far as possible, each type of labour was allotted to the most suitable gang, the strongest people doing the most strenuous jobs.

The figures given in Table 3 represent the wages paid for a day's labour to first and second gangs. Third-gang wages were proportionately lower. It cannot be claimed that these were the rates followed in every locality of every parish, but they indicate the general parochial and island wage movements through our period. There were three broad phases. The first, from August 1838 until the end of 1841, has already been described. It was the time of general dispute when the daily rate became widely established at one shilling and sixpence for first-class people.

This does not mean, however, that this sum was the maximum amount which could be earned by an agricultural labourer in one day, for there were other arrangements between workers and their employers. The two most important were task work and job work. In the former, the employer and worker agreed beforehand on a specified task to be completed in one day for a stipulated wage. A good worker might complete more than one such task in a steady day's work. In job work, the employer and a labourer contracted for the performance of a set piece of work to be completed for a stated sum of money; there was not usually any specified time limit on the job, nor was it necessarily performed single-handed by the labourer who had accepted the offer. Both these methods were commonly used in Britain, particularly in the mines and on railroad construction. The average daily earnings on task or job work in Jamaica usually exceeded the ordinary daily wage rate by about threepence to sixpence.

These conditions were maintained during the next five or six years, although in 1845 and 1846 there were occasional reports from stipendiary magistrates and others of slight decreases in one or two localities.[5] But there was still no evidence of any general decline. In Vere, for example, where the daily rate went down to 1/–, there had been extraordinary and prolonged drought; in the Falmouth district, near to a growing town in a parish whose soil was largely unfavourable to provisions growing, there was a similar decrease. On the whole, management-labour relationships continued happily. From 1847 to 1854, unfortunately, the half-yearly agricultural reports of the stipendiary magistrates were discontinued. By the latter year many of the original stipendiaries had died or left the island and had not been replaced, so the reports are not as comprehensive of Island conditions as they had formerly been; but the available information shows that a general decline of wages had occurred in the previous years. There is no doubt that the decline was related to the effects of the Sugar Duties Act, which reduced still further the planter's ability to pay. Faced with the impossibility of increasing wage rates in order to attract more labour, planters in the early 1840's set about finding solutions to the problem of shortage. They sought to increase the productivity of whatever labour was available, by the introduction of labour-saving implements and devices; and they initiated large-scale importations of indentured labour to increase the number of workers at their command.

The agricultural work is continuous on a sugar estate. Crop-taking cannot be allowed to interfere with the cultivation of canes for the following harvest. On the other hand, crop-taking, obviously, is seasonal. This is important. First of all it explains the increased demand for labour at crop time; secondly, it influenced the efforts of the planters to reduce their costs of production. In slave-days the stress had been on manpower rather than mechanical aids, and the machinery of an estate had been concentrated in the factory-yard where it was essentially needed. An estate simply had to have a mill, a boiling-house, siphons, coppers, and so forth. It did not have

5. For example: C.O. 137/284, Hall Pringle's report from Vere (June 1845), and C.O. 137/289, Gurley's report from Falmouth, Trelawny (May 1846).

to have ploughs and pitchforks, for the slave gangs, numerically sufficient to meet crop-time labour requirements, provided a superfluity of manpower which had to be employed throughout the year. When slavery was abolished and scarce labour had to be economized, the most obvious starting place was in the fields: both because field labour was continuous throughout the year, and because field labour was even more primitively employed than factory labour.

The value of the plough as a means of saving labour was obvious. It reduced considerably the need to employ expensive first-gang labourers to dig cane holes. Various makes of English and American ploughs, harrows, and other agricultural equipment came into general use, but they were not always suitable for the harder soils of Jamaica and some planters preferred to make their own. The locally built ploughs were said to have:

> a somewhat cumbersome appearance, but do much better work; make a deeper and cleaner Cane hole, and wider at the bottom than any I have seen done by the imported ploughs; those I have used have the mould boards made of copper, which possesses the advantage of admitting to be moulded with accuracy to such form as may be best adapted to the soil for which the Plough is required, for one particular form is not adapted to all soils. The share and socket were imported, as also the copper in plates, of the required dimensions. The double Mould-Board Ploughs made by the late Mr. Wright of Vere, are a considerable improvement on those which were before in use.[6]

Nonetheless, there were limits to what local ingenuity could do, and those estates which were topographically unsuitable for ploughing were gradually forced out of production either by the lack of sufficient hoe labour or by the great cost of that method of cultivation.

6. T. Henney, in *Eight Treatises on the Cultivation of the Sugar Cane,* Spanish Town, 1843. Henney's treatise won the first prize offered by Lord Elgin in November 1842 for such a paper. See also L. Wray, *The Practical Sugar Planter* (London, 1848), ch. 3.

During the early 1840's many planters submitted reports showing how much more cheaply the ordinary processes of cultivation could be done with the aid of the new implements. Not only was the actual planting of canes made less expensive, but there were subsequent benefits as well (see Table 4).

TABLE 4. *Comparative Costs of Cultivating Two Similar Cane Pieces*

By the Hoe	£.	s.	d.	By the Plough	£.	s.	d.
Cost of digging cane-holes and lining off (70 for 2/–)	27	9	1	Cost of plough-ing entirely, harrowing, and ploughing cane-holes	13	1	6
Picking plant tops and planting thickly along the rows	18	8	3	Picking plant tops and planting one every 3 ft. along the row	4	12	0
Weeding and supplying new tops to replace failures	20	4	6	Ditto	4	4	0
Cleaning till time of cutting	57	16	0	Ditto	20	19	0
TOTAL	£123	17	10	TOTAL	£42	16	6

Source: (W. F. Whitehouse), *Agricola's Letters and Essays on Sugar Farming in Jamaica* (Kingston, 1845), article entitled "On the Use of the Plough," written April 1841.

NOTE. W. F. Whitehouse was a planter and a rabid enthusiast for agricultural improvements. For those who used imported implements a good wrought-iron plough which could be worked by eight cattle cost "with duplicate socks, coulters, &c. and charges out, about £ 14": Whitehouse, in *Eight Treatises* (see n. 6).

Whitehouse showed that ploughing could be associated with, and productive of, other economies. Item 1 in the table of comparative costs reflects, above all else, the obvious saving of wages to cane-hole diggers. Once the land had been turned by the plough, the job became much easier. Item 2, however, indicates an incidental benefit. It had been the custom to plant canes very thickly. The practice was to place several pieces composed of the top joints of the cane stalk into each hole prepared for planting.[7] When the plough was introduced, two changes were generally adopted. In the first place the cane rows were spaced rather more widely, so as to allow ploughing between them; secondly, because the land became more productive with ploughing, it was no longer thought necessary to put quite as many cane tops into each hole in order to secure a suitable number of good shoots. It would appear, however, that Whitehouse was more assertive than were the majority of the benefits of such restrained planting as column two of the table indicates. Generally, although the rows were more widely spaced than they had previously been, planters continued to put two cane tops per hole. But even this brought a significant saving both in labour and in providing for suitable plants which were sometimes cultivated for this particular purpose.

The reductions in items 3 and 4 followed from the reduced number of plants and from inter-row ploughing. Weeding became easier. Fewer tops planted meant that there was less need for selective pruning of unhealthy or overcrowded shoots, and also that there were fewer stalks to be cleaned or "trashed" of dry foliage as they grew. These were all labour-devouring processes.

Whitehouse's remarks on the great advantages of ploughing were supported in the reports of the stipendiary magistrates. In 1841 most of them wrote of the widespread introduction of this and other labour-saving devices, and several compared the labour costs of the old and the new methods of cultivation. In January of that year, for example, Stipendiary Bell wrote from St. Dorothy: "The constant and improved use of ploughs in this neighbourhood has and will save almost a fourth of the money formerly disbursed for the digging part of the planting

7. Experiments in cane-growing from seed were carried out in Barbados in the late 1880's. See minutes, General Purposes Committee, of the W.I.C. for 10 April 1890. Seed-grown cane is now used for research purposes.

operations for canes, for instance, opening and preparing
15 acres with the plough £15; digging &c. 15 acres with the
hoe £60. This, of course, keeps much money out of the labourers' pockets, and accounts, with the dry weather, for the
anxiety to get work." [8]

In October, Stipendiary Brown wrote from Portland, on the
other side of the Island, that the plough was in use on some
estates; where it was being used, "the manual labour costs only
the sum of One Pound per acre, instead of Three Pounds eight
shillings . . . and by using the Plough in cleaning and mould-
ing the canes the work is performed for the sum of Four
shillings and sixpence per acre instead of from Ten to twelve
shillings." [9]

The use of agricultural implements, however, could not solve
all the difficulties. The trouble was that even with labour-
saving devices, the planter could seldom count on the local
population to provide all the labour he required exactly when
he required it.

The availability of local labour depended, for the most part,
on three factors: first, the position of the estate in relation
to population density and to the local alternatives to estate
labour. In Trelawny, or Vere, for example, where the soil was
not encouraging to provisions-growing, estate labour was
usually more available than, say, in Hanover or Clarendon.
Secondly, there was the policy of the sugar planter with regard
to local freehold settlement or the rental of idle estate lands.
By the early 1840's, when ejectment policies had obviously
backfired, many planters were trying to encourage settlement
either on or near to their estates, hoping in this way to have a
local reservoir of labour on which to call.[10] On Seville Estate,
in St. Ann, the proprietors had followed this policy from the
very beginning. Immediately after emancipation they had instructed their planting attorney, Charles Royes, to offer cottages and grounds on annual tenancies at the rate of 1/6 sterling per week, payable weekly. The cottages were to be kept in

8. C.O. 137/255, Bell's report of 3 Jan. 1841.
9. C.O. 137/257, Brown's report of 14 Oct. 1841.
10. C.O. 137/248, Metcalfe to Russell, No. 50, 30 March 1840, is a
very detailed exposition of the situation at that time.

good repair by the estate, and contracts were terminable at six-months' notice by either party. As Royes put it: "To this arrangement the labourers unanimously assented, and it is gratifying to state, that it has continued to the present period."

Wages were paid regularly every Friday evening by Royes himself, and he gave preferential rates to his tenantry. Most labour on the estate, except cane-cutting, and manufacturing, was done on the day-labour system, which by this time was uncommon on other properties and would seem to indicate a particularly good relationship between Royes and his employees. His wage rates were 1/6 sterling a day for those first-class people who were also permanent estate residents. Temporary settlers who came in during crop seasons got 1/3, and "strangers and others" were paid 1/–.[11]

On Montpelier and Ellis Caymanas, Lord Howard de Walden's attorneys were similarly instructed: "Every facility is to be given to those who desire to settle on the estate for a term of years, in regard to MONEY terms, provided they build suitable cottages, and efficiently enclose their grounds." [12] The interesting words are "for a term of years." He was trying to induce settlement by offering long leases, which were generally difficult to obtain, most planters preferring to rent only on a short-term basis, often as little as a week's notice each way.

However favourable or unfavourable these two factors (position of the estate and policy of the planter) might have been, the third factor was unpredictable and often baffling. It concerned the attitude of the local population towards the individual planter. People would sometimes go out of their way to offer labour to an employer they preferred, often refusing to give it on estates managed by unpopular planters or where long-established prejudices existed on the basis of past grievances.[13]

11. C.O. 137/284, report of S.M. Woofrys, May 1845.

12. Lord Howard de Walden, "General Instructions for Montpelier and Ellis Caymanas Estates in Jamaica," London, 1852.

13. For example, on Montpelier Estate in St. James, though the manager in the 1840's was personally liked. See C.O. 137/248, Metcalfe to Russell, No. 50, 30 March 1840.

In London the West India Interest, concerned over immediate post-emancipation reports of crippling withdrawals of labour from the estates, pressed for Government action. Their agitation led to the appointment in 1842 of a Select Committee of the House of Commons to enquire into the condition of the West India Colonies. After hearing a mass of evidence, the Committee, though pleased by reports of the material well-being of the ex-slaves, supported the requests of the planters for large-scale immigration schemes, provided that they were conducted by responsible officials. The immediate result was the provision by West Indian colonial governments for African immigration under a system of British Government supervision through the newly established Colonial Land and Emigration Commission.[14] On arrival in a colony, the immigrants were to be met by a responsible official. They would be required to contract with employers for labour, but no contract was to be made before arrival or to be binding for a period exceeding one year.

In 1843 the West India Interest sent a deputation to the secretary of state for the colonies. They complained that the African immigration was insufficient, and asked for the organization of Indian immigration. By the middle of the following year West India planters had been granted the right to import labour from India and China as well as from Africa.[15] In due course, Jamaica agents were appointed to Calcutta and Madras to supervise recruitment and embarkation. In the Island, an agent general for immigration and several sub-agents were responsible for the reception and subsequent welfare of arrivals. The agent general co-ordinated individual employer's requests for immigrants into an Island total which was submitted to the land and emigration commissioners for approval and action. The cost of the Immigration Department, the maintenance of agents abroad, and the costs of shipping were to be met by a direct tax of 20/– a year on employers for

14. See I. M. Cumpston, *Indians Overseas in British Territories, 1834–1845* (Oxford University Press, 1953), for the formation of this Commission and the early organization of immigration.

15. Ibid.

each immigrant they employed, and by annual votes from the general revenues.

The expense of bringing labourers from the Far East was great. The passage from India, excluding any other charges, was about £16 per person.[16] It was proposed that on their arrival the Indians should be distributed among those applicants for labour who offered them the best conditions of employment, and it was decided that the regulations which applied to Africans would be extended to the Indians. By these regulations, immigrants were to be paid the current daily wage of 1/6 for a day's labour of nine hours, or, at the usual rates for job or task work, which brought about 2/– for a good day's work. They were to be given, free of rent, a cottage with garden attached; and they were also to be provided with free medicines and medical attendance. These conditions would have put the immigrants in a far better position than the local people, who had to pay rent and taxes and subscribe towards medical attendance; but in fact the majority of people who applied for immigrant labourers offered money wages of 1/–, or just under, per day.[17] The first Indians arrived at Old Harbour on 9 May 1845. They numbered 261, and were dispatched to estates in Vere and Clarendon whose managers had offered to engage parties of twenty-five immigrants or more at wages not less than 1/– per day of nine hours, with free house, medicines, and medical attendance, and with rice supplied at cost price.[18] They were to remain as labourers under contract for a period of 5 years, at the end of which time they could apply for passage back to India at the expense of the Jamaica Government or, if they preferred, have their return passage commuted into a cash bounty and settle as ordinary residents in the Island.[19]

16. C.O. 137/352, Colonial Office minute on Darling to Newcastle, No. 63, 7 May 1861. See also Cumpston, p. 96.

17. C.O. 137/260, Elgin to Stanley, No. 130, 21 Nov. 1844 (enclosures).

18. C.O. 137/284, Elgin to Stanley, No. 49, 21 May 1845.

19. C.O. 137/315, memo to Sir John Pakington on B. W. I. immigration.

In February of the following year, at the request of the Indians themselves, their pay system was altered and a weekly ration of foodstuffs, prescribed by law, was substituted for part of their money wages. Similar ration scales were also laid down for the African immigrants.[20] There is no reason to suspect that in these first years of imported labour the immigrants were being imposed upon. Lord Elgin was taking a personal interest in the arrangements; Darling, the agent general of immigration, if we can judge from his frequent reports (and there is little else to go by), was careful in his supervision of the scheme and watchful over immigrant welfare.

Meanwhile news from Sierra Leone indicated that the voluntary exodus of free Africans from that country to Jamaica and other places was not likely to continue much longer. The people themselves were not generally inclined to emigrate and, besides, Sierra Leone employers were getting anxious about their own supplies of cheap labour.[21] The dependence on Indians was likely to increase.

At the end of 1845 a Committee of the House of Assembly conducted an enquiry into the condition of the Indian immigrants. They reported to the governor that the new labourers were efficient and of good character; that it appeared likely that many of them would decide to remain in the Island after their period of indenture; and that their presence had a settling effect on the labour market, tending to reduce any local demands by Jamaican workers for wages above the current rates. On the strength of this favourable report the Assembly pledged itself to finance the introduction of 5,000 more Indians in 1846.[22]

There were two advantages expected from immigration, the long-term and the short-term. It was hoped that when their periods of indentured labour were completed, the Africans and

20. C.O. 137/288, Elgin to Gladstone, No. 27, 4 Feb. 1846 (enclosures).
21. C.O. 137/283, Elgin to Stanley, No. 31, 25 March 1845 (enclosures).
22. C.O. 137/285, Elgin to Stanley, No. 6, 19 Nov. 1845.

Indians would decide to accept the settlement bounty and remain in Jamaica, raise families, and so swell the total population. This was the long-term, underlying, and less specific advantage. More to the point in the immediate business of sugar production was the fact that labourers on contract to estates provided a reliable nucleus of labour constantly at the planters' disposal.

The cost of immigration—in shipping, in the upkeep of the Immigration Department, in wages, and in return passages or commutation bounties—was unquestionably high, but it allowed the planters an advantage in a sort of dual labour-cost system. Basically, it was a question of marginal costs, in which the planter compared the amount which he would have to offer to tempt one more local inhabitant to work for him for, say, a year, and the amount in wages and taxes which he would have to pay to secure one imported labourer for the same period. In practice, the calculation would have been something like this: suppose a planter needed 130 labourers but could obtain only 100 at the rate of 1/6 per day and had to offer 2/– a day to tempt the other 30; in order to keep his workers, he would now have to pay them all at the increased rate of 2/– a day, a total daily cost of £13. But if he could get 30 Indians or Africans at a total cost (in wages and taxes) of less than £5 10s. a day, the immigration would be financially worth while. He would continue to pay the 100 local workers at 1/6 each, making £7 10s. a day; he would pay the 30 immigrants at the same rate, making £2 5s. a day, and still have just over £3 a day to spend on all the incidental costs of immigration without equalling the £13 it would cost to keep 130 local labourers.

Behind these paper calculations, however, there were other considerations: the way in which the local people would receive immigrants; the suitability of the immigrants for estate work; and, once the contracts had been signed, the behaviour of the weather, and the trend of prices in Britain.

Of the two main groups of immigrants the Africans presented the lesser problem. Most of them were placed in the eastern end of the island, especially in St. Thomas in the East. Their concentration there followed from the fact that vessels bringing them used to call first at Port Morant for directions.[23]

It must be remembered that in the 1840's there were still many ex-slaves in Jamaica who had been born and spent their youth in West Africa. A young person of, let us say, eighteen years brought over as a slave in 1800 would have still been under sixty in the 1840's. There would have been a great deal of common feeling and understanding between the Jamaican labourers and peasants and the African immigrants, and as the Jamaicans were economically well off, there was small chance of ill-feeling due to competition for employment. The employers also, because of their almost exclusive experience of dealing with labourers of African origin, would have found it easier to establish a working relationship with these people.

Not so with the Indians. These were strange people, speaking a language entirely new to the West Indies. The Jamaican workers, however, appear to have received them kindly, even enthusiastically, and any reluctance to fraternize seems to have come from the Indians. Of course there is a simple economic explanation: the Jamaicans preferred to grow provisions than to do estate labour, and the Indians, as well as all other immigrants brought in for the estates, would enlarge the market for provisions; but economic motives alone seem inadequate to explain the warmth of welcome which was sometimes evinced. Stipendiary Magistrate Hall Pringle, commenting on the Indians recently arrived in Vere in 1845, mentioned "the extreme kind reception they have met with from the Negroes, who have contributed to their comfort both in money and clothes. I sincerely hope this good feeling between them may last, and perhaps it will not, for they appear to have no very high opinion of the Negro."[24] On receipt of this report at the Colonial Office it was remarked that the same friendliness had

23. C.O. 137/306, Sir Charles Grey to Earl Grey, No. 13, 6 Feb. 1850. It may also have been influential that the agent general for immigration owned estates in that parish.

24. C.O. 137/284, report of S.M. Hall Pringle, June 1845.

been shown to the Indians on their arrival in British Guiana.

For the masters it was a different matter, and their main attitudes and problems were nicely stated by Richard Hill of Spanish Town in a letter to the governor.[25] There was, he said, a great lack of understanding, and a Special Magistracy, such as had been instituted immediately after the Emancipation to settle differences between ex-slaves and masters, would have been beneficial in the present circumstances. It is in fact questionable how much good such a panel of magistrates could have done, even if each member of it had been as intelligent and as sympathetic as Hill showed himself to be in this extract from his letter: "the employer who has had no previous conception of the quantity of trifling in Hindoo devotion can see only pretexts for indolence; while the Sirdar submissive himself to the same devotional Offices, perceives a diligent precision on the part of those he is superintending which in his view promises an exactness of character favourable to steadiness of work." But as Hill pointed out, there were more specific problems. The Indian was not always capable of doing the heavy manual labour that was expected of, and had formerly been exacted from, the estate gangs. Nor was he, because of his religious beliefs, always suitable for employment as a carter or herdsman. Above all, there was the matter of expense, for when seasons failed and the crops were poor, the immigrant still had to be supplied with his rations, his accommodation, and, if need be, medical attendance and medicines free of charge. In districts where seasons were unreliable the costs were high; when seasons failed, "it has become an unendurable burden."

Assuming a year of good weather, however—for drought or flood brought other losses besides the money spent on immigrant labour—we can roughly assess what the planters had gained by their use of agricultural implements and imported workers. From the various reports on the use of the plough and the harrow, it is apparent that the labour cost of planting and cultivation per acre was reduced by about 65

25. C.O. 137/296, Sir C. Grey to Earl Grey, No. 26, 6 March 1848 (enclosure).

per cent. One more illustration will make the point. Soon
after his arrival in Jamaica, Lord Elgin calculated that on
Shortwood Estate in St. Andrew, the property of Joseph
Gordon a well-known planter and estate attorney, the use of
the plough and harrow reduced the cost of planting and
cultivating one acre of canes from £6 12s. to £2 3s. 9d.[26]
Indeed, so impressive was the advantage that Captain Dillon,
one of the stipendiary magistrates, proposed in a speech to the
Trelawny Agricultural Society in December 1844 that the
House of Assembly should vote money to finance the purchase
of factory and field equipment rather than the importation of
immigrants. His speech was strongly recommended in an
editorial in the local paper, *The Falmouth Post*.[27] But Trelawny
was one of the better circumstanced parishes as far as the
supply of estate labour was concerned, and Dillon's proposals
did not receive wide support throughout the island.

Immigration schemes continued,[28] and by the end of 1847
there were about 5,000 imported labourers who would have
still been attached to various estates, concentrated where
local labour was least dependably available and where
planters could afford to maintain immigrants in accordance
with the prescribed regulations.

The discussion so far has centred around labour costs per
acre in cultivation, and on the supply of labour for general
year-round employment. The contribution of indentured labour to a solution of the crop-time labour problem was indirect. It is possible that by denying employment to some local
workers during the off season, the immigrants increased the
willingness of these people to accept crop-season employment.
More important, however, was the fact that their presence on
an estate meant that the planter could count on at least a
nucleus of steady labour for the crop-taking. But, unless sufficient local labour was also available, the exclusive application
of immigrants to crop-taking would inevitably lead to neglect
of current cultivation work.

26. Phillippo, *Jamaica: Its Past and Present State*, p. 96.
27. C.O. 137/289, report of S.M. Dillon, June 1846, with enclosures.
28. Full immigration statistics are given in Appendix 3, below.

The intermediary stage of cutting and carting canes, which came between the strictly agricultural and manufacturing processes, was the one which was least influenced by change during our period. There was talk of change, and there were proposals and plans, but these raised technical problems not possible of immediate solution. Thomas Henney, in his prize-winning essay on cane cultivation in 1843, submitted specifications of a cane-cutting machine of his own design. He also wrote of the necessity of careful cutting, for, as he pointed out: "if the cane is not cut even with or below the surface of the ground, the stump left above the surface undergoes fermentation, and particularly in dry weather the root perishes, or the eyes of the Cane which are left above the surface are the first to grow and obtain all the nutriment which is supplied by the earth to the root of the Cane, so that those which are below the surface germinate feebly, if at all. . . ." [29] There is no evidence that Henney tried machine-cutting but experiments were unsuccessfully carried out by another planter, a Mr. Shirley, who owned and managed Hyde Hall Estate in Trelawny.

The carriage of canes to the mill was another matter. Estate roads were notoriously bad and every crop season brought its measure of casualties to cattle and carts. Sometimes, when the rains were heavier than usual, the work was stopped as overladen wains bogged down to their axles in mud, or capsized over deep ruts. The answer, of course, lay in road-building, repair, and maintenance. Alternatively, there was the initially even more expensive possibility of estate railroads. One estimate, made in 1843, put the cost of buying and laying iron rails at 4/6 a foot.[30] But the idea of estate railways was generally advanced in connection with proposals for central factories, and only two estates appear to have been furnished with their own railways during our period: Mr. Shirley's Hyde Hall, and the Messrs. Price's "Worthy Park" in St. John.[31]

29. *Eight Treatises* (above, n. 6).

30. Biggs, *Observations on the Manufacture of Sugar and Rum in Jamaica,* p. 18.

31. Agricola (W. F. Whitehouse), *Letters and Essays,* in which see

There is a great deal of evidence of the awareness of planters that much could and should be done to improve intra-estate roads and transport, but apart from temporary repairs to cartways nothing seems to have been done by the majority. One explanation is that permanent, hard-wearing roads and railways were too expensive to be generally undertaken, especially in view of the estate-labour situation. Another is that planters gave priority to the more pressing demands for reform in agriculture and manufacture.

For the planter, who had to reckon his output in terms of sugar, reduced labour costs per acre of cane were only one, though a very important, aspect of his business. Ultimately, he was concerned with production costs per unit of sugar. Other things being equal, the new system of wider planting meant fewer canes and less sugar yield per acre. The alternative courses were either to extend the area of cane-field or to improve cultivation on the existing, or possibly a reduced, acreage. Basically these represented a choice between the application of more labour, for extension of plant, and the application of more capital, in the purchase of fertilizers and other aids to improved yield on a limited acreage. In the conditions existing in the early 1840's the second course was clearly the more attractive to most planters.

The successful planter of the 1840's, therefore, adopted certain guiding principles in his cultivation: he limited his acreage of cane to the area he felt confident could be harvested; to plant more canes than could be taken to the factory would clearly be wasteful. Secondly, he introduced the plough, the harrow, the wheelbarrow, the pitchfork, and other implements. Thirdly, he attempted to reduce annual planting by putting more emphasis on ratoon cultivation. These were all labour-saving devices. But it was also important to maintain

---

article dated 20 Sept. 1843, and "On the Manufacture of Sugar." C.O. 137/284, report of S.M. Hall Pringle (June 1845); Select Committee of 1848, Minutes of Evidence, 4911. Edward Thompson, custos of Clarendon and owner of Danks Estate, planned to have a railway on that property, but no evidence has been found of its construction.

sugar output, so he followed up the advantages to the soil of ploughing by an improved system of fertilization. Insofar as fertilizers had to be bought and applied there was an increased financial outlay, but the reward of healthier and better-yielding canes was greater.

Examples of the more general and improved use of fertilizers are numerous. In Chapter 1 mention was made of results obtained on Molynes Estate in St. Andrew. There were many other similar reports. David Smith, from whose letter to his brother in England we learn about the Molynes experiment,[32] wrote also of other planters, such as: "John Aris who has by adhereing [*sic*] to a principle he laid down some 5 years ago, of confining his cultivation to the quantity of land, which he could properly manure, made a small fortune out of Enfield Estate, in St. Thomas in the Vale, and which was considered one of the poorest in the district. He has lately bought Bowden in St. Thomas in the East." In his report of December 1845, Stipendiary Magistrate Ewart of St. Thomas in the East told of experiments with guano that were meeting with varying degrees of success.[33] The reports of the following May mentioned the use of guano and other manures at Twickenham Park and the three Caymanas estates in St. Catherine, and on estates in St. Ann.[34]

One of these St. Ann properties, Seville, will serve for a more detailed picture. Soon after the apprenticeship period this estate was yielding about 50 hogsheads of sugar a year and was thought to be a worthless, worn-out property. Then it was taken over by a new manager, Charles Royes, who was later to become custos of the parish. In 1844 the crop was 135 hogsheads; in 1845 an even greater yield was expected, and Royes said that after meeting all expenses the 1844 crop had brought a profit of nearly £1,700 to the owner. He was proud of his successful management but claimed credit for no more than employing "the ordinary modes of

32. C.O. 137/282, 15 July 1844.
33. C.O. 137/287, 15 July 1844.
34. C.O. 137/289, reports of S.M.'s Ramsay and Dillon.

cultivation, and implemental husbandry." He had relied chiefly on the estate's cattle for manure but had also used bone-dust, lime, and ashes.[35]

The new interest in fertilization had followed the general introduction of the plough. By ploughing, the soil was opened up to the air and made more permeable to roots, and the decomposition of vegetable matter in it was hastened. All this increased the nourishment to the canes and improved their appearance and quality. In addition, there was the indirect benefit that ploughing demanded more and better-fed cattle which provided more and better quality manure for use on the estates.

At the same time, the publication in Britain of various works on soil chemistry, particularly those of Professor Liebig of Giessen, and the first importation of guano manure from Peru in 1840, stimulated the interest of West Indians in scientific agriculture. Until then, little attention had been given by Jamaica planters to the condition of the soil. They had been content to apply to the cane-fields only the liquid and solid manures of estate live stock. The methods of application had been simple. The most popular was "fly-penning"— enclosing cattle and other stock on land soon to be planted in canes. The pens or enclosures were formed by temporary fencing that could easily be shifted from place to place.

The alternative to fly-penning was to pen the cattle permanently and employ people to carry the dung to the cane-field. The relative merits of "fly-penning" and "basket-dunging" as the last method was called, were controversial. The fly-penners argued that their method was cheaper and that in any case labourers did not like to carry dung.[36] This was understandable, since where the wheelbarrow was still unintroduced "basket-dunging" meant just what it said. Their opponents claimed that permanent penning kept the cattle safely away from growing crops and that it saved manure because

35. C.O. 137/284, report of S.M. Woodfrys, 1 May 1845.
36. Anonymous writer of one of the *Eight Treatises*. Another anonymous contributor recommended the use of wheelbarrows and gave a rough sketch of one.

only the cane rows were treated.[37] There was reason on each side, and of course the method used was influenced by other factors, such as whether the estate had a mill driven by animal or some other power. If it were animal power, during the crop season mules and cattle would be concentrated around the mill-yard and at least some basket-dunging would be necessary.

But in neither case had the planters given much thought to the building of compost heaps, or to advantages which might be derived from mixing various fertilizers to provide a variety of ingredients to benefit the land. In the 1840's the course indicated by the recent scientific publications was pointed out to them: "having ascertained, first, the constituents of the crop desired; secondly, to ascertain the constituents of the soil in which it is proposed to grow this crop; and, thirdly, to give to the soil such ingredients as, existing in the crop, either do not exist in the soil, or not in sufficient quantities; and lastly, to take care not to incur unnecessary expense, by adding materials in such excessive quantities as cannot possibly be used by the crop." [38]

Generally speaking, cattle manure provided all the necessary constituents for the cane, but not in sufficient quantities. It had, therefore, according to need from place to place, to be supplemented with other fertilizers.[39] Jamaica planters, according to their estimates of needs, set about this in three ways: first, they tried to make better use of estate manure by composting and by more effective application, though controversy still continued between the fly-penners and basket-dungers; secondly, they began to import various fertilizers, especially guano (see Table 5); and thirdly, they attempted to reduce the annual depletion of the soil.

When the canes were cut, it had been the practice to use the top leaves for cattle food. The stalks, when ground, were

37. R. W. Smith, in *Eight Treatises.*

38. P. Lovell Phillips, *An Essay on Tropical Agriculture* (3d ed. Glasgow, 1845), p. 13.

39. Sir H. A. Nicholls, *A Text-Book of Tropical Agriculture,* revised by T. H. Holland (London, 1929), p. 197.

used as fuel for the boilers and coppers in the factory. In short, little of the vegetable matter, except the dry trash taken off during growth, was returned to the soil. In the 1840's

TABLE 5. *Imports of Guano and Other Manures,
and Exports of Jamaica Guano, 1842–65*

Year	Imports			Exports
1842	109 cwts.			—
1843	—			—
1844 *	1,184 tons	2 cwts.		—
1845	1,509 tons	18 cwts.	65 hhds.	—
1846	7,950 tons	3 cwts.		—
1847	1,009 tons			—
1848	223 tons			—
1849	98 tons			—
1850	99 tons	6 cwts.		—
1851	155 tons	10 cwts.		—
1852 *	108 tons			—
1853	100 tons			—
1854 *	119 tons	5 cwts.		—
1855 *	568 tons			—
1856 *	928 tons			335 tons
1857 *	623 tons	5 cwts.		235 tons
1858	893 tons	5 cwts.		720 tons
1859	1,831 tons	61 hhds.	120 bags	—
1860	1,370 tons			—
1861	546 tons	5 cwts.		—
1862 *	893 tons	12 cwts.		—
1863 *	583 tons			40 tons 1 barrel
1864 *	764 tons			353 cwts.
1865 *	512 tons			160 tons

* Imports in these years included manures other than natural or manufactured guanos. For an explanation of the Export column see Chapter 3.

Source: Jamaica Blue Books.

several writers argued that although coal cost about 20/- a ton—excluding 6*d.* per ton per mile transport charge in the Island [40]—it would be advantageous to use coal or local timber for fuel and return the bagasse mixed with animal manure to

40. Biggs, p. 11.

the soil.[41] It is unlikely, however, that estates in the interior districts would have found this proposal profitable. Although the estates were certainly not the only users of coal in the Island, the increasing imports shown in Table 6 probably re-

TABLE 6. *Imports of Coal to Jamaica, 1849–65*

Year	Quantity		Year	Quantity	
1849	456	tons	1858	5,794	tons
1850	3,240½	"	1859	5,037½	"
1851	7,776	"	1860	4,612½	"
1852	8,479	"	1861	23,633	"
1853	8,861½	"	1862	19,776	"
1854	—	"	1863	18,130	"
1855	1,525	"	1864	34,107¼	"
1856	2,797	"	1865	33,886	"
1857	12,710½	"			

Source: Jamaica Blue Books.

NOTE. Imports before 1849 are not recorded although there must have been some coming in for the use of steamers and for the Jamaica Railway.

flect the new use, by some planters, of bagasse as a fertilizer, and also an expanding demand for fuel on estates which were converting their mills from animal, wind, or water power, to steam.

The interest in fertilization was very closely associated with the planters' attempts to reduce planting and increase and improve ratoon cultivation. According to the number of successive years of ratooning, canes grown in this way were known as first, second, or third ratoons, and so on, all of which were distinguished from the freshly put in "plant" canes. Ratoons matured in a shorter time than plants, so that ratoons allowed to develop from the roots of canes cut, say, in February 1841 would be ready, along with the plants established in the fall of 1840, for harvesting in the beginning of 1842.

41. For example, Fyfe, *Suggestions for . . . Establishing a Central Sugar Factory*, p. 8; W. F. Whitehouse, in *Eight Treatises;* Wray, *The Practical Sugar Planter*, ch. 3; and W. J. Evans, *The Sugar Planter's Manual* (London, 1847), p. 87.

The advantage of ratooning was, of course, that it saved the expense of fresh planting. The cost of cultivating an acre of ratoons was approximately one-fourth the cost of cultivating an acre of plants,[42] and the yield of sugar from an acre of ratoons was not necessarily much less than the yield from plants—provided that the ratoons were not too old or in poor condition. But the best ratoon soil was light and dry. Generally speaking, therefore, the north-east estates were high-cost estates, and as we shall see later, the Portland estates were rapidly abandoned during the 1840's.

Discussion, and adoption, of improved agricultural methods interested not only the few irrepressible enthusiasts such as Whitehouse, but the body of planters generally and the Island and parochial agricultural societies, organizations which, in turn, encouraged the planters: "The properties, and the nature of the growth of Plants, and the diseases, incident to them, all useful fields of enquiry for the practical farmer, all these are no longer neglected."[43] In June 1846, Stipendiary Magistrate Dillon summed up the factors which he thought had helped to improve production on the St. Ann estates. He wrote of the increasing use of machinery; the better system of wide planting; the use of imported manures such as guano and bone-dust; the improved use of home manures such as cattle dung, lime, ashes, seaweed, and ratbat dung; and: "a manifest desire of those interested in the management of Estates to increase their crops, not by extending their fields but by a better system of cultivation."[44]

These changes were not limited to Dillon's parish. The coming of the plough into general use, together with the condition of labour shortage and the new emphasis on soil fertilization, led to an intensification of agricultural method. There must be no confusion about this. The system of wider planting which was concurrently adopted did not mean an

42. J. Biggs, "On the Establishment of Central Sugar Works in the British Sugar Colonies," *The Colonial Magazine, 16,* Jan. 1849. C.O. 137/257, report of S.M. Brown, 14 Oct. 1841.

43. C.O. 137/284, report of S.M. Hall Pringle, 1 June 1845.

44. C.O. 137/289, Dillon's report of June 1846.

extension of the total area under canes. Thick planting, as practised in slavery, had given more canes of poorer quality. This had meant more labour in pruning, replanting, trashing, cutting, and manufacture, to obtain a given quantity of sugar. In slavery, first-class ratoons in Trelawny were proudly stated to yield 11.2 hundredweights of sugar per acre.[45] In 1848, first-class ratoons on a St. Catherine estate were said to give from 13.5 to 18 hundredweights of sugar per acre.[46] But local variations tend to invalidate such a comparison. In slavery, it had been estimated that 300 acres of suitable land in canes would give an average annual yield of 3,200 hundredweights of sugar—that is 10.66 hundredweights per acre.[47] In the 1840's the average yield for the island as a whole was said to be 16 hundredweights of sugar per acre.[48] The best illustration, perhaps, is in Table 7, which deals with a single estate over a period of twelve years. The Estate, Montpelier, in St. James, was regarded by its proprietor, Lord Howard de Walden, to contain only average quality sugar soil, certainly less productive than Ellis Caymanas in St. Catherine, of which he was part owner.[49] The table illustrates the reduced scale of planting after full emancipation in 1838, and the slight but noticeable improvement after 1841 in crop yields from a still reduced acreage. The hogshead measurement must be assumed to have been the 18 hundredweights hogshead commonly used in Jamaica in the 1840's, though it is possible, and the yield figures would support this, that Montpelier, an inland estate, used smaller hogsheads which were easier to transport.

Clearly enough, however, the quantity of sugar produced per acre involved manufacturing as well as agricultural techniques. The canes themselves might be juicier, and their sugar content increased, but unless the extractive processes

45. B. Edwards, *The History, Civil and Commercial, of the British West Indies* (5th ed. 5 vols. London, 1819), 2, 245.

46. Select Committee of 1848, Minutes of Evidence, 4598.

47. Edwards, 2, 290.

48. Biggs, "On the Establishment of Central Sugar Works."

49. Select Committee of 1848, Minutes of Evidence, 4480, 4596. Also see Biggs (previous note).

were adequate and efficient the sugar yield might still fall
short of the possible maximum.

Assuming that the planter found sufficient labour to cut the
canes, transport them to the factory, and carry out the manufacturing processes, there still remained the need for maxi-

TABLE 7. *Statement of Cane Field and Sugar Shipped from
Montpelier Estate, 1836–47*

Year	Acres in Canes	Crop Actually Shipped	Average Yield per Acre of Crop Shipped
1836	339	303 hhds.	0.88 hhds.
1837	382	171 "	0.45 "
1838	382	172 "	0.45 "
1839	212	76 "	0.36 "
1840	200	55 "	0.27 "
1841	171	149 "	0.81 "
1842	202	168 "	0.83 "
1843	236	142 "	0.60 "
1844	204	175 "	0.86 "
1845	201	150 "	0.75 "
1846	205	200 "	0.97 "
1847	225	275 "	1.22 "

Source: Select Committee, 1848, Minutes of Evidence, 4425–34.

NOTE. Although these figures are unquestionably useful it must be
borne in mind that they do *not* show any quantities of sugar which might
have been sold in the island. Nor can we assume that shipments in any
one year did not include produce carried over from the previous year in
storage.

mum extraction of sugar. There were two main sources of
loss in the factory: the waste of cane-juice, and the loss of
sugar by inefficient methods of boiling and curing. Changes
were necessary both at the mill and in the boiling- and curing-
houses.

The inefficiencies of the old mills arose out of several de-
fects. Where vertical mills were used, the canes had to be fed
into the lower part of the rollers rather than evenly along their
whole length. This put unequal stress on the machinery and
tended to move its parts out of proper alignment. If special

attempts were made to feed canes into the upper part of the rollers, much of the juice was lost as it trickled down the machinery and away from the conveyors leading to the siphons. Another and more general reason for inadequate grinding was that the mill power was simply not enough to exert the required pressure, and even the new steam mills continued deficient, though less so, in this respect.

The use of steam was no new thing in Jamaica. We are told, in fact, that John Stewart, a millwright on a sugar estate, was "the first to apply steam power to the operation of machinery in a manufacturing process." In 1768 he had invented a steam-driven sugar mill which he had built in England, and in 1770 it was put up on "Greenwich plantation in the Parish of St. Andrews" and appears to have given satisfactory service. There are a few records of other steam mills in Jamaica before 1800, but little evidence to show that any of them was successful.

These early experiments apart, the general use of steam in Jamaica may be said to have commenced in the first half of the nineteenth century. Between 1803 and 1852 Boulton and Watt of Birmingham exported 146 sugar-mill engines, of which fifty-six went to Jamaica. They were not the only suppliers. The first engine went in 1808 to an unspecified estate belonging to Sir Alexander Grant. In 1813 one was erected at Moneymusk in Vere, then the property of the Marquis of Sligo.[50]

It does not appear that the small steam-powered mill had any great advantages over a well-built water mill where the flow of water was dependable. Both these types were immeasurably superior to wind mills and far better than animal mills. When crop-taking was in progress and canes were arriving at the factory, they had to be ground within a few hours before the juice began to ferment. The wind was a

50. N. Deerr and A. Brooks, "The Early Use of Steam Power in the Cane Sugar Industry," excerpt from the *Transactions of the Newcomen Society, 21,* 1940–41. It appears that the documents are not sufficiently precise to allow a search for any remains of the first steam-mill, and it would seem that no one has stumbled accidentally across them.

capricious source of power which often failed the planter in
the course of his manufacturing operations, thus causing loss
of canes, fuel, labour, and time. Moreover, as the mill had to
be sited in the most convenient position to catch the wind,
it often led to a wasteful increase of distances between cane-
fields, mill-yard, boiling-house, and other estate buildings.
The cattle mill did not have this disadvantage but it made
heavy demands on livestock and even at its best was inferior
to a good water mill.

By 1854, as Table 8 shows, just over two-thirds of all sugar
mills in the island were driven by steam or water, and just
under one-third by steam. This is clear evidence of widespread attempts to improve manufacturing methods. Yet, as
the table also shows, steam power alone was by no means the
answer. No doubt it had its advantages. The figures for Westmoreland and Hanover indicate the superiority of water and
steam over wind and cattle. The figures for Vere, St. Dorothy,
and St. Catherine suggest, in the average production column,
a kind of healthy conformity in the performance of steam
mills. But in St. Thomas in the East, Metcalfe, and Westmoreland, the water mill was apparently holding its own.

It is relevant to point out, however, that these three are
river delta areas with abundant water power and first-class
sugar soils.

The essential point would seem to be that the early steam
mill, though an improvement, produced no revolutionary advance in the process of extracting the juice from the cane. This
is well borne out by a comparison between two statements
on the subject. The first was made by Bryan Edwards in the
late eighteenth century:

> A cattle or mule-mill on the old model was thought to
> perform exceedingly well if it passed sufficient canes in
> an hour to yield from 300 to 350 gallons of juice. The
> common return of [a new design of cattle mill, late
> eighteenth-century] is from 4 to 500 gallons. I have
> authority to say, that one of these mills in particular,
> which is worked with ten mules, produces hourly 500
> gallons: at this rate, allowing four hours out of the twenty-

four for loss of time, the return per diem is 10,000 gallons; being equal to 36 hogsheads of sugar of 16 cwt. for every week during the crop, exclusive of Sundays. Few water-mills can exceed this.[51]

TABLE 8. *Mills, Mill Power, and Average Production per Estate, 1854*

| PARISHES | TYPES OF MILL POWER | | | | TYPES OF ROLLERS | | AVERAGE Production per Estate |
	No. of Estates	Wind or Cattle	Water	Steam	Ver- tical	Hori- zontal	in Cwts.
Westmoreland	34	7	14	13	18	16	2,196
Hanover	34	16	4	14	18	16	1,044
St. Elizabeth	12	2	9	1	10	2	1,278
St. James	41	15	14	12	26	15	1,440
Trelawny	55	31	7	17	33	22	1,764
St. Ann	18	7	10	1	13	5	1,962
Clarendon	17	1	11	5	12	5	1,656
Vere	22	1	0	21	1	21	1,800
St. Dorothy	5	0	0	5	0	5	1,800
St. Catherine	3	0	0	3	0	3	1,980
St. John	6	2	3	1	4	2	1,746
St. Thomas in the Vale	12	6	4	2	10	2	1,350
St. Mary	21	2	16	3	13	8	1,674
Metcalfe	14	3	7	4	9	5	2,196
St. George	4	1	3	0	4	0	1,854
St. Andrew	5	0	4	1	3	2	1,188
St. David	3	0	2	1	2	1	1,260
St. Thomas in the East	21	2	15	4	11	10	2,934
Portland	3	1	2	0	3	0	486
SUMMARY	330	97	125	108	190	140	1,728

Source: C.O. 137/330, report of Richard Hill (1856).

NOTE. Of a total 216 estates in 1879, 160 had mills driven wholly or partly by steam-power (see *Handbook of Jamaica,* 1861).

When discussing the establishment of a sugar estate, Bryan Edwards remarked that the planter should have, if possible, a

51. Edwards, 2, 262 n.

water mill; if not, one wind and one cattle mill, or two cattle mills.[52]

The second statement was made in 1843 by John Biggs, an engineer resident in Jamaica:

> An 8 horse-power steam-engine, with a properly proportioned mill and average canes, is capable of grinding, if on the high-pressure principle, with steam at a pressure of 35 pounds on the square inch, 550 gallons of liquor per hour, which, working 12 hours per day, is $550 \times 12 = 6600$ gallons; allowing the yielding to average 1800 gallons to make a hogshead of sugar equal to 18 cwt. $6600 \div 1800 = 3 \frac{2}{3}$rd hogsheads of sugar per day, or 18 hogsheads $\frac{1}{3}$rd per week of 5 days, which might be effected during the crop, if all hands were employed cutting and carting canes on Monday, and the steam got up at daylight on Tuesday morning.[53]

Comparing the two statements the striking difference is not the output of liquor from the mill per hour, but rather the fewer working hours per week in time of freedom. Another, less obvious, difference is the reduced quantity of juice required to give a hundredweight of sugar. In Table 9 Bryan Edwards' figures for the improved-model mule mill are used to show not only the technical improvements achieved by 1843, but also the potential advantages which could not be achieved because of the shortage of labour that prevented the full use of capital equipment.

Had it been possible for the planter to keep his steam mill in action for the full twenty-four hours a day (Bryan Edwards' loss of four hours probably resulted from the need to relay the mules at the mill), he could have taken a far larger crop and

52. He was referring to the old-model cattle mills.

53. Biggs, *Observations on the Manufacture of Sugar and Rum*, p. 2. It is interesting to compare these statements with an extract from an account of Frome Estate in Westmoreland (the same area in which John Biggs spent most of his time) as it is today: "The mills (5 of them) are driven by two horizontal single cylinder steam engines, operating under a pressure of one hundred and fifty horsepower each." See *The West Indian Review* (Kingston, 5 July 1952), pp. 20–22.

produced about twice as much sugar as the labour shortage did in fact allow him to make. On the other hand, the greater power of the steam mill, a slightly improved cane quality, and improved methods of boiling and curing did bring some benefit. Using Bryan Edwards' canes and mill power with the shorter working hours of 1843, the planter could have produced only 288½ hundredweights per week instead of the 330 hundredweights which the improvements allowed him.

TABLE 9. *Cattle Mill Output and Sugar Yield about 1800, with Actual and Potential Figures of the Same for a Steam Mill in 1843*

MILL OUTPUT OF JUICE (galls.)

	per Hour	per Day (20 hours)	per Day (12 hours)	per Week (6 days)	per Week (5 days)	Yield of Sugar per Week (cwts.)	Gallons Juice to give 1 cwt. Sugar
Cattle (ca. 1800)	500	10,000	—	60,000	—	576	104
Steam, actual (1843)	550	—	6,600	—	33,000	330	100
Steam, potentential (1843)	550	11,000	—	66,000	—	660	100

In the boiling-house, interest, stimulated by the publications of chemists and sugar refiners in Britain,[54] centred around the various methods of clarification and filtration, the effects of heat on the cane-liquor, and the presence of impurities in the manufactured article. Of these, the controversies about the use of defecators—that is, the substances added to the juice in the clarifiers—are too specialized to detain us. The basic problem was that cane-juice refuses to crystallize until it is free of most impurities, and research was largely concerned with attempts to discover the most efficient means of removing such impurities. Various new methods of filtration were suggested and applied; but as far as the defecator itself is concerned, it is enough to say that although there have been improvements in the method of application,

54. For example, J. Scoffern, *On the Manufacture of Sugar*, London, 1849; and Evans, *The Sugar Planter's Manual*.

the commonly employed substance was then and still is milk of lime. The question of heat must be given fuller attention, and here the main point is that the chemists showed that heat was destructive to sugar, that "to produce brown sugar at all, is an evidence of bad manufacture," and that a great deal of produce was ruined in the actual process of manufacture. Muscovado (unrefined) sugar was wet because it was not properly drained of syrup, which was in fact uncrystallized sugar; and it was dark in colour because it contained impurities, the chief of which was burnt sugar. Wet, brown, raw sugar, therefore, was the product of an inefficient manufacturing process in which some of the produce was burnt and a great deal of it actually unprocessed.[55]

It was the work of the engineers to produce factory equipment which would, as nearly as possible, satisfy the theoretical demands of the chemists. This came in improvements of the size, shape, and alignment of the boilers, in methods of heating, in methods of juice and syrup conveyance, and in the vacuum pan and centrifugal drier.[56]

The vacuum pan, as its name implies, allowed the evaporation process to be carried on at a lower temperature by means of a reduction of pressure on the juice being evaporated. The centrifugal drier was designed to remove the molasses from muscovado sugar by the system of centrifugal rotation. Rapid rotation threw the wet sugar against the perforated walls of the container, thus sending the molasses through the perforations while the dry sugar remained in the centrifugal. The machine was efficient but it needed abundant motive power, which often was not available on the estates. An alternative method of drying, therefore, was proposed in the vacuum chest. This was a very large receptacle covered at the top with an inset tray of fine wire mesh on which the wet sugar was heaped. In a bottom corner of the receptacle there

55. Evans, *The Sugar Planter's Manual*, pp. 192 ff., 214.

56. W. Reed, *The History of Sugar and Sugar Yielding Plants* (London, 1866), pp. 83, 92, 93. N. Lubbock, paper on diffusion, as Supplement to *W.I.C. Circular, 1*, No. 9, Jan. 1887. Evans, *The Sugar Planter's Manual*, p. 146. Scoffern, *On the Manufacture of Sugar*.

was a valve connected to a suction pump which, when in operation, caused a strong current of air to pass through the sugar down into the receptacle. This air current speeded the drip of molasses from the sugar through the wire mesh, leaving dry sugar on the tray.

The new boiling-house equipment was not widely introduced in Jamaica during this period. As late as 1854, Governor Barkly observed that Jamaica planters had only just begun to show an interest in better sugar machinery and that the reduced scale of planting was not conducive to the introduction of expensive apparatus. The vacuum pan, for example, was so costly that even in British Guiana, where it had been in use for twenty-five years, it was thought unwise to install it on estates making less than 500 hogsheads of sugar a year. In Jamaica, at the time, only about three estates were producing that quantity. Jamaicans, in fact, were even reluctant to invest in cheaper substitutes for the vacuum pan (such as Gaddesden and Evans', or Schroeder's, disc pans). The unreliability of the labour supply, said the Governor, was the root cause of the lack of confidence.[57]

The dilemma of the Jamaica planter can be put briefly. Labour was scarce, dear, and unreliable. Therefore, he reduced his cane acreage and attempted to produce more sugar per acre. Moreover, because of his ultimate concern with cost per unit of sugar manufactured, he strove to improve his factory as well as his fields. But because there was little chance that new, more efficient, and very expensive equipment would be fully utilized, the planter, even if he had the capital, hesitated.

In 1843 John Biggs had remarked that proprietors who installed steam-engines were often disappointed, either because they had not proportionately increased the capacity of their boiling-house equipment, or because they had not a sufficient supply of canes for the mill.[58] But as we have seen,

57. C.O. 137/323, Barkly to Newcastle, No. 73, 26 May 1854. According to N. P. Burgh, *A Treatise on Sugar Machinery* (London, 1863), pp. 51–53, a nine-foot copper vacuum pan cost £ 1,000 in England.

58. Biggs, *Observations on the Manufacture of Sugar and Rum in Jamaica,* p. 1.

it was lack of cane supply that made planters reluctant to install improved boiling-house equipment.

In 1848 Lord Howard de Walden compared Ellis Caymanas, which was yielding an average annual net profit of £725, with Montpelier, which was showing an average annual net loss of £250:

> On the Caymanas estate we have had to contend only with high wages; and in keeping up the cultivation of the estate the proportion of loss was only affected by the rate of wages; whereas on the other estate, that being a larger estate, and much more expensive, the present cane-field not being proportioned to the establishment, of course the expenses were proportionately too great. The establishment was calculated for an estate producing from 400 to 500 hogsheads of sugar; and in order to yield a profit upon such an establishment, you must have an extensive canefield.[59]

Again it is the problem of labour to take the crop. The planter's estimate of his optimum scale of operations therefore had to be based not on the capacity of his land and capital equipment but on the number of people with machetes who would work for him during the crop season. In the agricultural side of production the problem could be met because there the units of equipment were small and relatively cheap. A planter would buy only that number of ploughs, harrows, and so on that he needed to cultivate the acreage which could be harvested. If the labour supply improved, a few more implements could be purchased. But in the factory it was a different matter. Improved machinery was often necessary; but it was expensive, and it combined greater efficiency with greater capacity. On a reduced harvest the economies of large-scale manufacture could not be realized.

By 1846 proposals were being put forward in an attempt to overcome this problem. If the individual estate could not profitably support improved machinery, there was no apparent

59. Select Committee of 1848, Minutes of Evidence, Lord Howard de Walden.

reason why a large and highly efficient factory should not serve a number of estates. Early in that year a very detailed prospectus for a Metcalfe Central Sugar Factory and Timber Company to be sited at Annotto Bay was issued by Alexander Fyfe, a stipendiary magistrate.[60] His plan consisted of the establishment of two completely up-to-date factories, each capable of producing eight tons of vacuum-pan sugar per day of twelve hours. The company would undertake to carry canes, make sugar, and cask and ship it at an inclusive charge of £10 a ton. It would be connected to surrounding estates by its own tramroads. It would burn timber from its own woodlands and use the cane trash from the mills in the manufacture of fertilizer. It would maintain horses and agricultural equipment to be hired out to estates at a fixed charge per acre. It would erect a saw mill to produce local lumber products to reduce imports. It might even, eventually, erect its own sugar refinery. The two main advantages to estate-owners would be that the division of labour would allow them to concentrate on agricultural improvements, and that the first-class equipment of the central factory would produce more and better quality sugar than the estates could do on their own resources. The benefit to the factory owners would be that when everything was going smoothly the centrals would be able to make sugar at a cost of about £5 a ton. Fyfe was ready to admit that this would leave a very high margin of profit; but he said that he wanted to begin on the safe side, since so much capital would be involved, and he offered half the shares in the company to local sugar-estate owners, "so that they may derive one-half of the profits which they themselves will furnish."

The cost would be high. Machinery for the two factories would cost £20,000 delivered on board in an English port. Freight, duties, buildings, the installation of plant, and the laying down of 32 miles of tramway would cost £60,000. The purchase of land, live stock, and agricultural implements for

60. Fyfe, *Suggestions* (above, n. 3). C.O. 137/292, Sir Charles Grey to Earl Grey, No. 44, 15 May 1847. C.O. 137/294, J. A. Gordon to Earl Grey (various dates in 1847).

the hiring scheme would be £20,000 more. The sum wanted for all this would be £100,000.

It was not until early 1847 that the Jamaica Legislature passed an act giving statutory recognition to the scheme and enabling "Alexander Gordon Fyfe and James Adam Gordon" to raise capital not exceeding £300,000 in shares of £50 each, and to carry out the project. Although Fyfe had received letters of encouragement from many prominent people in Jamaica, including planters and merchants, the governor, when forwarding the act to the Colonial Office for the Royal Assent, commented that he doubted whether the capital would be forthcoming in Jamaica. Even before the 1846 act it had not been easy to raise large sums in the Island, and, as always in the sugar industry, much of the financial support would have had to come from proprietors and merchants in Britain. It would appear that this had been Fyfe's reason for associating James Gordon, who lived in England, with the plan; but it seems that he had done so without securing the gentleman's support. During the course of 1847 Gordon corresponded with the secretary of state for the colonies, saying that he had given Fyfe no authority to use his name. Chiefly for that reason the act was disallowed.

In the same year Thomas Jelly of Westmoreland wrote: "Westmoreland within the last four years has done much, not only in her canefields, but in efforts at improved manufacture; larger boilers have been imported, furnaces on an improved scale constructed, and other minor adjuncts employed. She has much yet to undergo, viz., to get rid of her manufactories altogether, and learn how to subdivide, and thereby economise labour." [61] Jelly did not actually sponsor any particular scheme for a central factory, he simply put forward arguments to show how greatly his parish would benefit from centralization in manufacture. There were some estates, still using cattle or water power for their mills, on which cultivation could be extended; there was also good land which needed only to be drained, so that it could be planted in canes to support com-

61. T. Jelly, *A Brief Enquiry into the Condition of Jamaica* (London, 1847), p. 53.

paratively huge central factories. Centralization, by reducing the demand for factory labour, would tend to make more labour available for field work, and it would also allow the planter to specialize in the agricultural side of the industry.

Jelly suggested the establishment of several central factories, each at a strategic point in relation to the position of neighbouring sugar estates; the drainage of an area of 10,000 acres which could be planted; the dredging of the Cabaritta River as far up as Belleisle to allow the passage of "iron boats of 15 tons"; and the building of a wharf on that property to serve the produce of at least a dozen surrounding estates, including Frome. Similarly, other central factories were to be connected to the coast by road, river, or railway. The plan encompassed the whole Westmoreland valley from New Galloway estate to Negril Point, an area of over 100,000 acres on which there were forty sugar estates. The basis of the arguments about land and labour was that of this total acreage only about 6,000 acres were in cane, because of a deficiency of factory capacity or a deficiency of labour. The one would be remedied directly by the building of centrals, the other indirectly. John Biggs, the engineer, calculated that a single large factory capable of taking the crops of all the existing forty estates would need the services of 120 to 160 workers for three months. Under the current system, each estate employed about thirty-seven extra hands about the works for five months every year. Taking a twenty-day month as normal, the central factory would mean a saving of over 138,000 man days per crop year.

Following Jelly's arguments, a group of Westmoreland planters did actually set about to form a central works company, but failed to raise the estimated £40,000 for the project.

The interesting features of these proposals were their relative magnitude—their relation to the sugar district or area as distinct from the individual estate. Moreover, the very considerable saving of factory labour during crop, to be realized by the use of centrals, would probably have allowed the planters to extend their cane-fields.

But capital development on such a large scale demanded steady prices for the industry's products, and confidence among both planters and prospective creditors. The Sugar Duties Act of 1846, especially coming as it did in a time of commercial crisis in Britain, affected both prices and confidence in such a way as to render these proposals impracticable.

CHAPTER 3

Panic and Recovery

EVEN BEFORE the Act of 1846 it had become obvious that many estates could not hope to continue in production. The reasons behind the failures after emancipation have already been suggested. Hill-side estates, or those in the interior, could hardly survive. Respectively, they suffered from inability to introduce the plough and from high costs of transport to and from the wharves, which increased the prices of equipment and various estate supplies as well as the costs of sending produce for shipment.[1]

Disaster could also come from consistent over-planting beyond the possibility of harvesting; or, contrarily, under-planting when the labour supply for crop-taking was underestimated. Those planters, too, who did not, or could not, give greater attention and emphasis to ratoon cultivation found that labour costs of planting were too burdensome, or that sufficient labour was not always forthcoming.

Poor factory equipment, too heavy expenditure on more efficient new machinery, or heavy financial encumbrance in the form of debts or of fixed annual disbursements to claimants on the profits of the estate—these were all sources of failure.

It is worthwhile to review the situation statistically over a long period to show that estate abandonment was no new thing brought on by the events of the 1840's. Unfortunately, the records do not supply all the details we should like to see, such as the actual area of land under cane at different times, but they give a fairly useful picture (see Table 10).

1. In the very rich interior valleys, however, it generally required a combination of disadvantages to put an estate out of production.

A decline in the number of estates did not necessarily lead to a fall in the total output of sugar, for those remaining might increase their production. In fact, in the post-emancipation

TABLE 10. *Decline in the Number of Sugar Estates in Various Parishes, 1772–1854*

Parishes	1772	1791	1804	1834	1844	1848	1854
Westmoreland	73	66	68	48	48	46	34
Hanover	75	79	84	71	70	60	34
St. Elizabeth	32	23	27	17	20	12	12
St. James ⎫			90	80	74	62	41
⎬ 164	173						
Trelawny ⎭			94	76	86	68	55
St. Ann	32	31	41	30	32	22	18
Clarendon ⎫			62	40	41	23	17
⎬ 58	59						
Manchester ⎭			0	0	0	0	0
Vere	27	29	29	29	29	27	22
St. Dorothy	12	15	18	11	10	10	5
St. Catherine	6	4	11	5	5	5	3
St. John	20	19	23	11	10	9	6
St. Thomas in the Vale	36	33	46	23	24	23	12
St. Mary ⎫							
Metcalfe ⎬	83	87	95	86	79	59	39
St. George ⎭							
St. Andrew	25	24	24	14	18	5	5
Port Royal	4	3	4	3	3	2	0
St. David	12	13	16	10	10	8	3
St. Thomas in the East	90	85	94	67	61	54	21
Portland	26	24	33	25	24	13	3
TOTALS	775	767	859	646	644	508	330

Sources: 1772 and 1791—B. Edwards, *The History of the British West Indies* (5th ed. 1819), *1*, 312–14. *1804, 1834, and 1854*—C.O. 137/330, report of Richard Hill (1856). *1844*—Jamaica Census. *1848*—by subtracting the number of estates abandoned 1832–48 from estates existing in 1834, thus slightly inaccurate. The total number of estates in 1848 was 513. See N. Deerr, *History of Sugar, 1*, 174–77.

NOTE. It is impossible to claim exact accuracy for these figures, especially for the earlier years, but their indication of main trends is useful.

period the labour shortage did curtail production, at least temporarily, in most of the West Indian colonies.

At the same time, the sugar output of other British possessions and of foreign sugar production was rapidly increasing, so that in 1850, the West Indians produced only about one-ninth of the world's sugar, as against nearly one-half in 1828 (Table 11).

TABLE 11. *World Production of Sugar, 1828 and 1850 (cwts.)*

Output in 1828	Source	Output in 1850
4,210,000	British West Indies	2,590,000
(1,363,960)	(of which, Jamaica)	(592,487)
516,000	Other British Producers	2,200,000
1,300,000	Cuba & Puerto Rico	5,920,000
560,000	Brazil	2,200,000
400,000	Louisiana	2,480,000
1,700,000	Other Foreign Producers	5,260,000
140,000	European BEET Sugar	3,800,000
8,826,000	TOTALS	24,450,000

Sources: (1) J. Davy, *The West Indies before and since Emancipation* (London, 1854), pp. 31–32. (2) The Jamaica figures: *1828*, N. Deerr, *History of Sugar, 1*, 198; *1850*, Jamaica Blue Book. (3) The total B.W.I. figure for 1850: statistical returns to Parliament.

NOTE: As Table 13 shows, the 1820's seem to have been a good crop period for the B.W.I. and a poor one for other producers. The contrast illustrated above is, thus, somewhat exaggerated.

These changes in the pattern of production, coming chiefly in the later 1830's and the following decade, at a time when the policy of free trade was gaining strength in Britain, encouraged the British Government gradually to abandon the principle of protection to colonial sugar production.

Changes in the sugar duties, which first of all in 1826 and 1836 had removed protection to the West Indies against other British producers,[2] and then, in the 1840's, whittled down protection to British as against foreign producers, encouraged

2. Mauritian and British East Indian, respectively.

the entry of competitors into the British market and altered the pattern of British sugar imports (Table 12). The non-West Indian and, even more, the foreign producer came to play an

TABLE 12. *Duties on Sugars Entering Britain, 1840–65 (per cwt.)*

Dates	British Colonial Muscovado		Foreign Muscovado			All Refined Sugars
1840	25/2		66/1¾			168/4
1841	25/2		66/1¾			176/5
1844			*Free-Grown*	*Slave-Grown*		
(Nov. 10)	25/2		35/8½	66/1¾		176/5
1845	*e.w.c.*	*n.e.w.c.*	*e.w.c.*	*n.e.w.c.*		
(March 15)	16/4	14/–	28/–	23/4	63/–	166/–
1846			*Foreign Muscovado*			
			e.w.c.	*n.e.w.c.*	*e.d.r.*	*n.e.d.r.*
(Aug. 18)	16/4	14/–	24/6	21/–	31/6	28/–
1847						
(July 5)	16/4	14/–	23/4	20/–	30/–	26/8

July 1847–July 1854: annual decreases until the discrimination ended.
All Sugars Entering Britain

	n.e.b.c.	*n.e.w.c.*	*e.w.c.*	*Refined*
1854				
(July 5)	11/–	12/–	14/–	17/4

July 1854–April 1857: slight increases to help finance the Crimean War. In 1857 reductions begin.

	n.e.b.c.	*n.e.w.c.*	*e.w.c.*	*Refined*
1857				
(April 16)	12/8	13/10	16/–	18/4

	n.e.b.m.	*e.b.m*	*n.e.w.c.*	*e.w.c.*	*Refined*
1864					
(April 16)	8/2	9/4	10/6	11/8	12/10

Source: N. Deerr, *History of Sugar*, 2, ch. 27, gives history of the sugar duties.

NOTES. e.w.c. = white-clayed
e.b.c. = brown-clayed
e.b.m. = brown-muscovado
e.d.r. = double-refined
n. = Not

All Jamaica exports would have come under the classifications n.e.w.c., e.b.m., n.e.b.c., and n.e.b.m.

increasingly important part in the once lucrative preserve of the West Indians (Table 13).

The activities of the Jamaica planters in the post-emancipation years had been stimulated primarily by labour shortage, but they also reflected a growing awareness that the industry

must be made competitive. Without a reasonable assurance of
profit, the capital needed to finance the reorganization of
production would not be forthcoming.

By far the greatest part of the sugar produced in Jamaica
was consigned by the planters to merchants or commission

TABLE 13. *Annual Averages over Decennial Periods of Sugar
Imports into Britain, 1800–63 (cwts.)*

Years	B.W.I.	Mauritius and Brit. East Indies		Foreign	Total
1801–10	3,600,000	76,000		260,000	3,950,000
1811–20	3,700,000	123,000		230,000	4,050,000
1821–30	3,900,000	680,000		185,000	4,400,000
		Mauritius	B.E.I.		
1831–40	3,400,000	550,000	240,000	480,000	4,700,000
1841–50	2,300,000	790,000	1,250,000	1,260,000	6,000,000
1851–60	3,140,000	1,200,000	1,100,000	2,670,000	8,200,000
1861–63 *	3,400,000	1,200,000	500,000	4,600,000	10,000,000

* Three years only.

Source: L. Levi, *On the Sugar Trade and Sugar Duties*, London, 1864.
The figures are obviously very rough approximations.

agents in Britain, who arranged the marketing of it. Proceeds
of sales did not all accrue to the planter. First, the agent deducted his advances for customs duties, freight, landing, and
marketing, together with interest and commission. Then he
deducted the cost, with interest, of such supplies as he had
shipped to the planter in advance of the crop to be received.
Also, there were the claims of other creditors, mortgagees, and
various others, such as those who had been granted perpetual
annuities by wealthy proprietors when their estates had been
enormously profitable in the eighteenth century. Even when
sugar prices were well above 30/– a hundredweight, exclusive
of duty, heavily indebted or encumbered estates might
scarcely show a profit, and for those which were least indebted
and encumbered the possibility of saving was limited.

In 1847 a Committee of the House of Assembly enquired
into the state of the Island's sugar industry, and after receiv-

ing much evidence prepared a report. According to the governor, Sir Charles Grey, who was sympathetic to the planters, it showed "a very remarkable variety in the condition means and prospects," and although some individual proprietors were optimistic the governor agreed that distress was widespread and "ruinous." Of the evidence itself, he advised: "All statements of the cost of production must be received with caution. . . . The fact is that even the real and unavoidable cost varies widely on different estates and in different parts of the Island and that in the estimates given by different witnesses it is impossible to guess without strict cross-examination what expenses are improperly included."[3] In a later dispatch the Governor again stressed the same point: "Examination of costs of production statistics shew that average costs have been worked out on total expenses divided by total product irregardless of large sums invested in machinery or of years of small crops due to drought etc."[4]

Mr. McKinnon, a prominent attorney and planter in the Clarendon area, for example, had shown the average costs of production on one estate as £16 sterling per hundredweight in 1844, and 9/7 per hundredweight in 1847. Another attorney, John Stirk, of New Yarmouth Estate in Vere, submitted figures of 8/8½ per hundredweight in 1842, 28/– per hundredweight in 1843, 117/9 per hundredweight in 1844, and 11/9 per hundredweight in 1845. The explanation is that in 1843 the estate purchased a steam engine which was installed in 1844. Thus in 1843 his account of costs includes the full price of a steam engine; and in 1844, apparently due to the hold-up for installation, the estate produced less than 40 hogsheads of sugar instead of its usual 330.[5]

Nevertheless, in their final summing up the Committee do not appear to have greatly overstated the case.[6] They con-

3. C.O. 137/295, Sir C. Grey to Earl Grey. No. 17, 7 Feb. 1848.
4. C.O. 137/295, Sir C. Grey to Earl Grey, No. 21, 21 Feb. 1848.
5. C.O. 137/295, see Grey's dispatch, No. 21, of 17 Feb. 1848, and enclosures.
6. See the Committee's report and also evidence given by Jamaica planters before the Select Committee of 1848 on Sugar and Coffee Planting in the Colonies.

cluded that for the island as a whole the average cost of
production of a hundredweight of sugar, after deducting any
proceeds from the sale of the by-product (rum), was 22/7½.
This figure did not include capital charges or the costs of
marketing produce.

According to Sir Charles Grey, the comparable figure on
some of the Island's best estates was about 15/- per hun-

TABLE 14. *Sugar Prices, Duties, and Marketing Costs,
1840–47*

	1840	1842	1844	1846	1847
Average price per cwt. (including duty)	74/3	62/1	58/10	48/5	42/3
Freight, dock rates, brokerage, insurance, etc.	7/6	7/6	7/6	7/6	7/6
Import duty per cwt.	25/2	25/2	25/2	14/10	14/
TOTAL of these charges per cwt.	32/8	32/8	32/8	21/6	21/6
BALANCE to cover costs of cultivation and manufacture, charges on capital, and any encumbrances	41/7	29/5	26/2	26/11	20/9

NOTE. Freight, dock rates, etc. have been given at 7/6 throughout, for
there is no record of variations, which were probably slight during these
years. The figure quoted is based on estimates of these charges given by
the governor in his dispatch covering the 1847 report (C.O. 137/295),
and by various planters in evidence before the 1848 Select Committee of
Parliament.

dredweight. With these figures in mind, Table 14 will indicate
the trend from 1840 to 1847.

A few planters might have been able to put something by
in the period of relatively high prices between emancipation
and 1842, but for the industry as a whole, capital accumula-
tion could not have been significant. Another source of capital
was the compensation money paid by the British Government
to the owners on the emancipation of their slaves. In fact,

however, much of this had gone straight into the hands of creditors in settlement of outstanding claims. But in a few instances at least, estate owners did receive all or part of their compensation money and applied it to estate development.[7] In any case, the total compensation to Jamaica slave owners had been over £6,000,000, and insofar as this reduced the indebtedness of planters it would have helped to restore their credit-worthiness. Still another source of money was the sale or rental of idle estate land to speculators or to small settlers. Sales of this sort represented a liquidation of fixed assets into cash which the planter could use to improve the remainder of his property. On Seville Estate in St. Ann the owner realized about £200 a year from rents,[8] not an inconsiderable sum in hard times.

There is little doubt, however, that the greater part of the capital development described in the previous chapter was financed by advances to the planters from merchants and other creditors in Britain. Jamaica planters who owned property in Britain, or elsewhere beyond the sugar estates, were sometimes able to borrow on the security of that property, or perhaps had accumulated savings out of the profits from it, which might be applied to sugar estate development. It is possible that improvements on Montpelier and other estates were financed in this way. In 1848 Thomas Price said that he and other trustees of Worthy Park Estate in St. John had borrowed £30,000 on their securities, to be spent on re-equipping the property.[9]

When news of the Sugar Duties Act reached Jamaica, the planters' immediate reaction was panic. In expectation of a price fall they cancelled their orders for immigrants. In October 1846 Mr. Darling, the agent general for immigration, informed the acting governor:

> It was impossible to foresee this change in the views of the Planters—as I stated in my General Report of last

7. C.O. 137/194, letters from John Nelson Bond and S. M. MacLeod to Lord Sligo, Dec. 1834. See also West India Committee Minute Books, Acting Committee, 27 Jan. 1854.

8. C.O. 137/284, report of S. M. Woolfrys, 1 May 1845.

9. Select Committee of 1848, Minutes of Evidence, 4911.

year, I had at that time applications for Eight Thousand Coolies in my Office. The imposition by an Act of the last Session of the Legislature, of a Tax upon Employers of Two pounds per Annum, in respect of each Coolie above eight years of age in his employment—the severe illness occasioned among the Immigrants by the unusual wet weather which immediately succeeded their arrival, producing as it did, a great deficiency of labour: but above all, the serious apprehensions which appear to be so generally entertained of the effect of the new Sugar duties arrangements at home, are no doubt the causes which have produced this sudden change in the views of those who are conducting the cultivation of Estates.[10]

At the end of the following month, November 1846, the Assembly sent a message to the Colonial Office "intimating their desire to abandon Asiatic Immigration" because the Island could no longer afford it. In reply, the secretary of state for the colonies hoped that the new sugar duties would not be as ruinous as the planters anticipated, but he agreed that the expense of Indian immigration was too much for Jamaica. Steps had been taken to reduce the number of Indians sent in accordance with Mr. Darling's request, and after that there would be no more.[11]

As Darling had said, the prime reason for the abandonment of the scheme was the Sugar Duties Act. The annual charge of £2 on each Indian over eight years of age was not a completely new thing, but it was an increase of the previous rate.[12] It might have brought about some reduction in the demand for Indian labourers, but hardly so drastic a reduction as Darling mentioned; and it certainly would not have led to the immediate cessation of import. Nor is it likely that illness among the Indians, would have led to so drastic a move. The selection of healthy and efficient labourers was a matter which

10. C.O. 137/289, C. H. Darling to the acting governor, 22 Oct. 1846.
11. C.O. 137/289, Berkeley to Earl Grey, No. 44, 21 Nov. 1846, and Colonial Office draft reply.
12. The tax of 20/– per immigrant payable annually by employers.

could be brought under stricter control by the Jamaica agents in Madras and Calcutta.

In October 1847 the governor informed the Colonial Office [13] that there was no sign or desire for the renewal of Indian immigration, and in fact recent comments in the Assembly had suggested that "there is no decided wish at present even for African immigrants." He asked, therefore, that no more arrangements should be made to bring in Africans unless there was some fresh request.

In March 1849 the Jamaica Act for the Encouragement of Immigration, which provided funds and made provision for an agent general and sub-agents of immigration, expired and was not renewed. From then until 1854 there was no immigration into Jamaica at the Island Government's expense.

In Britain the Sugar Duties Act brought a sudden cessation of advances from the merchants. This meant that the ordinary processes of cultivation were obstructed, because planters generally obtained estate supplies on credit in advance of crop; it also meant that the introduction of machinery was severely curtailed. The results were serious. The governor informed the Colonial Office:

> the plain truth is that the whole body of planters and their subordinate agents here who depend on advances of money or credit from London are in a deplorable way. The dead loss from the mere fall of price between January and August of this year being commonly estimated at nearly ten pounds per ton, and being in reality as near as I can form a calculation and judgment nearer seven pounds than six: one consequence of which and of other circumstances of the moment is that London houses are refusing to make for the future any further advances otherwise than by allowing bills to be drawn on them for their own estimate of the net proceeds of cargoes consigned to them, and the recent failures in London are

13. C.O. 137/293, Sir Charles Grey to Earl Grey, No. 105, 23 Oct. 1847.

exciting alarm amongst the Consignors that they cannot be secure even of those bills being accepted.[14]

As the governor said, the caution of the merchants resulted from other circumstances as well as the sudden fall of sugar prices. From 1845 to 1847 British capitalists invested close to £100 million pounds in railway building and amalgamation. This was long-term investment because it would be some time before the railways were completed and begin to yield returns. This sobering consideration did not, however, prevent an orgy of speculation in railway shares. At the same time there was a series of potato crop failures in Ireland and poor wheat harvests in England, which increased food prices, and incidentally settled the repeal of the Corn Laws. There was also a short cotton crop in the United States, which increased raw material prices. In 1847 commercial panic was added to industrial depression because the Bank of England, after a tremendous drain on its resources, ceased to make advances on bills of exchange submitted by merchant houses and others. Then, sudden improvements in the wheat crops brought the price of wheat crashing down (from 102/– to 48/– per quarter), with accompanying ruin to grain houses that had stocked up in the previous year of high prices. Not until the Bank Act was suspended and the Bank of England had resumed advances, though at a higher rate of interest, did the panic slowly begin to subside.[15]

Obviously the crisis was not unconnected with the West Indian distress. In fact it contributed to the failure of eighteen West Indian Merchant Houses in the United Kingdom, and the West India Bank which had its headquarters in Barbados.[16] But just as the misfortunes of the grain houses had been

14. C.O. 137/293, Sir C. Grey, No. 99, 22 Oct. 1847.

15. See: H. N. Hyndman, *Commercial Crises of the 19th Century* (London, 1892), pp. 57–62; J. H. Clapham, *Economic History of Modern Britain. The Early Railway Age (1820–50)* (2d ed. Cambridge, 1930), chs. 9, 13; G. P. Jones and A. G. Pool, *A Hundred Years of Economic Development* (London, 1948), pp. 129–30.

16. W. L. Mathieson, *The Sugar Colonies and Governor Eyre* (London, 1936), p. 53.

emphasized by a sudden increase in supplies and low prices due to improved harvests, so the sugar houses had been affected by a sudden increase in supplies and a fall of prices following the Act of 1846.

A clear example of the effects on newly begun attempts to enter into large-scale production is given in the case of Smith's Agricultural Society for Jamaica. The Company, formed in Liverpool in 1846, planned to acquire estates, reestablish them on improved methods, and restore them to profitability.[17] The founders were the brothers William and David Smith, of whom mention has previously been made. The necessary capital was readily subscribed, and in 1846 the Company bought Retreat Estate in Westmoreland for £5,050, and leased Cornwall Estate in the same parish for seven years at £400 per annum. Retreat covered 2,500 acres, of which about 250 were in canes and another 350 suitable for cane and pasture. The remainder was rocky. Cornwall contained about the same acreage of suitable cane-land. New machinery was ordered for the estates, a Lincolnshire farmer named Thomas Dickon was sent out as manager to work under David Smith in Jamaica, and the Company began to negotiate for other properties. To quote the Directors, "Circumstances, however, then occurred which induced the Directors to pause, and ultimately to terminate altogether their negotiations for more West India property." The "circumstances," of course, were the Sugar Duties Act and the accompanying fall in the prices offered for sugar in Britain. Despite the termination of further investments the Company had, by the end of 1848, spent a total of £22,940. Of this sum, £6,330 had been paid for machinery and livestock—a vacuum pan for Retreat had alone cost £3,000.

The directors declared that it was impossible to carry out the original plan, and proposed that the two estates should be continued as economically as possible, at least until the end of the lease on Cornwall; or, if even that was impossible, that

17. For details see *Smith's Agricultural Society for Jamaica* (Manchester, 1848), report of the board of directors, 1848. Also Select Committee, 1848, Minutes of Evidence, 6519–6797.

the Company should be wound up slowly so as to avoid the entire sacrifice of capital. The Company had recently obtained ninety African indentured labourers who would form a reliable labour nucleus; Mr. Dickon, who had proved unsuitable, had been replaced by another manager; and the chance still remained that they might pull through if the share-holders were willing to meet further calls up to £1 a share. The directors admitted to having made some mistakes in the past administration of the Company: "Mr. Dickon and all connected with him was the main one, and that we all entertained too sanguine views as to speedy returns . . ." But even though Mr. Dickon, not entirely through his own fault,[18] had been in a difficult position, and even though there had been some trouble in finding sufficient labour, it seems clear that the death blow had come with the Sugar Duties Act.

One other specific case may be cited, that of the proposed Clarendon Tramway.[19] Clarendon is a large parish in which the interior estates were handicapped by long, difficult, and expensive transportation to and from the docks. In some cases it cost £2 in carriage alone to send a hogshead of sugar to a shipping point. In addition there was the wear and tear on carts, cattle, and goods. The idea of a tramway had originated in 1846, but was not formally presented until the following year, when the accompanying Memorial to the secretary of state pointed out: "Believing that we have still a chance of success if the Tramway be made, we are willing to use all our energies and expend all the means we can in effecting it." But, it went on, the financial assistance of Government was needed.

In Jamaica the individuals chiefly concerned were Edward Thompson, William Rose, Gilbert Shaw, and Louis McKinnon, all of them estate attorneys of repute and themselves estate-owners. Edward Thompson, custos of the Parish, owned five

18. From his evidence before the 1848 Committee it is clear that he was allowed to exercise very little independent judgement in managing the estate.

19. C.O. 137/291, Sir Charles Grey to Earl Grey, No. 27, 25 March 1847, and enclosures.

estates, including Danks, one of the largest in Clarendon. Between them the four men supervised the affairs of thirty of the forty-one estates involved in the scheme. The tramway was planned to begin at a point just north of Chapelton, going south-east past Danks and along the Dry River as far as Chatteau Estate. From there the route went easterly to Palmetto, south to the Longville Park Pen area, and on to the coast at a point about midway between Long's Wharf and Burkefield Wharf in Old Harbour Bay. This would have given the Upper Clarendon Estates not only an improved outlet to the sea but also a connection with the proposed South Midland Railway from Spanish Town, through Old Harbour Market, to a terminal just west of the mouth of Bower's River.

But both the South Midland Railway and the Clarendon Tramway failed to materialize. The proposers of the tramway had asked for a loan from the British Government. The answer was a definite refusal. The governor, who had anticipated the Colonial Office's reaction, made an alternative suggestion to the sponsors of the tramway. If they would agree to have their lands taxed at, say, one shilling per acre, the tax could be applied to interest on a loan to be subscribed in England or in Jamaica. If they wanted to be a constituted Joint Stock Company with transferrable shares, the Tramway prospectus and all relevant information would have to be sent to England for approval, and the Company would have to submit to regulations governing railway companies. If, on the other hand, they were only to be a private partnership, they could probably be regarded in the same way as owners of Colliery Railways in England.

Nothing definite has been found to tell why the scheme was abandoned. It would seem, however, that the proposers wanted a public railway that would not only serve their estates but also yield a revenue from use by the people of the numerous Clarendon settlements. If so, Colliery Railway status would not have been enough. As for the governor's proposals, the memorialists might have felt that the suggested tax would have fallen too unequally among them, or that the chance of raising the necessary loan, especially at that time, was too slight to warrant the trial.

Such facts as have been discovered about the imports into the Island of agricultural implements, factory machinery, and fertilizers are also illustrative of the post-1846 loss of credit and confidence (see Tables 5 and 15).

Table 15 is most unsatisfactory, but it is the best that can be compiled. We have clear and abundant evidence [20] that between 1838 and 1848 considerable quantities of agricultural and factory equipment were sent out to Jamaica. But the official records (the Jamaica "Blue Books") give hardly a hint of these imports. Nevertheless, the broad pattern is shown of an increased volume after 1856. This, together with the general evidence of the early 1840's, suggests that the pattern of imports shows a noticeable bulge at each end—1838–48, and later, 1857–65—with a considerable decline in the middle ten years. This is borne out by Governor Barkly's comment in 1854 that the planters were turning to machinery now that all hope of protective duties was lost.[21]

In 1848 a Parliamentary Select Committee, under the chairmanship of Lord George Bentinck, met to enquire into the condition of sugar and coffee planting in the colonies. West Indians pleaded for an extension of colonial preferences, and the exclusion of foreign slave-grown sugars, against which they said they could not compete, from the British market. By the casting vote of the chairman the Committee supported a recommendation that British sugars be given a preference of 10/– per hundredweight for a period of six years. The Government, however, refused to accept the recommendation; but the date of equalization between the duties on colonial and foreign sugars was postponed two years, from 1852 to

20. For example: evidence of Thomas Price, Lord Howard de Walden, S. B. Moody, and others before Select Committee, 1848; *Smith's Agricultural Society for Jamaica*, the directors' report in 1848; and reports of the governors and S.M.'s, some of which have been quoted in the text.

21. C.O. 137/323, Barkly to Newcastle, No. 73, 26 May 1854.

1854; and a British guaranteed loan of £500,000 was offered
to be shared by Mauritius, British Guiana, Trinidad, Barbados,
and Jamaica.

The Jamaica Assembly, which at the time was suffering
from violent internal disagreement, rejected the offer. It had,
since 1846, instituted a policy of financial retrenchment.
Lower sugar prices, it was argued, meant a collapse of the

TABLE 15. *Recorded Imports of Agricultural Implements
and Various Machinery into Jamaica, 1840–65*

| | AGRICULTURAL IMPLEMENTS | | MACHINERY | | *Estimated Value* |
YEAR	Specified	Unspecified	Specified	Unspecified	(£)
1840	—	50 pcs.	1 sugar mill	7 cases	277
1841	—	—	—	9 cases, 4 pcs.	1,824
1842	—	—	—	1 box	1
1843	—	2 pcs.	—	—	6
1844	2 ploughs	—	—	—	25
1845	2 ploughs	—	—	—	4
1846	29 ploughs	—	—	—	37
1847	1 plough	ad. val.	—	—	201
1848	—	26 pcs.	—	—	87
1849	—	ad. val.	—	—	166
1850	—	ad. val.	—	—	1,345
1851	—	ad. val.	—	—	322
1852	—	ad. val.	—	—	225
1853	—	ad. val.	—	—	15
1854	—	ad. val.	—	ad. val.	234
1855	—	—	—	ad. val.	173
1856	—	—	—	ad. val.	111
1857	—	—	—	ad. val.	3,255
1858	—	12 pcs.	—	1,587 pcs.	12,436
1859	8 ploughs	—	—	2,158 pkgs. 5 pcs.	18,729
1860	14 ploughs	—	2 sugar mills	various lots	29,998
1861	4 ploughs	11 pkgs. 15 pcs.	—	various lots	25,275
1862	2 ploughs	10 pkgs.	3 mills	2,254 pkgs.	

YEAR	AGRICULTURAL IMPLEMENTS		MACHINERY		*Estimated Value* (£)
	Specified	Unspecified	Specified	Unspecified	
1862 (*cont.*)		9 pcs.	35 sugar pans, 1 stm. engine 3 stills	1 piece	16,010
1863	10 ploughs	10 pkgs. 13 pcs.	—	1,327 pkgs.	7,831
1864	40 ploughs 3 cane-top cutters	636 pkgs.	6 sugar pans 10 sugar mills	—	5,645
1865	15 ploughs	57 pkgs.	3 mills, 5 sugar pans 1 still	3 pcs.	3,687
1840–65	TOTAL ESTIMATED VALUE (sterling)				*£ 128,019*

Source: Jamaica Blue Books.

NOTE. The information has been put in as much detail as is convenient, but some simplification of classifications has been necessary.

sugar industry, a decline in the government revenues, and lack of funds for the administration of the Island. In 1847, and afterwards, the Assembly passed bills reducing the salaries of public officials. The Legislative Council, of which many of the members were officials, refused to countenance these bills and in retaliation the Assembly threatened to vote no supplies, unless Parliament granted compensation to the planters and also altered the constitution so as to make the Council an elected body.[22]

These demands, neither of which was met, illustrated the attitudes of the two main groups in the House. They agreed on the retrenchment policy, but for absolutely opposed reasons. According to Sir Charles Grey, who had succeeded Lord Elgin as governor, the Planter or Country party openly declared their ambition "to bring about a crisis: and to have both

22. C.O. 137/301, Sir Charles Grey to Earl Grey, confidential, 21 Feb. 1849; and C.O. 137/302, No. 31, 9 March 1849.

Council and Assembly done away and some new form of Government established." They knew that political instability in Jamaica was a great deterrent to increased and improved sugar production, insofar as it made the island unattractive as a field for further capital investment. They would have liked financial compensation, for it would have provided at least some of the capital which was now hardly obtainable from merchants or agents in Britain.

The Merchant or Town party, on the other hand, sought to increase the power of the Assembly by making the revenue almost entirely dependent on annual votes and by asserting all the ancient claims to rights and privileges. It was said that they advocated salary cuts because they hoped to make the public offices less attractive to Europeans and so more open to themselves.[23] Their growing strength in the Assembly would have led them to demand that the Council, too, should be an elected body. Their businesses were based on the export of minor crops rather than sugar, and on import of consumer goods. As long as the small farmers were productive and the general demand for imports remained effective, they could make their profits. It is hardly possible that they could have been unaware of the importance of sugar-estate wages as a source of purchasing power; but there were few people in Jamaica in 1847 who were optimistic about the continuation of sugar production, whatever might be the political situation.

In these circumstances the governor was practically helpless, and it would appear to be of great credit to Sir Charles Grey that the Government continued to function at all during these seven years, and that he was able to win the respect, if not the support, of both parties in the Assembly.

Across the Atlantic matters were coming to a head. The Colonial Office, in the early 1840's, had wanted a strong executive in Jamaica to protect the newly emancipated from measures designed by a planter-controlled Assembly to increase their dependence on estate wages. During the ad-

23. C.O. 137/316, Sir Charles Grey to Newcastle, No. 40, 10 May 1853.

ministrations of Metcalfe and Elgin this motive had been undermined by the great material advancement of the ex-slaves and the concurrent optimism among sugar planters and other employers of labour.

After 1846 the situation had deteriorated. The 1848 investigation by the Select Committee had brought more evidence about the high costs of labour. Planters had stressed the importance of lower wage rates and a reliable supply of labour. The myth of the "lazy negro" was being cultivated. The accomplishments of the small farmers in Jamaica passed unstressed and uncredited. The understandable reluctance of peasants and labourers to work longer than was necessary to provide their immediate wants, or to abandon their own cultivations in order to serve the estate planters, was attacked on moral grounds:

> Whatsoever prohibits or prevents a man from this his sacred appointment to labour while he lives on earth—that I say, is the man's deadliest enemy; and all men are called upon to do what is in their power or opportunity towards delivering him from that. If it be his own indolence that prevents and prohibits him, then his own "right" he has—poor indolent blockhead, black or white, —is, that every *un*-prohibited man, whatsoever wiser, more industrious person be passing that way, shall endeavour to "emancipate" him from his indolence, and by some wise means, as I said, compel him, since inducing will not serve, to do the work he is fit for . . . but if your Nigger will not be induced? In that case, it is full certain, he must be compelled; should and must; and the tacit prayer he makes (unconsciously he, poor block-head), to you, and to me, and to all the world who are wiser than himself, is, "Compel me!" For indeed he *must*, or else do and suffer worse,—he as well as we. It were better the work did come out of him! It was the meaning of the gods with him and with us, that his gift should turn to use in this Creation, and not lie poisoning

the thoroughfares, as a rotten mass of idleness, agreeable to neither heaven nor earth.[24]

By 1854 the Colonial Office had decided that the frustration of the governor must now be overcome by a limitation of the powers of the Assembly. The crisis of 1847 and subsequent years had followed from matters which had directly affected the sugar industry; the importance of that industry to economic and political stability seemed only too clear, and thus it might be advantageous to put some pressure on the labouring population. Towards the end of 1853 the secretary of state in his instructions to the new governor, Sir Henry Barkly, pointed out that much of the public revenues was derived from the negroes, who could afford to buy dutied goods though they did not give regular estate labour. A renewal of immigration would be a good thing because "the Negroes themselves would be greatly benefited by a competition in the labour market which should enforce from them some moderate amount of industry." And, looking to their permanent welfare, it would be no misapplication of the produce of taxes paid by them to import labourers who would by competition reduce wage rates. Finally it was emphasized for the new governor that "there are at your command available sources of revenue still productive, capable of being drawn upon without deranging trade or discouraging industrious habits."

The retiring governor, continued the letter of instructions, had asked that Parliament should give him emergency powers to secure the permanent revenues; the West India Interest in Britain had pressed for the abolition of the Assembly and the institution of Crown Colony Government. But although there was much to be said for these suggestions, the British Government preferred to maintain the Assembly, which might function well under more favourable circumstances, "containing as it does the germ and organisation of a more com-

24. The quotation is from Thomas Carlyle, *Occasional Discourse on the Nigger Question,* first published in *Frazer's Magazine,* Dec. 1849, reprinted as a pamphlet in 1853, and later included in *Latter Day Pamphlets* by Carlyle, London, 1858.

plete representative system . . ." Certain essential reforms were, however, necessary. Above all, it must relinquish its executive authority and modify its dominance over the Council in legislative affairs. If satisfactory reforms were introduced, the British Government would guarantee a loan of £500,000 to the Island for the purpose of consolidating the public debt at a lower rate of interest. Also, a further loan of £50,000 would be allowed to provide compensation for public servants who might be put out of office by the retrenchment programme.[25]

On 18 October 1853 Barkly put these proposals to the Jamaica Legislature in his speech opening the session. The Assembly were not immediately receptive, but by the end of the year a Committee on Political Reform provided what seemed to be a satisfactory plan for constitutional change.[26] The essential features of the new political organization were as follows: the Legislative Council was to consist of seventeen nominated members, of whom only five might hold any "office of emolument"; each of the others had to own a freehold in the island of not less than £300 annual value. This enlarged Council was given power to originate bills not involving taxation or the appropriation of revenues. Secondly, the governor was empowered to select three assemblymen and one councillor to form a committee to assist him in his duties.[27] This Executive Committee was to have all the powers of the old Assembly boards and committees, and in the future money votes were to be proposed in Assembly only on the recommendation of the Governor-in-Executive-Committee. Thirdly, various sources of revenue, especially the newly scaled import duties, were to be set permanently against the costs of the civil establishment and the costs and liquidation of the British guaranteed loan.[28]

25. C.O. 137/319, Newcastle's instructions to Barkly, Oct. 1853.
26. C.O. 137/319, Barkly to Newcastle, No. 6, 22 Oct. 1853; and No. 36, 26 Dec. 1853.
27. In practice the choice seems to have been limited to two from the Assembly and one from the Council.
28. C.O. 137/323, Barkly to Newcastle, No. 46, 10 April 1854.

The second half of the 1850's was a period of temporary political stability under the new constitution, which came into effect in 1854. There was also economic improvement. Faced with the actuality of free trade and competitive production, the Jamaica planters abandoned their demands for renewed protection and turned once more to attempts to improve and cheapen their production of sugar.

The desire for immigration had, in fact, been renewed even earlier. Since 1849 Africans liberated from slave-trading vessels had been brought into the West Indian colonies at the expense of the British Government. It was a measure intended to bring some relief to the planters. The inflow varied, however, with the volume of the foreign slave trade; it was heaviest from 1848 to 1850 and then declined, until there was a short revival in 1860–63.[29] In 1850 Jamaica suffered from a terrible outbreak of cholera, which began in Port Royal and Kingston and spread rapidly throughout the Island. Its progress was widened and accelerated by the filthiness of these and other towns, by the inadequacy and maladministration of public health services, and by the movements of people who, without realizing their own infection, hurried away to other parts of the Island in attempts to escape.[30] The epidemic gradually abated in the summer of 1851; but although there were later sporadic outbreaks, the main damage had already been done. It is impossible to say with complete accuracy how many people lost their lives, because even in ordinary circumstances there was no proper machinery for the registration of births and deaths in the Island, and in such a period of crisis the tabulation of statistics was no doubt affected by fright as much as by fact. Nonetheless, there is no doubt whatsoever that the human loss was extremely heavy. The not wholly reliable figures given [31] show a total

29. See below, Appendix 3.
30. *Report Made by Dr. Milroy to the Colonial Office, on the Cholera Epidemic in Jamaica, 1850–51*, London, H.M.S.O., 1854.
31. C.O. 137/313, Sir Charles Grey to Earl Grey, No. 5, 28 Jan. 1852, provides the statistics, with the following comments: (1) in St. George, Metcalfe, and St. Ann, the records are incomplete, so the

of 30,590 deaths in a total population of about 377,500—that is, about 8 per cent. Of the casualties, it was estimated that 10,000 were able-bodied men and women.[32]

When, in 1852, offer of another British loan was made, a delegation from the Assembly[33] visited the Colonial Office. They proposed that greater action be taken to stop the slave trade to foreign competitors. The Colonial Office replied that this was already being done and the trade was not increasing. They proposed that all restrictions on the importation of free labourers from Africa should be removed. This was refused by the Colonial Office because of the danger that West Indians might again become involved in the slave trade if they tried to obtain people from slave-dealing areas. They proposed that because of the diminution of the Island's labour force by cholera, the decision of many Indian immigrants to return home rather than settle in Jamaica, and the great cost and difficulty of getting labourers for Jamaica in competition with other labour-seeking countries, all Africans captured from the slave trade should be sent to Jamaica and their contracts of indenture extended from one year to three or five years. The Colonial Office replied that the entire immigration problem was under consideration by the secretary of state, that it would be unfair to other colonies to send all captured Africans to Jamaica, and that in any case the total number was small; but permission was given to extend the contracts of those delivered to three years.[34] The delegation also proposed that

---

number of deaths is partly estimated; (2) in St. Catherine, probably a considerable overestimate; (3) in Westmoreland, Hanover, St. James, and Trelawny, more deaths since these returns were compiled.

32. See Cumpston, *Indians Overseas*, p. 143, where she refers to a dispatch from the governor, dated 31 Dec. 1851.

33. Edward Thompson, planter, planting attorney, and custos of Clarendon; W. Smith, landowner and a director of the Jamaica Railway; and W. Girod, a planter.

34. Liberated Africans, whose passage to the Colonies was paid by the U.K. from 1849, had been indentured for only one year because it was considered that they had less to "pay off" in the type of labour which all immigration was intended to provide, namely labour on estates.

the British Government should give "concurrence and support" to the imposition of increased taxes upon the Jamaican peasants and labourers, to support expenditures on existing social welfare institutions. Some general levy such as a tax on houses was suggested. This, which had in fact been an idea of the previous secretary of state,[35] was accepted by the Colonial Office provided that the enabling Act of Assembly gave security that the money thus raised would in fact be spent in this way. A fifth proposal was that a guaranteed loan of £100,000 then being considered should be applied to immigration purposes. The delegation pointed out that the interest and amortization charges of this debt were to be met by export duties on staple products which would fall "exclusively upon the Planting interest." The Jamaica Immigration Act, 15 Vic., cap. 39 (1852), had established export duties to be applied to immigration purposes. In the following year an Act of Parliament allowed the use of the British loan as the delegation had requested. Finally, the delegates asked the British Government to secure the effectiveness of all these measures by temporarily "averting the rapidly approaching equalization of the Sugar Duties." This last suggestion passed swiftly through one ministerial ear and out the other.[36]

By this time the secretary of state could quote figures in support of an argument that other sugar colonies had received no permanent injury from the Act of 1846. At the end of 1853 he wrote to Governor Barkly: "There can be no doubt that Jamaica in common with all the other Sugar Colonies, suffered greatly by the change of policy adopted in this Country on the subject of the Sugar duties . . . But in all the principal Sugar producing Colonies except Jamaica the difficulties of the time have been almost entirely surmounted." [37] He then proceeded to analyse the "peculiar

35. In a dispatch from Earl Grey to Sir C. Grey, governor, dated 15 July 1851.

36. C.O. 137/315, contains all details of the delegations' proposals and Colonial Office minutes on Jamaica immigration and the £100,000 guaranteed loan.

37. Ibid.

causes of adversity" affecting Jamaica. He mentioned the great density of population in Barbados, which had made immigration unnecessary. Where there had been no idle cultivable land the ex-slaves had been denied the alternative of freehold settlement and had been compelled by circumstances to remain as estate labourers earning about 9*d.* sterling a day, with free cottage and about a quarter acre of garden land.[38] In an industry in which wages were so significant an element of costs this meant that Barbados planters had a great advantage over planters in Jamaica, Trinidad, and British Guiana. But, continued the secretary of state, the two last named colonies had availed themselves of the British offer of a loan in 1848 and had applied it to immigration. They had thus been able to increase their sugar output, and so had "compensated themselves for the reduction of prices by increase of quantities." Jamaicans, on the other hand, had been wayward; the Assembly had rejected the loan. Although it was right to question the prudence "under ordinary circumstances" of bolstering industry with public money managed by Government agency, this had been a time of transitory crisis, and a loan then would have, as in the case of British Guiana and Trinidad, put the colony back on the right road to prosperity. In other words, Jamaicans had missed the boat, and for those who might yet catch up with it the way would be harder and more expensive.

These observations only went part way towards the whole truth. It was also important that Barbadians, with their limited amount of land area, had long been more careful agriculturalists than Jamaicans. That does not mean that they had been readier, or even as ready, to use better agricultural implements, because they had no problem of labour shortage to spur them on. It does mean that they were more considerate of their land, more experienced in the use of fertilizers, tidier and more compact in their estate organization, and more concerned with the details of management. A Barbadian who

38. For general accounts of Barbados and other islands see J. Davy, *The West Indies before and since Emancipation,* London 1854; and W. Sewell, *Ordeal of Free Labour in the British West Indies,* New York 1861.

went to Trinidad in the early 1840's had something to say on this score. He gave a very high opinion of the fertility of the Trinidad soil and remarked that with proper attention and care Trinidadians could make as good sugar as Barbadians and "plenty of it," "but that the cultivation and manufacturing processes are most dirty and slovenly; and this is so apparent that it struck me on my first visit, and must be evident to the most superficial observer." [39]

Another Barbadian feature, arising out of the predominance of sugar-planting and the non-emergence of any new group of small, independent freeholders, was that the Island Legislature, unlike that of Jamaica, was almost exclusively concerned with the welfare of the sugar industry. There was no apparent alternative as in Jamaica, where, for example, some of the coloured people had visions of an island of small farmers and the development of an internal commerce.

In Trinidad and British Guiana there was the same almost exclusive concern with the sugar industry. These were "new" colonies, acquired at the turn of the nineteenth century, and when they had come into British hands they were relatively undeveloped. Four essential consequences of their later acquisition and development are important. First, the estates in these colonies, compared with those of the "older" island territories, were relatively unencumbered by the numerous claims of annuitants and beneficiaries whose rights dated from the ill-founded generosity of ancient owners. Thus it was more possible to finance capital development out of savings, a particularly important condition when, after 1846, the merchant houses restricted credit. At the same time, because they were relatively unencumbered, they were more attractive borrowers. Secondly, these colonies, from the time of their acquisition, had faced a labour shortage. The development of their sugar industries under British rule had hardly begun when the slave trade was abolished in 1807. Thus there must always have been a tendency for planters to economize labour and to adopt labour-saving devices.

39. W. H. Burnley, *Observations on the Present Condition of the Island of Trinidad,* London, 1842.

Thirdly, the establishment of new estates came just when industrial development in Britain was providing tropical agricultural equipment, steam-engines, vacuum pans, and the rest. Fourthly, these two colonies had no ancient and powerful elected assemblies. Because they were recognized by the British Government as "sugar" colonies they were governed as such, and were the "colonies of experiment" in the eyes of the Colonial Office. They, for instance, were allowed first participation in the attempt to introduce Chinese indentured labour. For all these reasons, Barbados, Trinidad, and British Guiana were less severely affected than was Jamaica by the Sugar Duties Act.

The £100,000 loan made available to the Jamaicans in 1852 was immediately disposed of: £35,000 went to settle the claims of Indians already in Jamaica who had completed their terms of indenture for five years and were claiming return passage to India or their promised cash settlements; £40,000 was put aside for the importation of 2,000 Chinese labourers from Hong Kong; and £25,000 remained to be used, partly in the recruitment of labourers in Madeira or West Africa, provided that they would come without contracts for return passages.[40] The Chinese immigration, which had been authorized in 1844 had, up to this time, been unproductive because of a lack of people willing to emigrate to the West Indies. In the 1850's it failed because of too great expense.[41] In 1854 one shipload of Chinese arrived from Hong Kong. Of 310 embarked, forty-three had died at sea and fifty-seven were sent to hospital when they arrived in Jamaica. Later in the year another vessel brought 197 Chinese from Panama, where they had been railway labourers.[42] In the same year the proposed immigration from Madeira had brought in 167 people.[43] The total number for the year was therefore 631. The

40. C.O. 137/317, Sir C. Grey to Duke of Newcastle, No. 66, 24 June 1853.

41. C.O. 137/323, Barkly to Earl Grey, No. 86, 10 July 1854.

42. C.O. 137/324, Barkly to Earl Grey, Nos. 91, 111, 10 Aug. and 8 Nov. 1854.

43. Land and Emigration Commissioners, *15th General Report*, London H.M.S.O., 1855.

cost had been about £9,500.[44] The results had not come up to expectations. Between 1854 and 1860 the search for other sources of immigrant labour was both increasing and unrewarding (there was even a proposal that the Indian mutineers should be sent to Jamaica as labourers). Canada and the United States had already been tried unsuccessfully. There was no further significant entry until the renewal of Indian immigration in 1860.

This last inflow was made possible by the numerous Jamaica immigration acts of 1858 to 1861. The Act of 1858 continued the old regulations and included some new sections which provided that a proportionate number of women should be brought in; that families should not be separated; and that contracted labour should be given for a period of five years, though not necessarily to the same employer. It also established special immigration funds and empowered the governor to borrow money from time to time not exceeding £50,000 a year, or a total of £100,000 at any time, for purposes of immigration. The later acts introduced certain amendments required by the British Government and some new provisions. These affected the introduction of women and children; the length of the period of contract with the immigrants' first employer; and the financing of immigration which, after 1861, was to be borne one-third by the general Island revenue and two-thirds by an export duty which would fall on all planters as a class.[45]

In the beginning of 1858 the new governor, Mr. Darling, who had once been agent general for immigration in the Island and since been abroad as governor of other colonial territories, wrote to the secretary of state for the colonies to ask if Jamaica would be included in new proposals for Indian and Chinese immigration to British Guiana and

44. C.O. 137/340, Darling to Bulwer Lytton, No. 156, 24 Dec. 1858, gives the cost of the 1854 Chinese immigration, to which is added the expense of the Madeira immigration at the rate of £7 bounty per head.

45. These acts whose provisions have been so lightly touched on were: Jamaica Acts 22 Vic., C. 1, 2, 3, 4, 8; 23 Vic., C. 30, 31; 24 Vic., C. 16.

Trinidad. The attitude of the Colonial Office was not encouraging. Jamaica had "committed gross breaches of faith" in the matter of repatriation of immigrants who had not wanted to settle after their indenture. Jamaicans had frequently changed their mind about the desirability of immigration, and new schemes could hardly be tried with such "shifting counsels." Crown colonies were far better suited for experiments of this sort, and if the plan worked in Trinidad and British Guiana and if Jamaica still wanted immigrants and would observe the conditions, the Island would then be included in the scheme.[46]

There was much truth in these observations. The Jamaica Assembly had certainly vacillated in its attitude towards immigration, and breaches of contract with the Indians had been committed. Indeed, if the Island had not obtained the £100,000 immigration loan in 1852, part of which was spent on repatriation and the commutation of return passages into settlement grants, the immigrants would probably have fared even worse. A statement of August 1858, prepared by the Jamaica Immigration Office, was illustrative (see Table 16).

Lack of precise information reflected the breakdown of the efficient administration of immigration before 1849 and the subsequent failure to re-establish it. In 1850, 1851, and 1852, various groups of immigrants had become due for repatriation or commutation of their passages home; but with the exception of four repatriates, neither repatriation nor commutation was undertaken until 1853, by which time the first comers were two to three years beyond their period of indenture. It is also significant that the repatriations and commutations of 1853 were paid for out of the British loan of the previous year. The obvious implication is that the Jamaica Legislature had not made any other provision to meet its obligations to these people.

Before the new arrivals of 1860, attempts were made to reorganize the old system of control. The duties of the agent general were restated and eight of the few remaining stipendi-

46. C.O. 137/337, Colonial Office comments on Darling's dispatch, No. 59, 21 April 1858.

ary magistrates were appointed as sub-agents. They were to visit each estate in their districts once every three months, irrespective of other visits required by special circumstances which might arise. Quarterly returns of each estate were to be submitted to the agent general, as well as general reports of the agents on their entire districts. These were all to be summarized and laid before the governor.

TABLE 16. *Record of Indian Immigration, 1845–58*

Years	Entered	Repatriated	Commuted	Unaccounted for
1845	261			
1846	1,851			
1847	2,439			
1851		2	nil	
1852		2	nil	
1853		1,167	664	
1854		429	442	
1855		nil	459	
1858		126	18	
TOTALS	4,551	1,726	1,583	1,597

Source: C.O. 137/338, Darling to Bulwer Lytton, No. 115, 30 Aug. 1850 (enclosure).

NOTE. The Repatriates and Commuters included 355 children born in Jamaica. Of the 1,600 missing immigrants, some no doubt had died of the cholera and other afflictions, and some had deserted the estates.

On paper it was sound enough, but in practice it was a hopeless arrangement. The average age of the magistrates must have been well over fifty, for they had all been appointed at the time of the apprenticeship, 1834–38. Their districts were large.[47] The roads were bad. They had other

47. C.O. 137/343, Darling to Bulwer Lytton, No. 16, 26 Jan. 1859. The sub-agents, the dates of their original appointments, and their districts were as follows: Mr. Chamberlain (Jan. 1836), Trelawny, St. James, Hanover. Mr. Willis (Sept. 1835), St. Thomas in the East. Mr. Bell (Nov. 1834), Clarendon, Vere, St. Dorothy. Mr. Laidlaw (May 1835), St. Elizabeth and Manchester. Mr. Fyfe (Aug. 1835), St. George, Metcalfe, St. Mary. Mr. Hill (April 1836), St. Catherine, St. Thomas in the Vale, St. John. Mr. Kelly (Nov. 1835), Westmoreland. Mr. Ewart (Nov. 1835), agent general, also responsible for St. Andrew.

duties to perform. All were magistrates in Petty Sessions; most, if not all, had parish appointments of one sort or another (as vestrymen, and such like); some had special appointments: Hill was secretary of the stipendiary magistracy and until the end of 1862 a privy councillor; Fyfe was inspector of island prisons. By 1863 the organization and the entire immigration scheme were once more ineffective.[48] That was the last year of any significant immigration in our period.

Except for the years 1860 to 1863, when a total of 6,482 immigrants were brought in, Jamaica immigration schemes produced little result between 1846 and the end of our period. Nonetheless, the eager searching for places of recruitment and the passage of many acts and regulations by the Island Assembly followed from the renewal of confidence after 1854.

The main reason for this was the improvement of sugar prices after the expected slump in 1854, the year of duty equalization. Between 1855 and 1857 prices rose from 26/4 to 35/2 per hundredweight, in both cases exclusive of duty.[49] Then there was a decline, but not until 1861 was there any reversion to the low levels of the early 1850's. From the previous tables showing imports of estate equipment and fertilizers it is apparent that the price improvement was accompanied by a restoration of credit to the planters.

It is also clear that although Britain still remained the chief source of capital for sugar industry development, the local body of merchants in Jamaica was becoming increasingly important in that respect. Records of the late 1840's contain direct evidence of the purchase, or lease, by local merchants of the estates of planters who were going out of produc-

48. C.O. 137/374, Eyre to Newcastle, No. 202, 24 Aug. 1863 (enclosures).

49. This improvement, which coincided with the period of war in the Crimea, was in rough conformity with the general level of prices in Britain, which tended to remain fairly steady or to rise. The very sharp increase of sugar prices in 1855, however, was associated with speculative buying based on shortages caused by West Indian crop failures. See Reed, *The History of Sugar and Sugar Yielding Plants*, ch. 8.

tion. In 1847 and 1848, for example, George William Gordon, a Kingston merchant,[50] bought three properties, in St. Thomas in the East and Portland, for a total of £5,200. Their previous valuations were said to have amounted to £160,000.[51] In 1854 Governor Barkly mentioned the Tharp Estates, in Trelawny, seven of them covering 20,000 acres. In "old times" they had been "reckoned to be a little Principality," averaging 2,500 hogsheads of sugar and clearing it was said, in some years, upwards of £50,000. At the time of Barkly's visit the whole seven were leased to a "Mercantile Firm in Falmouth" for £800 a year, of which £200 were to be laid out in repairs.[52] By 1865 there is frequent mention of the wealthier merchant-proprietors such as Robert Nunes, George Henderson, Michael Solomon, and George Solomon. But it is not at all clear that merchants who acquired sugar estates invested much money in improvements. Some, apparently, intended to subdivide the land and sell or rent it to small settlers; others seem to have gone into pen-keeping and cattle-breeding; some continued in sugar production, but they are not specifically mentioned, nor is there any reason to think that they were eminently successful.

The more important aspect of the situation is the description by the governor, in 1853, of the Country party in the Assembly as made up of "planters and of proprietors of impoverished estates, and of merchants closely connected with the planting interest." [53]

A possible interpretation is that there was a group of merchants who did not own estates but who were closely allied with the sugar interest as creditors. This explanation seems even more likely in view of the failure in 1848 of the Planters' Bank in the Island.

The Planters' Bank, which had been formed in 1839,[54]

50. The G. W. Gordon of Morant Bay rebellion fame.

51. Hon. E. Stanley, *Claims and Resources of the West Indian Colonies*, London, 1850.

52. C.O. 137/323, Barkly to Newcastle, No. 73, 26 May 1854.

53. C.O. 137/316, Grey to Newcastle, No. 40, 10 May 1853.

54. C.O. 137/245, Mr. Calvert to Lord Normanby, 16 Aug. 1839; C.O. 137/240, James Franklin to the governor, 16 Dec. 1839.

listed 130 (later 140) shareholders, and though primarily intended as a Loan Association it had soon extended its activities to include "all the Legitimate Transactions of a Bank of Deposit, Discount, and Circulation." There was, of course, unlimited liability of the shareholders, who, on the backing of their personal fortunes, printed and issued notes which had no right of legal tender. The notes were, however, accepted by most people except the labourers, who usually demanded their wages in silver coin. There were certain essential estate supplies, such as lumber, staves, foodstuffs, and other goods from the American mainland, which planters were unable or found it more expensive to purchase through their agents in Britain and had therefore been accustomed to buy from local merchants engaged in the American trade. It is very probable that these merchants accepted the Planters' Bank notes in payment, using them later to purchase agricultural produce for export.

As long as people had confidence in the ability of the Bank to meet its obligations, all went well, and it would seem that even some of the labourers eventually overcame their early reluctance to accept the notes. After 1846, however, the sudden fall of sugar prices and the planters' shouts of ruinous competition destroyed confidence and initiated a demand by the holders for redemption of the Planters' notes. The demand could not be met. Briefly, the situation was this: liabilities included about £43,800 in notes in circulation and £26,000 in deposits; assets were almost entirely in the form of loans by the Bank which totalled about £180,000 of which only £40,000 were in any way secured. Even so, the security was the signatures of three guarantors of each loan, and these were found to be so frequently repeated that they offered little real guarantee. The Jamaica Assembly refused a request for Government assistance, and the Colonial Office, when given the details, commented severely on the "rotten edifice" of the Bank.

In subsequent dispatches the governor emphasized the need of the planters for a sound system of credit within the Island, and told of plans to form a Government Bank, but the

Assembly's proposal to raise capital by a loan on the credit of some fixed branch of the Island revenue was not acceptable to the Colonial Office, and the matter was dropped.[55]

Insofar as island merchants had been shareholders, or had held the notes of the Bank, or had been depositors in it, the planters' obligations to them would have been significant. The failure of the Bank and the fact that no other credit organization succeeded it would seem to indicate that after 1848 the merchants became a more important source of local credit to the sugar planters.

Other factors also point to a growing connection between the local mercantile and estate-proprietory groups. There was, for instance, the guano trade of the 1850's.

The exports of guano shown in Table 5 indicated a new enterprise in Jamaica, especially among the Kingston merchants. Around the island are scattered many small uninhabited islets or "cays" which are the habitual resort and resting-place of sea-birds. These places, consequently, are rich repositories of guano. In the mid-nineteenth century they were suddenly descended upon by Jamaicans and Americans, all in search of the new manure, and there were occasions when competition for the excrement of sea-gulls almost precipitated international dispute. The Americans had got there first as guano-diggers. Jamaicans had visited the cays in search of turtles and booby eggs. In 1855 the rights of the Americans to dig guano on the Pedro Cays was questioned by the governor, Sir Henry Barkly,[56] and in 1863 and 1864 the Pedro and Morant Cays were formally declared to be British territories and the property of the Crown in Jamaica.[57] It was proposed that they should be leased out by the Island

55. C.O. 137/297, Sir C. Grey to Earl Grey, Nos. 75 and 81, 19 Aug. and 16 Oct. 1848; and C.O. 137/298, Nos. 96 and 107, 4 Nov. and 6 Dec. 1848.

56. C.O. 137/327, Barkly to Labouchere, No. 119, 22 Dec. 1855, complaining of the infringement by Americans of lawful rights of the British owner of the Pedro Cays. In a later chapter the activities of Jamaica merchants in the guano trade will be mentioned more particularly.

57. C.O. 137/381, Eyre to Newcastle, No. 125, 15 Aug. 1864.

Government. By September 1864 one Kingston merchant and ship owner, Mr. Astwood, said that he had removed 1,000 tons of guano from the Pedro Cays. There were competitors in the field and Astwood wanted to secure sole rights, but he did not want to lease the islands, probably because the guano supply was already nearly exhausted.[58] It is very probable that some Kingston merchants supplied guano to island planters, but there is no evidence to suggest how much was sold locally. The price of imported guano in the 1840's ranged from about 20/– per hundredweight for natural guano re-exported from Britain, down to about 10/– per hundred-weight for British manufactured guano,[59] and it is likely that the former was, as far as possible, replaced by local supplies.

Finally, but not least important, was the consequence of property transfers which had been going on since the emancipation. Many of the sugar estates passed into the hands of island residents, some of whom had not previously been engaged in sugar production and whose financial and commercial arrangements had always rested with local merchants rather than with agencies in Britain. In 1854 Governor Barkly, in his diary of a tour through the Island, reported that over half the sugar estates belonged to absentees, but there was nonetheless, a "rapid transfer of the smaller properties to practical Planters which it will be perceived from my journal is going on." [60] A few years later, a visitor to the Island commented: "Nor are the new class of resident planters who have appeared in Jamaica within ten years past by any means to be ignored. They work their estates with prudence and economy, though they lack the advantages that latter-day science has given to American and Cuban proprietors." [61]

Property transfers, however, were limited until near the end of our period by the extremely complicated nature of

58. C.O. 137/384, Eyre to Cardwell, No. 253, 8 Sept. 1864.
59. Anonymous writer of one of the *Eight Treatises*.
60. C.O. 137/323, Barkly to Newcastle, No. 73, 26 May 1854.
61. Sewell, *Ordeal of Free Labour in the British West Indies*, p. 242.

title-deeds and by the fact that on so many estates returns were subject to the prior claims of creditors and annuitants.

It was not always easy for owners to persuade claimants that the estate would no longer yield their expected annuities and should be sold to avoid further loss; nor was it easy to interest prospective buyers in properties which were burdened, or of which the titles were so complicated as to present doubt of their validity.

To ease the situation, an act was passed by Parliament in 1854 to enable the application of the Irish Encumbered Estates Act to West India property;[62] but before it could be put into operation in any colony the Colonial Legislature would have to petition the Crown to bring the act into local effect. The Irish Act, which dated from 1849, made it possible for an encumbered estate to be summarily sold by judicial decree, on the application of the owner or any encumbrancer. The price received would be divided, by a competent tribunal, among the various parties entitled by their claims to a share of it. Finally, the new purchaser would receive the estate free of any encumbrances by means of a special Parliamentary title.

At first, the Jamaica Legislature declined to petition for the application of the act to that island. As most Jamaica estates were owned by people living in Britain, and most of their encumbrancers were also in the United Kingdom, the Jamaican opposition is explainable. Colonial lawyers did not fancy the idea of so much Island business going to lawyers in Britain, and potential buyers resident in Jamaica feared that they would have little opportunity to make offers for encumbered property put up for sale in Britain. Not until March 1861, when the act had already been applied to St. Vincent, Tobago, the Virgin Islands, and St. Kitts, and after several amendments had been introduced to meet West Indian conditions, did the Jamaica Legislature petition for it. Three months later a local Encumbered Estates Court was established in the island, and between that date and the middle of 1864 over thirty estates were disposed of under its regulations.

62. R. J. Cust, *A Treatise on the West Indian Incumbered Estates Acts* (London, 1865), and *Supplement to a Treatise* (London, 1874).

There is little doubt that some Jamaica merchants came
to play a significant part in the financing and marketing of
sugar in the mid-nineteenth century. After 1865, when the
British market for West Indian sugar declined in the face of
increasing importations of subsidized European beet-sugar,
the long-standing American connections of many of the local

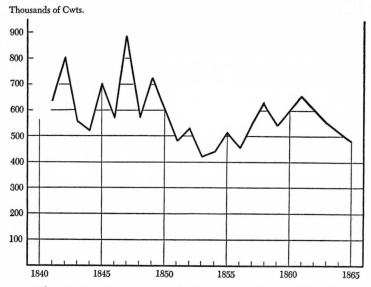

Thousands of Cwts.

Chart 2. Jamaican sugar exported from the Island, 1841–65.

merchants would have served to increase their importance
still further. In the later part of the century the United States
became the chief market for British West Indian sugars.

The Emancipation Act and the Sugar Duties Act both had
deep effects on Jamaican sugar production, but the conditions were quite different. The former brought about a forced
liquidation of capital, for the slaves had been the significant
capital equipment of the estates. On emancipation, the
planter could more easily make the immediate decision to
abandon production, or to re-invest in new capital equipment
in the form of agricultural implements and better factory
machinery. But because sub-marginal estates had already been
forced into abandonment by problems of slave shortage after

the end of the legitimate slave trade in 1807, and by the low prices in the depression following the Napoleonic Wars and lasting into the 1830's, the majority chose to continue production, though on a greatly reduced acreage. There was, accordingly, a sudden great diminution of sugar output, followed by a slow increase which reflected improved agricultural techniques.

The 1846 Act did not present such clear alternatives. The planters who had remained in production, and those who had newly taken over the estates of owners who had sold out after emancipation, now faced a price decline which threatened to prohibit the possibility of further development and also to render recent investments unprofitable. Immediate abandonment or sudden further restriction of the scale of planting would clearly result in great financial loss. The wisest course, as the Directors of the Smith's Agricultural Society pointed out, was to wind up the estate by a gradual restriction of operations as capital equipment became obsolete or unusable and was not replaced.

There was, accordingly, no such immediate and enormous decrease of sugar output as had followed the emancipation; and although many estates did eventually go out of production, the better-circumstanced properties remained to enjoy the improved conditions of the later 1850's. To such estates, which had weathered the relatively low price period between 1848 and 1855, the higher prices of the later 1850's provided an adequate stimulus to renewed capital investment and increased production.

To complete this comparative analysis of conditions in the sugar industry during the 1840's and the 1850's, it is necessary to discuss the movement of sugar prices with an eye to the general trend of prices in Britain during these decades. During the 1840's prices, on the whole, tended to decline, and during the 1850's they rose.[63] But it is the normal behaviour of the prices of basic agricultural products, such as sugar, to

63. Clapham, *The Early Railway Age* (*1820–50*), ch. 13; also the subsequent volume in the series, *Free Trade and Steel, 1850–1886* (Cambridge, 1932), ch. 9.

move more violently than the prices of other commodities in these broad cyclical fluctuations.[64] The reason is that alterations in the price of a basic agricultural product do not produce great changes either in the supply or the demand. Sugar planters, for example, cannot either rapidly expand output or divert their resources to the production of some alternative and currently more profitable commodity. Sugar buyers would be hard put to it to find a suitable substitute for sugar, nor are they likely, when the price falls, to consume enormously increased quantities of it. Sugar prices are therefore liable in free market conditions, to fall relatively low or to rise relatively high as general price levels move downwards or upwards, and the sugar planter prospers in a period of rising prices. To this extent, therefore, the 1850's were better years for the planters, and this followed from conditions beyond the narrower consideration of circumstances peculiar to the sugar industry and the sugar market.

On the other hand, the gloomy aspect of the 1840's must not be overworked. It has been shown that although sugar prices had been declining since 1840, the really severe deterrent to production came only in 1846, when the price fell below thirty shillings per hundredweight, excluding duty. Moreover, though the price of his own produce was declining, the sugar planter, in a period of general price decline, was paying less for the goods of which he was a purchaser. This was true not only of goods bought in Britain but also, as will be shown in a subsequent chapter, of island produce, such as provisions which planters bought for themselves and their indentured labourers.

Nonetheless, the abandonment of sugar production by many planters, the availability of capital or credit after 1834 by the granting of slave-compensation awards, the diverse activities of the mass of the ex-slaves, and the increasing wealth of the local merchants which accompanied the post-emancipa-

64. Today, by way of illustration, we have industrial stabilization schemes in wheat, sugar, cocoa, and other basic agricultural industries, designed to protect producers from the consequence of severe price falls.

tion growth of local trade, had all subscribed since 1834 to a diversification of the economy. There was a spreading out of agricultural interests, which added to the importance of the minor export staples; and there was also an interest in new industrial ventures.

CHAPTER 4

Capital Enterprises other than Sugar

ATTEMPTS to diversify the economy fell under three general headings. First, there were the efforts made to revive old agricultural industries, but the very fact of their earlier decline or abandonment augured slight chance of success. Secondly, there were attempts to develop quite new enterprises, and here the key factor was the availability, or otherwise, of hitherto unworked resources. Thirdly, and largely dependent on conditions in other existing industries, were the proposals to launch ancillary or service industries.

In any of these attempts the scarcity of labour and of capital, which so obviously affected the sugar industry, might offer serious handicaps. In the formation of new or the revival of old ventures the attraction of private capital was extremely difficult, not entirely because of the wide range of investment opportunities in Britain, in the larger colonies, and in foreign territories, but also because of the conditions imposed by existing company law. In 1855 only a very few British industrial ventures, by exceptional grant of privilege or by incorporation under an Act of Parliament, enjoyed a limited liability, and for another ten or fifteen years unlimited liability remained the common condition of business enterprise.

But these were not absolute deterrents to industrial development. They might or might not retard it, depending on the nature of the individual project; and so too, might other occurrences, such as accident, delay, mismanagement, or a change in the general economic environment.

The main sources of capital for industrial development were

private investments by people in the colony or in Britain who would become shareholders. British financial institutions were not concerned with long-term financing of development, and Government, both in Britain and Jamaica, provided funds only for specific projects that did not attract private capital and were in the category of public services or public works.

In Jamaica, the main body of investment was made by planters who sought to spread their assets, by ex-planters looking for new interests, and by the merchants and professional groups. Labourers, small settlers, craftsmen, and others of the general population who accumulated cash reserves generally tended to hoard. A few were depositors in the savings banks which were maintained in several of the parishes, but these deposits were lent to the Island Treasury and were not therefore available for private enterprise.[1]

The interest of British investors had to be aroused by consistent canvassing, and the total response was relatively meagre. We know that the £222,250 spent in building the Jamaica Railway was raised in Britain. Later, some thousands more, perhaps £150,000, were put into mining ventures, and in the early 1860's a few thousands were raised in London and Manchester for cotton-growing projects.

It is important to observe that British capitalists invested in a Jamaica Railway when there was a railway boom in England; in Jamaica mining enterprises when the gold rushes had begun in California and Australia; and in cotton-growing when there was a cotton famine in England. In each case there was an external stimulant. Those who were classed as the West India Sugar Interest, it is true, provided a considerable stream of capital, at any rate until 1846, but it was capital for the sugar industry rather than for new undertakings.

Two other sources of capital—other empire and foreign capitalists, and money brought in by immigrants—are mentioned only to be dismissed as of little importance. The rest of the empire and the United States, which is today the chief

1. See the accounts in various years of the *Jamaica almanac*. That for 1846 is particularly helpful. These were private banks and in themselves, therefore, were a form of private enterprise.

foreign source of capital for the British West Indies, were then all capital-importing areas, and this of course reminds us of Jamaica's lack of attractiveness to the British who were exporters of capital. There was some American investment in copper-mining in the 1850's, and perhaps there were a few American share-holders in the Jamaica Silk Company; but that appears to have been the limit. As for immigrants' capital, throughout the period there were incoming settlers with some money, chiefly political refugees from Haiti and Cuba, but they were relatively few. The majority of immigrants were indentured labourers from India and elsewhere.

The conclusion must be that, all sources taken together, there was very little capital available for economic development in Jamaica during these twenty-five years. The reason was of course the greater probability of high profits from enterprises elsewhere and, in the immediate post-emancipation months, the uncertainty about life, labour, and property in the new system of free labourers. But as the teething troubles of freedom were overcome a measure of confidence was restored, during the governorship of Lord Metcalfe, and was encouraged under Lord Elgin into that exuberance which was the note of our opening chapter. Moreover, in those years when Lord Elgin and many influential Jamaicans voiced their belief in the ultimate economic recovery of the Island and in the wealth of resources other than sugar which awaited development, the curiosity and the participation of British capitalists was revived.[2] As Elgin told the Legislature in October 1845: "There is reason to believe that the exertions which the colonists have made of late in improving the resources within their reach, have attracted the attention of British capitalists, and that investments in Jamaica are regarded by them with increasing favour." [3]

Apart from the larger enterprises, which we shall discuss in some detail, there were investigations and small beginnings made in a variety of undertakings, many of which were purely

2. C.O. 137/284, Elgin to Stanley, confidential, 23 Sept. 1845.
3. C.O. 137/285. Elgin's speech opening the Legislature, Oct. 1845; enclosed in Elgin to Stanley No. 89, 21 Oct. 1845.

experimental. The fact that most of them were abandoned
does not detract from the importance of their commencement.
There was, for example, a short-lived attempt to grow tea, and
a sample was sent to London, but it would have had to compete on equal terms with the China leaf, and that was impossible.[4]

The production of fibres,[5] though continuously proposed by
a few enthusiasts, came to nothing. In 1835 a "Colonial Fibre
Company" received a charter enabling it to operate in Jamaica
and British Guiana.[6] But in Jamaica, at any rate, no more was
heard of the matter.

The large-scale cultivation of tobacco of which Governor
Metcalfe had told the Assembly in 1841 does not appear in
the records, and subsequent reports tell of it as a small-scale
peasant production mainly for the local market.

The whole dismal story of the new industries which, until
1846 at any rate, were regarded in Jamaica and in Britain as
the first shoots of a new economic structure, can be illustrated
in reviews of the larger enterprises in cotton-growing, silk
production, copper-mining, and railway development. Between
them they illustrate not only the various effects of the post
1846 troubles but also the peculiar difficulties which would in
any case have been encountered by their promoters.

In the eighteenth century cotton had been one of the main
export staples of the British Caribbean colonies, surpassed in
importance only by sugar and coffee. By the 1840's it had long
been forced out of production by the overwhelming output
of the southern United States (see Table 17).

In view of the existing market situation, any attempt to
reintroduce this cultivation on a large scale in Jamaica in the
1840's would have been a rash and defiant indiscretion, unless
the intention was to produce a particularly fine type of long-

4. C.O. 137/252, Board of Trade to James Stephen, 9 March 1840.
5. From banana, plantain, penguine (of the American aloe genus),
and other plants, but not including cotton, which is separately discussed.
6. C.O. 137/328, West India Committee to Lord John Russell, 8
May 1855.

stapled sea-island cotton. The sample sent by Sir Charles Metcalfe and reported on by the Liverpool brokers in early 1842 was from the experimental plantation of a Mr. Gourgues who had cultivated some land near Kingston.[7] But sea-island cotton is a difficult plant to cultivate,[8] and, even if the market had been favourable, these were years of unreliable weather and unsettled labour conditions in the island. It is not surprising that Mr. Gourgues' attempt was eventually abandoned and

TABLE 17. *Imports of Cotton into Britain,*
1786–1850 (percentages of total)

Years	U.S.A.	Brazil	B.W.I.	Mediterranean	East Indies	Sundries
1786–90	.16	7.87	70.75	20.44	.78	——
1796–1800	24.08	11.43	35.23	18.47	8.9	1.89
1806–10	53.14	16.07	16.23	1.28	12.79	.49
1846–50	81.13	3.76	.12	2.04	12.76	.19

Source: T. Ellison, *The Cotton Trade of Great Britain,* p. 86, quoted by G. P. Jones and A. G. Pool in *A Hundred Years of Economic Development in Great Britain* (London 1948), p. 95.

that cotton did not again become an important staple product.

From this time on, any serious interest in the possibility of cotton cultivation in Jamaica emanated from the British rather than from Jamaicans. At first the British interest was almost entirely academic. It arose out of a fear that if Britain's supplies of any essential import came largely from a single foreign country and any disaster should befall that country, or British relations with that country should deteriorate, extreme hardships might result. The argument was summed up by one writer as follows:

> When a nation derives the whole or any considerable portion of any important article from abroad, it is necessarily exposed, especially if the supply come from only

7. W. J. Gardner, *A History of Jamaica* (London, 1873), p. 413.

8. Edwards, *The History, Civil and Commercial, of the British West Indies,* 2, 309–24, deals with cotton cultivation, especially in Jamaica. See also the account of the Jamaica Cotton Company given below.

> one foreign country, or but a few, to the risk of more or
> less inconvenience, from any interruption of the friendly
> intercourse subsisting with it or them. When such impor-
> tant articles are furnished by a colony, their supply is, of
> course, comparatively secure; and in such cases colonial
> possessions may be of peculiar value.[9]

Theoretically this was sound, but it was hardly translatable
into practice, because as long as the single foreign country
remained the cheapest source no buyer, in a system of free
trade, would be likely to buy dearer colonial goods as a sort of
insurance against misfortunes which might not occur during
his lifetime.

At the same time this theory was being put forward, however, there were a few people in Britain who were seriously
declaring that the resources of the British Caribbean were
not being sufficiently exploited, and that if they were, the
Colonies would be hard competitors with the foreign producers of sugar, cotton, and other British imports. Among
them was Stephen Bourne the ex-stipendiary magistrate who
had spent much of his life in Jamaica and subsequently in
British Guiana. He was a well-meaning, hard-working man,
with a sincere desire to promote the welfare of all classes in
the West Indian colonies. He spent much of his time, after his
return to Britain about the mid-nineteenth century, speaking
and writing on economic conditions,[10] and on many occasions
his theme was the industrial development of the British Caribbean. One such address, delivered at the London Coffee
House, Ludgate Hill, on 15 June 1853, prepared the way for
the formation of the British West Indian Association for encouraging and extending the growth of cotton and sugar, and
establishing industrial schools in the British Colonies.[11] The
argument was mainly in support of the need to develop British

9. J.R. McCulloch, *A Descriptive and Statistical Account of the
British Empire* (4th ed. London, 1854), 2, 530.

10. S. Bourne, *Trade, Population and Food,* a series of papers on
economic statistics, London 1880.

11. The address was published in the same year in pamphlet form.

Guiana by drainage of the coastal strip, by improved mechanical farming, and by the unrestricted migration of workers from the more densely populated islands,[12] and of capitalist settlers from Britain and elsewhere. His account of the agricultural potential of the British Caribbean was exaggerated, perhaps mistakenly, possibly deliberately in order to excite the support of his audience.

But the pronouncements of the theorists and the labour of Mr. Bourne failed to produce any real result until Civil War threatened in the United States and the main supply of raw cotton for the industry of Lancashire was obviously in danger of being shut off. In the autumn of 1860 the governor of Jamaica was asked about the possibilities of cotton-growing in the island. He replied that his informants, the Jamaica Society of Arts, did not hold out any expectation of success in such a venture.[13] There was no reason why they should have. But by 1862, when the cotton famine was reaching its height in Lancashire, there were experimental cotton plantations in several parts of the Island, especially in the parishes of Hanover and St. Thomas in the East.[14]

Most of these plantations were sponsored by companies or associations in England, but some of the resident planters and small settlers were also engaged. Mr. Eyre thought that their chances of success were probably better than those of the overseas companies whose agents in Jamaica were not always well chosen. One company formed in Kingston with lands

12. The possibility of importing labour from densely populated islands such as Barbados had also been considered by the sugar planters. The idea had, naturally, been opposed by Barbadian employers and also by the Colonial Office. In 1864 (C.O. 137/384; see minutes on Eyre to Cardwell, No. 245, 7 Sept. 1864) Henry Taylor pointed out that it had been held that Her Majesty's Government could not be a party to measures taken by one W.I. colony to appropriate money to withdraw labourers from another W.I. colony. The Government of Barbados, or any other colony, he said, would have a right to legislate with a view to defeating any such emigration.

13. C.O. 137/351, Darling to Newcastle, No. 139, 10 Oct. 1860.

14. C.O. 137/367, Eyre to Newcastle, No. 86, 1 Oct. 1862.

near to the city was able to get boys' labour from the Kingston Reformatory and so at least had found no labour problem.[15]

There is very little ready information about any of these
efforts, and there is little temptation to search out the details
because none of them succeeded. The most important was the
Jamaica Cotton Company,[16] founded in London apparently
sometime in 1861. It was the child of Stephen Bourne, launched
"at length and after much toil and disappointment." [17] There
can be little doubt that it had required the American Civil
War as well as Mr. Bourne to set the enterprise going.

The original number of shares issued by the Company was
2,000, of which all but 100 had been taken. The price had
been £10 each. In 1862 the directors had been authorized to
increase the capital to £50,000. The money had been spent
in buying 5,000 acres in St. Thomas in the East.

Only a small part of the total 5,000 acres were actually
planted in cotton because of the lack of capital. It had cost
£10–15 to fence, drain, and plant each acre; and if, eventually,
3,000 acres were brought under cultivation, there would be a
need for buildings and machinery costing £30,000. The Company was short of funds by about £20,000.

Even in 1865, Bourne claimed, all was going well. His son,
who had spent much of his youth in Jamaica, was back in the
Island with his family and was managing the business there.
The estates had been visited by Mr. Whitelock, the custos of
Hanover, where other cotton plantations had been started in
1851, and he had expressed confidence in the venture. If cotton
prices held for a few years longer at 1/– a pound for good
quality, the Company ought to pay handsomely. But even if
suitable cotton could not be raised successfully, the Company
was aware of the possibilities of a diversified production of
sugar, cotton, arrowroot, coffee, and fibres for cordage and
paper pulp. Sea-island and the other long-stapled cottons were

15. C.O. 137/384, Eyre to Cardwell, No. 256, 10 Sept. 1864.

16. C.O. 137/398, Bourne to Cardwell, 27 Nov. 1865.

17. It was a limited-liability company, probably the first such to
operate in Jamaica.

very delicate and the last crop had failed badly. As a result, only 200 people were irregularly employed, whereas, if the Company could only find capital to continue its development, it would eventually provide constant employment for at least 600 people.

The plea that such a great enterprise should not be allowed to fail roused no financial support from the British Government. It was hardly to be expected that it could have, when it was the policy of Government to steer clear of interference with supply, demand, and the employment of private capital. And in any case, the American Civil War and the cotton famine were drawing to a close. The Jamaica Cotton Company and the panic expired together.

The attempt to reintroduce this industry when circumstances favourable to its existence had long disappeared illustrates the way in which a disruption of normal international trade could, and still does,[18] encourage investment in the establishment or expansion of ventures which previously might not have been attractive. After the brief experiment by Mr. Gourgues in 1841 very little was heard of cotton in Jamaica until in the panic of the 1860's the Cotton Supply Association in Lancashire began to search wildly for other sources of raw material. The West Indies was only one possibility: India, Egypt, the Mediterranean—all figured in the search, and with more successful results. That was all the more reason why, when normal trade with the Southern States of America was resumed, Jamaica fell right out of the picture.

Jamaicans had not managed to summon up much enthusiasm for the attempted revival of cotton, but the new industries, understandably, aroused greater interest. The Jamaica Silk Company[19] was established on 27 October 1840. The

18. In this respect we may wonder about the stimuli given to industrial development in the sterling area by the present scarcity of dollars—for example, the encouragement to sterling sugar producers to expand output while dollar producers every year produce surpluses which they cannot sell.

19. *Jamaica Almanac*, 1846: trustees, Hon. Joseph Gordon, John G. Vidal, Charles Mackglashan; chairman, Hon. Edward J. Panton; deputy chairman, B. S. Moncrieffe; auditors, George Barnett, James Allwood;

person responsible for its formation was Samuel Whitmarsh, an American from Boston. Since about 1830 Whitmarsh had been employed in silk production in the United States, but in 1840 he decided, for reasons unstated but probably connected with the unsuitability of the New England climate, to change his location.[20] He paid a visit of inspection and enquiry to Jamaica.

What he found in the island obviously satisfied him for soon after his crop of July 1840 he left Boston for Jamaica, bringing with him thirty Bostonians and a suitable supply of silk-worm eggs.

The site chosen for the mulberry plantation, together with the silk factory and cottage accommodation for the immigrants, was called Metcalfeville, a few miles to the east of the main road from Claremont to St. Ann's Bay, in the Parish of St. Ann. Whitmarsh was obviously keen, energetic, and of considerable ability in his business. He set about the work promptly and by the end of February 1841, not more than six months after his arrival at Metcalfeville, he was able to send a full account of progress, as well as a sample of the first silk produced in Jamaica, to Sir Charles Metcalfe.

He was convinced that, once the industry was properly established and in full production, Jamaica silk would be of first-class quality, superior even to that of India or China, and yet the cost of production in Jamaica would be no greater—

directors, Hon. Edward J. Panton, Hon. Joseph Gordon, B. S. Moncrieffe, John W. Davis, J. C. Vidal, Charles Mackglashan, Charles Stewart, Thomas L. Bayley; register, Beng. Walker; solicitors, Messrs. Barnett, McNeil, and Minot.

20. Whitmarsh was the manager of the Company; and although it seems certain that he was also a considerable shareholder, it is obvious that the greater part of the capital had been subscribed by Jamaicans. The Company executives were resident in the Island, some of them Jamaican-born. (Mr. Moncrieffe was a distinguished coloured barrister-at-law.) Attempts to produce silk in New England were handicapped by climatic conditions and lack of cheap labour, but about the 1840's New England factories were set up to manufacture silk cloth from raw silk imported from the Far East (see H. Faulkner, *American Economic History*, 7th ed. New York, Harper's, 1954, p. 252). It was probably Whitmarsh's intention to supply these factories with raw silk from Jamaica.

perhaps even less. In his last crop in the United States the
silk-worms with proper care and attention and warmed by
artificial heat had not commenced to spin cocoons until forty
days after their emergence from the eggs. This was the normal
period in France and Italy too, but in Jamaica even in the
crude surroundings of the half-built establishment the worms
had begun to spin on the twenty-sixth day from the eggs. This,
he said, was most important, "as the expense is thus reduced,
and as it is an established fact, that the quantity of Silk from
a given number of worms will be increased in proportion to
the shortness of the period of *Natural* feeding . . ." The cocoons had then been left in the frames for three days for the
worms to finish winding, and on the twenty-ninth day the
sample of silk had been on its way to Spanish Town.

The Company owned about 400 acres of which 100 had
already been cleared of timber and were being rapidly planted
in mulberry trees, 5,000 to the acre. A steam saw mill was being
installed to prepare lumber off the estate for the various factory buildings and cottages for his American immigrants who
were in excellent health. Metcalfeville promised to be "a prosperous little village of farmers and mechanics," and for the
silk industry in Jamaica there was "every prospect of future
success." [21]

News of the silk company and the sample of silk forwarded
by the governor were duly received in London, and there
followed an interesting little correspondence between Lord
John Russell, then secretary of state for the colonies, and
Whitmarsh, with Governor Metcalfe acting as intermediary.
The secretary of state informed Whitmarsh that an attempt at
silk manufacture was also in progress in Montserrat, passed
on some details of methods followed in that island, and asked
particularly if Whitmarsh was aware of the necessity of cold-
storing the silk-worm eggs. To this Whitmarsh replied, a little
indignantly, but justifiably so, for he had been in the business
for a long time, that he had long been aware of this necessity.
In Jamaica "Our eggs are now at the ice house in Kingston,

21. C.O. 137/255, Metcalfe to Russell, Nos. 188 and 198, 12 &
28 Feb. 1841.

from whence we shall withdraw them as we need them." He
concluded by saying that he would gladly exchange information with the Montserrat people, and remarked once again
on the good prospects of his own company. The first export
would be made in a few months' time, and would be followed
by regular monthly crops as the mulberry trees increased in
strength.[22]

During the next months, however, although Whitmarsh's
optimism increased, the Company began to find itself short
of money. On 30 April 1842 he reported progress to the directors of the company in a manner which reads like a pep talk.
By that time the paid-up capital amounted to £30,000, but
more was needed "to pay off all the Bonds of the Company,
furnish Cocooneries and carry out our plans in full . . ." In
view of the excellent results of all experiments to date and the
promise of immediate and large profits to be derived from the
plantation, he respectfully proposed to the directors "that the
unpaid calls should forthwith be paid up to meet the current
expenses and that all the unsubscribed Scrip Shares of the
Company be filled up and signed and forwarded to an Agent
in London to be disposed of at not less than £20 per share
paid up in full."

This confident proposal was based on his detailed analysis of
the Company's condition. There were now 200 acres in mulberry trees and more were being planted, so that eventually
350 of the whole 400 acres would be in plant. Each acre
yielded 10,000 pounds of mulberry leaves every three months,
and 80 pounds of leaves would make one pound of silk. There
would therefore be a yield of 500 pounds of reeled silk per
acre per year, making a total output of 175,000 pounds of silk
annually from 350 acres. This quantity, moreover, would increase as the mulberry trees grew older and stronger. The costs
of production, per pound of silk, were as follows: (a) gathering 80 pounds of leaves, 3d.; (b) feeding them out, 2d.; (c)
gathering cocoons when finished, 2d.; (d) reeling one pound
of silk, 1/3. This added up to 1/10, and making allowances
for interest on the paid-up capital of £30,000, the average

22. C.O. 137/256, Metcalfe to Russell, No. 237, 11 Aug. 1841.

cost of production of one pound of silk would not exceed 2/6. There was no doubt that this was highly satisfactory,[23] and now all that was needed was the large iron cocoonery which he proposed to order from England for immediate delivery at St. Anns' Bay.[24]

Whitmarsh's appeal was favourably received, and although some observers were full of criticism of what they called, for no apparent reason, a "frivolous and contemptible" enterprise, the shareholders in the Island, who numbered about twenty, raised no objection to the plans for financial expansion. Whitmarsh himself sailed for England in May to further the business, taking with him the sample of which Durant in London was to speak so enthusiastically. It is possible that English capitalists took up the outstanding scrip shares at £20 each; but from then on, things began to go badly.

Until the essential building was complete, there was no possibility of production on a significant scale. It had been hoped that the prefabricated iron cocoonery,[25] together with proper reeling machines, would arrive in September 1842, but they did not, it seems, reach Metcalfeville until the following year; for when Lord Elgin, the new governor, stopped at the plantation during his tour round the Island in March–April 1843 he found the workers putting up the building. Whitmarsh told him that little labour was required to put it up and the cost was comparatively moderate.[26] In the meantime three other important tasks had been given preference: completing the workers' cottages, supplying and planting the mulberry trees more closely so as to reduce weed-growth, and accumulating a large quantity of silk-worm eggs to eliminate the need to import supplies.[27]

The cocoonery was not ready for use until May 1843, when

23. For an estimate given in 1843 of the price which Jamaica silk might raise in England, see above, p. 33; below, p. 134.

24. C.O. 137/257, see reports of S.M.'s Woolfrys and Bell. C.O. 137/262, Metcalfe to Stanley, No. 125, 6 May 1842 (enclosure).

25. C.O. 137/281. There were several other British exports of iron "prefabs" at this time, some to West Africa.

26. C.O. 137/273, Elgin to Stanley, No. 112, 20 April 1843.

27. C.O. 137/264, report of S.M. Woolfrys, 1 Nov. 1842.

a most favourable report was sent to Lord Elgin by the local stipendiary magistrate. He described it as being 225 feet long, 68 feet wide, and 35 feet high, together with an iron reeling-house 100 feet by 50 feet. There was also a wooden building which housed a steam engine to propel the reeling machines. All these buildings with their various fittings, which included a small railway (the exact purpose of which he did not state), would be completely ready in two or three weeks, when Whitmarsh would begin production. It was anticipated that by the end of July the plantation would be producing about 200 pounds of silk daily.[28]

But when the buildings were at last completed and Whitmarsh sent to the Kingston Ice House for a supply of eggs, he discovered to his dismay that about 1,600 ounces of eggs were spoiled because they had been too long in storage, and another seventy ounces had also been ruined as a result of some failure in the Ice House. This meant another long delay as well as the expense of ordering a fresh supply. The loss both of time and of money was severe. Certainly, there was now no prospect of a silk crop in 1843. Enough was gathered "to test the skill of some young females in acquiring the art of reeling . . ." The young females proved their dexterity and a small quantity of silk was shipped to London.

Whitmarsh cannot possibly have been happy, but he was not yet prepared to surrender. Benjamin Walker, a Kingston solicitor who was the register [29] of the Company, gave Lord Elgin news of it in October 1843. He credited Whitmarsh for having "every regard to improvement and economy" and re-iterated the chant of faith: one ton of mulberry leaves would yield 20 pounds of reeled silk, five or six tons of leaves from one acre would thus yield a gross return of £100 to £120 if silk sold at 20/- a pound.[30]

There was some contraction here, however, from the claims of Whitmarsh before the Company directors some eighteen

28. C.O. 137/274, report of S.M. Woolfrys, 1 May 1843.

29. This was the word used in contemporary accounts, probably meaning "registrar."

30. C.O. 137/275, Elgin to Stanley, No. 162, 4 Oct. 1843 (enclosure).

months previously. The expected yield of silk from a given quantity of leaves is less, and there is no mention of four crops of leaves per year.[31] Nonetheless, a gross return of £35,000 a year, if 350 acres were in production, was still a considerable reward, considering that labour costs were small and the total capital outlay by this time probably did not exceed £50,000.[32]

The problem now facing the Company was that with all its share capital expended, it would have to sit through another long period of waiting while fresh supplies of eggs were arriving from abroad—probably from the United States. In the interim money would be needed to pay the labourers who must continue to tend the mulberry plantation, to meet interest charges on capital, to maintain buildings and fittings in good working order, to pay wages to the thirty Bostonians, who might otherwise wander off into other employments, and to allow Whitmarsh a salary.

By November of the following year, 1844, there had apparently been no change for the better, and although Whitmarsh had declared himself still confident of ultimate success, the majority of the shareholders had for many months been thinking differently.[33] The project was now four years old and their investments had still yielded no return. Appeals were made to the Jamaica Legislature for financial assistance. It is very probable that Benjamin Walker's letter to Lord Elgin in October 1843 was part of a softening-up process before the request for help. The Legislature did, in fact, respond with a loan of £3,000. But it was of no avail; the eggs did not arrive until 1845 and the remaining history of the venture can be summarized in two further reports from Stipendiary Magistrate Woolfrys,[34] who had faithfully watched its progress from the beginning. On 1 November 1845 he

31. Cf. with figures on p. 132, above.

32. Eighteen months previously the paid-up share capital had totalled £30,000. We assume that the shareholders had met Whitmarsh's appeal to pay up the remainder in full, and it is also possible that some of the £20 scrip shares had been accepted in London.

33. C.O. 137/279, report of S.M. Woolfrys, 1 May 1844: C.O. 137/283, report of S.M. Woolfrys, 1 Nov. 1844.

34. C.O. 137/287, and C.O. 137/289, Woolfrys' reports.

wrote to Lord Elgin: "I regret that I cannot report any thing favourable of the Silk Company's Establishment or hold out any prospects of its ultimate success to the Share holders." In May of the following year he penned the obituary: "The Silk or Mulberry plantation, I regret to say, has totally failed and since abandoned . . ."

The silk company came and went before the Sugar Duties Act of 1846, and its decline cannot in any way be attributed to changes in British tariff policy. It was a completely new enterprise in Jamaica, introduced by a man who was apparently honest, capable, and enthusiastic. It was also the type of industry that would have been extremely well-suited to Jamaica at the time, because it required the services of few labourers, it need have made no exorbitant demands on capital, and it would have served to stimulate the growth of industrial skills in the Island. If documents can be trusted, there were no obstacles presented by soil or climate, although it is possible that the long and widespread drought of late 1845 and the beginning of 1846 may have served to hasten the Company's failure. On the basis of the available evidence, that failure must be attributed to factors both beyond and within the control of the promoters.

The main factor would seem to have been the costly accident of delay in the arrival of the iron prefabricated cocoonery from Britain. It may be important that by the time the essential building was completed, the spring rains were over and several months of comparatively dry weather lay ahead. It was certainly of disastrous importance that by the time the buildings were ready 1,600 ounces of silk-worm eggs had perished from having been kept too long in storage, and that replacements were so long arriving. For these misfortunes Whitmarsh cannot be held responsible.

The second factor leading to the abandonment of the project was the inability of the Company to survive delay, for it must be remembered that as early as May 1844 the shareholders were beginning to throw in the sponge. There are, of course, explanatory features. The Company had already been in existence for some years and had shown no returns on capital, and as early as April 1842 there had obviously been some financial embarrassment. It seems a fair criticism to say that if Whitmarsh had canvassed the scheme more widely before actually embarking upon it, he might have won support from a larger number of Jamaicans with capital. A larger issue of shares might then have been distributed more widely, and the unpaid calls would have been available to meet emergencies such as eventually arose. As it was, the project was not sufficiently popular in the beginning to ensure even the taking up of the whole issue of shares, and by the financial arrangements of 1842 the Company had called in all its capital reserves. When later disaster came there was little chance of recovery. The great speed with which Whitmarsh had established the Company, though admirable from the point of view of physical and technical accomplishment, was unsatisfactory from the aspect of financial organization.

In contrast to the small number of the supporters of the silk enterprise, the copper-mining industry attracted many people. During the 1850's almost every important landowner dabbled, or would have liked to dabble, in prospecting. At the beginning of our period there had been an attempt to work lead on Hope Estate in St. Andrew; and a copper mine then actually at work in the same parish promised to be a great success.[35]

In 1839 reference had been made to the lead mine, and other mineral possibilities: "The lead ore of Jamaica is extremely rich, and heavily impregnated with silver; several varieties have been found, and, indeed, worked at Liguanea, where striated antimony is obtainable; in the lower mountains of Liguanea every variety of copper ore is in profusion . . ."[36]

The Hope lead mine hardly figures in official letters and dispatches to England. A good deal of money appears to have been spent bringing water along an aqueduct and in erecting

35. J. M. Phillippo, *Jamaica: Its Past and Present State*, p. 72.
36. *Jamaica Almanac*, 1839, p. 48.

machinery to crush the ore, but unfortunately the lode seemed to be fragmentary, and although the business dragged on from year to year, there appeared to be nothing in it.[37]

In the early 1840's another company had been formed to work a copper mine in the Port Royal Mountains. This was the Mount Vernon Mining Company.[38] There were some notable people among the officials. Mr. Dallas, speaker of the Assembly, was vice president, and Edward Jordon and Charles Lake, two coloured men of distinction, were directors. At first all went well, and, as told in Chapter 1, the samples of ore sent to Britain for analysis received high commendation. But there were still some questions to be answered before the enterprise could be called a success. First, were these samples typical of the whole deposit? Secondly, how large was the whole deposit? Thirdly, was there enough capital and skilled labour available to work the mine? And fourthly, as Jamaica had no coal and the ore would have to be shipped to England for smelting, could this be done profitably? [39]

In January, March, and April of 1842 the answers were implied in three reports to the president on the condition of the Company.[40] There were now four galleries or stations, at each of which the prospects were most encouraging. The locality of the veins allowed a comparatively easy approach to them, and "were these prospects offered in Cornwall they would be seized and prosecuted vigorously." In the middle of April progress was stopped in order to ventilate the mine, and when this was done it was proposed to push forward on

37. F. Cundall, "An Historic Jamaica Estate" published in *West India Committee Circular*, London, 1927.

38. *Jamaica Almanac,* 1846: president, James Ward; vice president, Hon. Samuel Jackson Dallas; directors, Andrew Johnson, Samuel Murphy, Charles Dewdney, John Harvey, John Burger, Edward Jordon, John Nunes, Edward Lewis, Charles Lake, Henry Hutchings; managing director, J. Drew; hon. secy., E. C. Lewis; bankers, Colonial Bank.

39. C.O. 137/259, Mr. Roderick Murchison, president of the Geological Society to R. V. Smith, M.P., 6 March 1841.

40. C.O. 137/262, enclosures in Metcalfe to Stanley, No. 123, 29 April 1842. Although John Drew was the managing director, these reports were made by a Mr. J. Street. It is possible that he was a practical miner employed to supervise the operations.

one large good lode in one of the galleries. To do more than that would require more labour than was available. The present force consisted of four skilled miners and a few labourers; to sink the mine farther would call for more than twice as many workers. As for machinery, the need would be "trifling" and "the probable cost of proving the mine" would be £5,000 at most. Before all that was spent, however, there should be some financial returns to the promoters which might be ploughed back.

Although the wording was optimistic, the probability of failure can be read between the lines. Some good ores had been found, and that was the limit of success up to date. To say that such prospects would be "prosecuted with vigour" in Cornwall did not necessarily mean that the same enthusiasm would be merited in Jamaica. Though Cornish ores were less valuable, according to their copper content, they were known to exist and were being worked in quantity, and the Cornish mine owners did not have to ship the ore to smelters across the Atlantic Ocean. In addition, the Jamaica Company, before their mine could even be proved sucessfully, would have to import several thousand pounds worth of machinery as well as skilled personnel to use and maintain it. The local people would provide the unskilled labour, but only if they were paid at a rate competitive with their earnings on provision grounds or estates, and only if they were paid promptly. These would have been considerable disadvantages even to a company well-established and long-experienced in the mining industry. For novitiates, even with a qualified employee at their elbow, the difficulties were increased.

The venture apparently struggled on, for a year later Mr. Kent, the local stipendiary justice, reported to the governor that mining operations at Mount Vernon had drawn off a few labourers from the neighbouring estates; [41] and the Census of 1844 listed forty-one miners in its record of occupations.[42] But there were no exports, and although the mine was kept open, work in it eventually ceased altogether. In his report

41. C.O. 137/274, report of S.M. Kent, 1 May 1843.
42. See below, Appendix 1.

on the Blue Books for 1847 and 1848 the governor, Sir Charles
Grey, remarked that although mineral deposits were known
to exist in Jamaica no mines were being worked. He mentioned
"an open mine of copper in the Port Royal mountains which
was worked only a few years ago and was abandoned as it
is said only from a want of capital." [43]

But this was not the end of mining in Jamaica. California
and Australia were to have their gold rushes and Jamaicans
were soon to have a copper rush—in the excitement of which,
unfortunately, very little copper was found.

In 1851 a fever of prospecting broke out: Rumours wove
magic circles round copper, lead, antimony, graphite, mer-
cury, iron, and even coal. By the end of 1852 not only Jamaican
but British and American capital as well was engaged in
searching out the mineral wealth of the Island. So keen was
the activity that the governor began to consult the Colonial
Office about the rights of the Crown over mineral deposits.
According to the opinion of the Colony's attorney general, all
gold and silver mined was the property of the Crown; but all
the other ores belonged to the subject, who must, however,
pay the Crown a royalty of one-twentieth of the gross proceeds.
This raised several important questions. Under such regulations there would obviously be no inducement to private individuals to work any gold or silver which might be found,
and also very complicated issues would arise if, in mining for
other metals, companies were to extract ores which contained
percentages of gold or silver. Secondly, if royalties did, in fact,
begin to accrue to the Crown from the extraction of metals
other than gold or silver, how would the Crown propose to
use this revenue? Thirdly, what would be the best way to
give licenses or agreements to prospectors under the present
circumstances? Fourthly, what about foreign prospectors who
were coming into Jamaica, especially from the United States?
According to existing regulations a foreigner who took out
naturalization papers in Jamaica was a British subject only
in Jamaica and its dependencies.[44] If these people left Jamaica

43. C.O. 137/304, report on Blue Books.
44. Cayman Islands, and the Turks and Caicos Islands. The Cayman
Islands north-west of Jamaica, had since the mid-seventeenth century

they presumably reverted to their original nationalities and rights in their own countries. What would happen, then if, say, an American naturalized in Jamaica should become an extensive purchaser of land in trust for a New York Mining Company? These were all problems which required the opinion of Her Majesty's Government. As for the more immediate matter of royalties, the governor suggested that it might be possible to give various companies rights as lessees, agents, or profit-sharers with the Crown, and thought that some arrangement might at once be made with one of the larger concerns, the Port Royal and St. Andrews' Mining Company. He recommended, however, "that the agreement should not be of so permanent a character nor so favourable to the Mining Adventurers as to afford any topics of reproach in case the Colonial Legislature should propose as they would be sure to do if the Mines became valuable, some appropriation of them to local purposes."

There was still very much doubt as to the real extent of the Island's mineral resources, but from various accounts it appeared that rocks "strongly impregnated with copper" existed in a general line running northeasterly from St. John, through St. George into Portland.

It was Sir Charles Grey's opinion that even if the copper existed in workable quantity and profits were possible with all the expense of transportation of the ore, the many small companies already in existence would simply "worry each other to death" without accomplishing anything. He would like to see the formation of a single, strong, well-capitalized company holding the sole right to mine in Jamaica.[45]

The resident and absentee owners of abandoned estates dreamed of vast deposits of valuable minerals beneath their

---

been under the control of the governor of Jamaica. They were formally annexed in 1863. The Turks and Caicos Islands were politically separated in 1848 from the Bahamas (of which they are geographically a part) and brought under the control of the governor of Jamaica. Formal annexation did not come until 1874. See Sir Alan Burns, *History of the British West Indies* (London, 1954), pp. 668–9.

45. C.O. 137/317, Sir Charles Grey to Newcastle, No. 65, 18 June 1853.

overgrown cane-fields—excavations appeared here, there, and
everywhere. Mining companies, some of them hardly deserv-
ing the title, were at work in Portland, St. David, Port Royal,
St. Andrew, Metcalfe, Clarendon, Hanover, and Westmoreland. According to Sir Henry Barkly, the new governor, these
were the principal localities of prospecting, "but rumours of
all sorts are rife as to rich indication in other spots many of
which are made matters of mystery out here . . ."

He stressed, however, that he knew of no illegalities being
practised, for, generally speaking, the people connected with
all these schemes were too highly respectable to indulge in
law-breaking. It is possible that he was right. In any case,
he made the important point that "a complete and systematic
Mineralogical Survey" was needed immediately "were it only
to prevent money being squandered fruitlessly in unscientific
attempts and unfit locations." The Jamaica Legislature were
considering such a survey, he explained, but the political situation was so unsettled and the revenues so small that there was
little chance of "a speedy appropriation of funds" for the
purpose. In illustration of this need there was the case of the
Job's Hill Mine in the Parish of Metcalfe. Once its shares had
stood at a premium of £18 in the London Stock Exchange,
but now they were almost at a discount. The reason was that
although many of the companies had employed experienced
mine captains and competent assistants, the reports of these
people varied so greatly, even upon the prospects of a single
venture, that confidence was impossible.[46]

The largest and apparently most heavily capitalized of all
the companies was the Port Royal and St. Andrew's Mining
Company.[47] A brief survey of its operations will indicate the

46. C.O. 137/319, Barkly to Newcastle, No. 32, 22 Dec. 1853.
47. C.O. 137/320, Port Royal and St. Andrews' Mining Company, a
joint-stock company formed in London for the purpose of mining
in Jamaica. Capital: £25,000 in shares of £1 each, with payable
deposit of 5/– per share. Trustees: John Hodgson, John Diston Powles.
Directors: W. Gladstone (merchant), John Anderson, Francis Pegler,
Thomas Ogilvy. Auditors: J. E. Koch, Frederick Partridge. Secretary:
J. H. Koch. Solicitors: Messrs. Baker, Ruck, and Jennings, Lime St.,
London. Bankers: Messrs. Smith, Payne, and Smiths, Lombard St.
Office of the Company: 44 Lombard St.

methods followed and the problems encountered by its competitors.[48] The company was formed in London in 1852 with a first issue of 25,000 shares of £1. The first payment was 5/– per share. The main area of operations was to be in the two Jamaican parishes named in the title of the Company, and the directors secured mineral rights over several estates for a total sum of £3,500 paid out in shares of the Company. In some cases mining leases were acquired for a period of ninety-nine years subject to a royalty to the landowner of one-sixteenth of the net profits. The estates were all within about fifteen miles of Kingston, the roads were all serviceable, and there was no difficulty in obtaining labourers.

The first issue on which the Company sought settlement was that of the Crown rights in minerals. They appealed, both by letter to the Board of Trade and by a memorial to the Queen, that the Crown would waive its rights to all gold and silver because these rights

> would in all liklihood [*sic*] be of no value whatever to the Crown inasmuch as the rights are only to the gold and silver in its natural state embedded in the ore, and the probable produce of gold and silver in Jamaica would not pay the expense of extraction, unless such process were at the same time applicable to other metalic produce —but the exercise of any such rights on behalf of the Crown would seriously impede the operations of your Memorialists.

The request led to a keen enquiry by the British Government into the London personnel and organization of the Company, and letters to successive governors Sir Charles Grey and Sir Henry Barkly asking about the Company's affairs in Jamaica. On the matter of royalties there was divided opinion. The colonial land and emigration commissioners in London had suggested an absolute grant of the precious metals for ten years, but no change in the royalty on the base metals. Sir

48. C.O. 137/320, C.O. 137/317, C.O. 137/319, C.O. 137/321, C.O. 137/322, C.O. 137/324, and C.O. 137/326 provide the information upon which the following account of the Port Royal and St. Andrews' Mining Company is based.

Charles Grey had recommended that the present royalties be left in abeyance by the Crown until the Jamaica Legislature should discuss the business and come to some decision. Sir Henry Barkly, the third to express an opinion, preferred an immediate surrender of its rights by the Crown to the Island Government as a good way to stimulate the Assembly into voting money for an immediate mineralogical survey.[49] Moreover, he would give an assurance to every duly registered company that for a period of years, say ten, no claim whatsoever would be preferred, and that no duties of any sort would be levied on mineral products.

While these exchanges were going on in government circles, the Port Royal and St. Andrews' Copper Mining Company continued to develop its organization. In August 1853 a staff of miners, with contracts for three years, were sent out to Jamaica. Early in the following year stipendiary magistrates told of events in their respective parishes. Mr. Kent, in Port Royal, reported the opening up of shafts on three or four estates and much prospecting, but, he said, there was little reported success.

The other companies were also at work. Charles Lake, in Portland, said that there were signs of deposits all over the parish. Two companies were at work, and they too had brought miners from England. Excavations were extensive and prospects seemed favourable. In Clarendon, the "Wheal" and the "Clarendon Consolidated" were prospecting on lands owned by Edward Thompson, custos of the Parish. There was considerable copper, but there was also uncertainty as to the size of the deposit.

The debate over the Crown's rights continued for another year, and it was not until the end of December 1854 that the secretary of state for the colonies dispatched a proposal by which the Crown would cede all its rights over minerals in Jamaica to the Island Government—provided that certain conditions were fulfilled. In April 1855 Sir Charles Barkly informed the Colonial Office that the Legislature had accepted

49. This concession, with others, was to be granted by the British Government in return for the reform of the Jamaica Constitution.

the British Government's proposal with its conditions, one of which had been the exemption of the mining interests from all imposts for a period of six years. The Jamaica Legislature had, in fact, given them an exemption for a period twice as long.[50] Now at last, after two years of uncertainty, the mining companies knew where they stood in regard to royalties and the rights of the Crown. They could begin to dig, but where? This was a high-cost industry, largely because of the difficulty and expense of transporting ore to Britain, which could only afford the extraction of good quality ores. As far back as December 1853 Governor Barkly had been informed that in the case of good ores the expenses would be about 50 per cent of gross income, without any allowance for rents and royalties, and for this reason he had stressed the need for an immediate mineralogical survey. Now the royalties were removed for a period of twelve years, but the costs of production including rents still were too high to permit the working of inferior-grade ores.

A second period of delay now ensued while the British Government and the Island Legislature pondered and discussed the need for an immediate survey. The big question was who would pay for the survey. Should it be the mining companies, the Jamaica Legislature, or the British Government? There were certain very real obstacles preventing private surveys by the companies. The expenses would be considerable, and the lack of roads and extremely mountainous nature of the country would make the work a long and arduous one. If the companies pooled resources to finance a general survey, there would be immediate problems—for example, should they subscribe equally or proportionately, and, if the latter, on what basis should the proportions be established; or another, where should the survey begin so as to give no unfair advantage to any particular company? On the other hand, it would have been both expensive and ridiculous, in such a small island, to have half a dozen or more surveyors on separate surveys but quite unable to keep out of each

50. An early, but not the first, instance of legislation to encourage what are now called "pioneer industries."

other's way. The companies made no move. They waited the outcome of the deliberations of authority. The best solution would be a Government-financed survey, which would not only bring no direct cost to them but would probably, in view of previous analyses of samples, bear a certain prestige encouraging to capital.

The Jamaica Legislature, still obsessed with the need for financial retrenchment and having already made two important concessions to the mining companies, sat tight and waited for the British Government to do something. Eventually, in November 1855, it accepted a suggestion by the Colonial Office that a geologist and mineralogist should be appointed to survey the mineral resources of such of the West Indian Colonies as should be willing to contribute £1 a day towards his salary.[51] But the acceptance was to have no immediate result because the surveys would be undertaken in the various colonies in the order of their acceptances, and the Government of Trinidad had taken up the offer before the Government of Jamaica.[52]

In the spring of 1856 Sir Henry Barkly left Jamaica and Lieutenant General Bell, O.C. Troops in Jamaica, was deputy for a year until the arrival of Governor Darling. In October, Bell received a memorial[53] from the various mining companies deploring the long delay in the arrival of a geologist to make a survey and the fact that they must wait until Trinidad had been served. They pointed out "That several mines of undoubted promise have failed and many other discoveries of Minerals Marbles, & c. have not been worked for want of the public confidence necessary to induce the investment of Capital in mining enterprise; a confidence only to be secured to an adequate extent by an authoritive report, under Government sanction, on the economical Geology of this Island."

The memorialists proceeded to give a list of the various

51. C.O. 137/327, Barkly to Sir George Grey, No. 110, 26 Nov. 1855.
52. This was not the only occasion on which Jamaica took second place for this reason. It also happened in the matter of immigration.
53. C.O. 137/332, Bell to Labouchere, No. 51, 25 Oct. 1856.

Companies in Jamaica, showing how the long delay had frus-
trated capital and stifled enterprise. The following, all of which
were English joint-stock companies, had had to suspend operations altogether: the Metcalfe General Mining Company,
the Jamaica Copper Company, the Sue River Mining Company
(in Metcalfe), the St. Andrew's Liguanea Company, and the
Port Royal and St. Andrew's Copper Mining Company. There
were some companies still engaged in operations of a sort:
the Clarendon Consolidated Company, the Ellersie Bardowie
Mining Company, the Rio Grande Mining Company (in Portland), the Wheal Jamaica Copper Company (in Clarendon
and St. Andrew), and the Mt. Salus Mining Company (in St.
Andrew); but the extent of these operations can be judged
from the fact that throughout the entire Island only two mines
were actually being worked—Silver Lead at Hope Estate in
St. Andrew, and Copper at Orange Brook.

When the memorial was received at the Colonial Office, it
went the usual round. Henry Taylor remarked that he was
opposed to Government direction of commercial enterprise
and that what the memorialists were eager for "is not so much
scientific survey as Govt. sanction; & they will take that sanction to market and sell it high." The second comment was Mr.
Merrivale's. He thought that Taylor's observations were very
true but he supposed that the Government's decision to send
a geologist to the West Indies was based "on the principle
that their precarious condition justifies Government assistance
of some sort, & that this is at once the least onerous & the most
likely to promote ultimately, productive industry." Finally,
Mr. Labouchere endorsed the views of Merrivale, adding that
if Jamaica wanted an immediate survey the Island would
have to pay extra for it, and further, that the memorialists
must not expect the survey to say precisely which mines were
best fitted to be worked, or "to supply the need of knowledge
& practical skill in working existing mines." That was the gist
of the Colonial Office dispatch which was eventually sent in
early December 1856, in answer to the memorial.

The survey geologists arrived in Jamaica in April 1859,[54]

54. C.O. 137/344, Darling to Bulwer Lytton, No. 55, 6 April 1859.

nearly three years after the complaint of their delay in Trinidad. There were two of them: Lucas Barrett, the chief, who received £740 a year; and Mr. Sawkins, his assistant, who got £640.[55] But work could not commence immediately, for the geologists wanted more instruments and more pay. The instruments arrived within the year and the pay demand was met by an extra allowance, included in the figures given above, of £75 a year allowance each for horse and servant. These matters having been settled, there began a long professional dispute between Barrett and Sawkins on the way in which the survey should be carried out.

In Trinidad the chief geologist had been a gentleman named Mr. Wall, and he and Sawkins had worked harmoniously and, according to the Colonial Office and Sir Roderick Murchison of the Department of Economic Geology, to good effect. Wall had then resigned. No one had recommended Sawkins for promotion and Murchison had informed the Colonial Office that a bigger salary would have to be offered to get a really good man to fill his place. The secretary of state for the colonies had not been prepared to grant the increment, however, and the position had been given to Barrett, a young man of apparently adequate recommendation but unknown to Sir Roderick Murchison.

Sawkins, older, more experienced in mining geology, and accustomed to the respectful treatment he had been given by Wall, resented this appointment of a younger man to the superior position. Moreover, he thought that Barrett, who was reputedly a good paleontologist, had neither the right qualifications nor the right idea of how to set about the work. One particular argument between them concerned the way in which the surveyed areas should be mapped. Barrett wanted straight geological maps indicating geological formation but omitting topographical features. Sawkins argued that the lat-

55. C.O. 137/375, Eyre to Newcastle, No. 244, 23 Oct. 1863. Salaries were made up as follows: British Govt., chief, £300 p.a.; assistant, £200 p.a. Jamaica Govt., £365 p.a. to each, as well as horse and servant allowances of £75.

ter should definitely be given. A letter from him to Barrett, dated 30 January 1860 illustrates this point as well as the state of feeling which then existed between the two gentlemen: "I am surprised at being called on by you, the Chief of the Survey, to instruct you in 'the advantages of laying down the mountains and the hills' to do so 'as briefly as possible'. I must refer you to that excellent elementary work of Sir H. de la Beche . . ." [56] The argument was settled by the temporary posting of Sawkins to the Island of Anguilla, leaving Barrett free to work as he wished. He began in Portland. In a letter to the governor he insisted that it was necessary to examine the geological structure before reporting on actual mineral veins.[57] It is easy to understand the impatience with which the mining companies must have watched this thorough young gentleman descending cliff faces and the deep shaft of one of the mines of the Wheal Jamaica Company [58] in order to observe fossils. Governor Darling observed that despite Barrett's obviously good qualifications he thought Sawkins the better man for Jamaica's purpose.[59] When news of the altercation reached Sir Roderick Murchison, he commented that though making topographical maps was certainly not the work of geological surveyors, and especially so in a mountainous and thickly wooded country, he thought a sketch map of the most important features "would be of practical utility to the Colony." He reminded the Colonial Office that he had not recommended Barrett for the job, but also remarked that he seemed to be doing his work very competently.[60] In short, Sir Roderick preferred not to commit himself in any way.

In a subsequent letter to the Colonial Office Sir Roderick gave news of the actual findings of the survey to date. Barrett had ascertained

56. C.O. 137/348, Darling to Newcastle, No. 33, 24 Feb. 1860 (enclosure).

57. C.O. 137/349, Darling to Newcastle, No. 69, 17 May 1860 (enclosure).

58. The deepest shaft in Jamaica, then 390 feet.

59. C.O. 137/349, Darling to Newcastle, private, 21 May 1860.

60. C.O. 137/352, Murchison to Fortescue, 24 April 1860.

the important fact that the Copper Mines of Jamaica occur in deposits of much younger age than those which contain the same ore in Northern Europe. But as we know that the rich Copper Ores of Cuba and a part of Tuscany occur in rocks of like age, which have been perforated by certain eruptive rocks, there is good reason to hope, that the mines in Jamaica may also prove to be highly remunerative, if worked with talent and perseverance.

This at least was encouraging, but, as far as the speculators were concerned the damper was contained in a following paragraph: "Mr. Barrett is a clever geologist but as he is not a Miner, he cannot be expected to give opinions as to the probable relative value of this or that lode, so as to re-assure the public and impart confidence to those who speculate in Mines." If that sort of research was to be made, Barrett and Sawkins would need the assistance of yet a third person "who is well skilled in the practical working of Copper Mines." [61] In other words, the survey was to produce no direct results for the mining companies.

The remaining history of mining enterprises in Jamaica up to 1865 deals not with companies, all of which were fast fading out of existence, but with personalities. It concerns the comings and goings of gentlemen engaged in the survey. By the end of 1862 Barrett reported to the governor that he had completed surveys of Portland and St. George, and Sawkins, now returned from Anguilla, had done St. David. Metcalfe and Port Royal were partly surveyed. The year had been unfavourable for field work because of an unusually wet summer. A collection of rock and ore specimens and illustrative maps were being sent for display at the International Exhibition of 1862.[62] Nobody, it seems, took much notice.

By the end of that year Barrett was dead—drowned while

61. C.O. 137/352, Sir R. Murchison to Mr. Rogers, 6 July 1860.
62. C.O. 137/364, Darling to Newcastle, No. 2, 7 Jan. 1862.

experimenting with a diving suit off Port Royal. Sawkins lost no time in applying for the vacant position. His application was supported by Governor Eyre, who claimed that the general public and the Island Assembly all felt that Sawkins had done most of the practical work in the field as well as the map-making, "tho' hitherto the credit due for these has not been given to him." [63] He eventually was offered, and accepted, the leadership of the survey.[64] The assistantship was filled for a short time by a Mr. Lennox, who resigned for reasons of health and was succeeded in November 1864 by a Mr. Brown.[65]

The mining companies had long ago folded their tents, but the survey dragged on, and eventually in 1869 the surveyor's report was published by the British Government. It contained little information of the sort to revive any interest in mining. The copper and other deposits, though some rich veins existed, were said to be so distributed as to make profitable extraction generally impracticable (see Table 18).

TABLE 18. *Exports of Jamaica Copper Ore*

Year	Tons	Cwt.	Year	Tons	Cwt.
1851	1	—	1857	178	5
1852	2	6	1858	38	—
1853	85	—	1859	22	3
1854	184	10	1860	48	2
1855	35	—	1861	4	10
1856	63	—	1862	5	5

Source: Jamaica Blue Books.

To present-day Jamaicans the speculations in lead, copper, and the rest are especially significant, for mining companies are now showing interest not only in bauxite, which in the 1860's was still undiscovered, but also in lead and zinc at Hope, manganese in Portland, copper in St. Mary, and de-

63. C.O. 137/368, Eyre to Newcastle, No. 128, 24 Dec. 1862.
64. C.O. 137/372, Eyre to Newcastle, No. 159, 9 June 1863.
65. C.O. 137/385, Eyre to Cardwell, No. 294, 8 Nov. 1864.

posits of various minerals in Manchester and other parishes.[66]
The failures of the nineteenth century were apparently due
primarily to a lack of capital and a lack of confidence by the
mining companies, the latter of course tending always to encourage the first. In these circumstances the long delay over
the survey was fatal. But there was more to it than that. Even
if the survey had been rapidly completed, its findings would
have given little encouragement to mining companies of the
last century. Today, when surveys can be made more accurately, when technical improvements have made it possible
for low-grade ores to be worked profitably, and when new
discoveries have shown us both new minerals and new uses
for old ones, mineral wealth is easier to assess and capitalists
are readier to put their more efficient machinery to work.
Today, moreover, shipping facilities are greater and cheaper,
and whereas, in the nineteenth century, lack of coal made
the shipment of raw ores unavoidable, there is now the possibility of using hydro-electric power for smelting.

Nonetheless, had the burst of speculation in the first half
of the 1850's been met by an immediate survey, some money
and a good deal of effort would have been saved, for the
documents clearly indicate that the prospectors were all aware
that only large deposits of high-grade ores would yield a
profit.

The explanation of the delay is to be found on both sides of
the Atlantic. In Jamaica the psychological depression which
followed the Sugar Duties Act, and the long drawn out political disturbances which it engendered, made it impossible for
the Island Legislature to decide a firm policy on any subject,
especially on matters calling for an expenditure of public
funds. In Britain the laissez-faire attitude, so well illustrated
in Taylor's minute, could allow Government financial assistance to private enterprise only in the guise of a sort of poor
relief such as Merrivale indicated.

The final industry selected for review, railway construction,

66. *Colonial Geological Surveys:* directors report for 1951–52. Summarized in *West India Committee Circular*, April 1953. J. G. Sawkins
et al., *Reports on the Geology of Jamaica*, London, H.M.S.O., 1869.

differs from the others. Designed to produce a service, its expansion depended primarily upon the demands made by other industries for its development. From all that has gone before it is evident that the story will be short, and the main point of this small section will be to illustrate once again the sudden disappearance of the optimistic note after 1846. The enthusiasm which accompanied the laying down of the thirteen miles from Kingston to Spanish Town was general. Lord Elgin proclaimed the railway to be an important public utility which should be given every encouragement. Hall Pringle, stipendiary magistrate for Vere and Clarendon, in June 1845 referred to its near completion and the intention of the promoters to carry it on to Old Harbour, about twelve miles beyond Spanish Town,[67] and in December, Richard Hill, secretary of the stipendiary magistracy, referred to "the Railway now being built across the island" as a coming aid to mountain settlements.[68] By the end of 1846 the numerous proposals for new lines and extensions were no longer significant. Several acts were passed by the Jamaica Legislature between 1846 and 1865 authorizing the formation of joint-stock companies to build and maintain various lines: Spanish Town to Old Harbour and Bower's River; Kingston to Stony Hill; Annotto Bay to Montego Bay with branch lines into the interior up to a length of seven miles each branch; and others, doubtless, which did not progress even as far as the passage of the enabling act. Many of these acts were returned by the Colonial Office for amendment before they could be given the Royal Assent, and these comings and goings took up a great many months; but it really did not matter, for however much the promoters might have liked to build, and the public to see the Island netted with railroads, there was no capital available either in Jamaica or abroad for the projects. There was no further construction during our period, and even the extension from Spanish Town to Old Harbour, so confidently expected by Hall Pringle and Hill in 1845 was not undertaken until 1867.

67. C.O. 137/284, Hall Pringle's report on 1 June 1845.
68. C.O. 137/287, Richard Hill's report, 23 Dec. 1945.

We have seen the collapse of four industrial undertakings between 1840 and 1865, and have examined some of the circumstances peculiar to each. There are, however, some general conclusions with which the account may be drawn to a close. The lack of local experience in financial and industrial affairs was important.[69] Some criticism has already been made of the financial organization of the Jamaica Silk Company. In conjunction with this, there was a lack of experience in the framing of legislative acts concerning the establishment or the regulation of industries. We have seen that many of the acts enabling the formation of railway companies were returned to Jamaica for amendment because they were in some respect deficient or unworkable. An act to regulate mining companies had actually been disallowed by the governor (a rare occurrence in those days) because it was so confused that it would have presented "the most effectual bar that could well be imagined to the development of the mineral resources of Jamaica." [70]

There was, also, only a limited supply of capital available for investment, so that even when local enthusiasm for a particular project was great—as in the case of mining or railway or tramway development—there was no hope that it could be undertaken without the support of overseas capital. This factor entered into the account of each of our chosen industries, and we have seen how important were the external stimuli to investment in particular ventures. The renewed vitality of the sugar industry in the early 1840's undoubtedly played a large part in furthering the cause of the Jamaica Railway Company, but as sugar cultivation retreated towards the coast, railways into the interior became less important to that industry.

69. The financial aspect of sugar production had for the most part been a matter for the planters' agents in Britain. Planters in Jamaica had been content to keep estate account books of a sort, but the raising of money, the paying of bills, and the exact adjustment of estate balance sheets had been generally left to the agents.

70. C.O. 137/317, Sir Charles Grey to Newcastle, No. 65, 18 June 1853.

Thirdly, there was the danger that even the most promising enterprise could be ruined at an early stage by accident or by delay. The accident of Mr. Whitmarsh's silk-worm eggs is a case in point. If we also include the slow deliberations of political authorities, the troubles of the mining companies in their long wait for surveyors are brought to mind.

Fourthly, it is important to remember that in the nineteenth century, scientific research, techniques of production, and methods of discovering, building up, and supplying markets were far less efficient than they are now.

But lack of skill, capital, and speedy communications were hindrances, not serious obstacles, as the history of other areas during the same period illustrates. Jamaica's troubles lay deeper. In the second half of the nineteenth century there were continents yet unopened, the days of the small island were apparently gone, and if, as in Jamaica after 1846, the island was also the home of a depressed and squabbling Legislature, there was little chance that the attention of capitalists abroad would be attracted.

By the 1860's the interests of local investors in attempts to establish new enterprises had quite disappeared, and Government loans at 6 per cent for public works that could not be financed out of ordinary revenues had become the favourite investment. In 1864–65, for example, it was proposed to build a slip-dock in Kingston harbour. Private enterprise proved reluctant, but when the Government decided to borrow £40,000 to carry out the project, which it claimed would be of public benefit, the governor told the Colonial Office: "There would be no difficulty in obtaining this sum, as whenever a loan is taken up there are always more offers of money in the Colony itself than the Government can accept." [71] That was a significant comment on the lack of private industrial enterprise and confidence.

The failure to build any large-scale industrial alternatives

71. C.O. 137/390, Eyre to Cardwell, No. 88, 15 April 1865. The Colonial Office was at the time objecting to the extravagant borrowing of the Island Legislature.

to sugar had its consequences for both rural and urban development. Industrial growth, by increasing purchasing power, would have encouraged trade and fostered the local production of consumer goods, bringing, among other benefits, expanding markets for the produce of the small freeholders and renters of land, whose condition we now turn to examine.

CHAPTER 5

Peasants and Rural Labourers

AT THE TIME of emancipation there were 218,500 predial slaves in Jamaica.[1] The majority had been attached to estates; some, about 19,500, had been "jobbing-slaves" hired out by their owners to estate employers. The domestic economy of the majority had been simple. They had occupied cottages for which they had paid no rent and given long labour for which they had received no money wages, but their owners had provided at least the subsistence minima of food, clothing, and household utensils. They had cultivated provisions and sometimes reared pigs, poultry, and other live stock, on land for which they had paid no rent. The products had been used as food for themselves and surpluses had been sold for money or bartered in local markets. The money received from such sales had been used to buy supplementary items of food, clothing, and household goods; to contribute to the various dissenting missions to which the majority belonged; or simply hoarded in an attempt to accumulate enough to buy their freedom. Because they were generally liable to be sold or transferred from one estate to another, slaves can have had little inducement to invest their money in goods which they could not easily carry with them if the occasion arose. The important feature, for the present argument, is that the bare necessities of life had been provided by their owners, but extras had been earned by the production of supplies for the local markets. Production for exchange had been an important feature in the life of the

1. R. Hill, *Lights and Shadows of Jamaica History* (Kingston, 1859), p. 144, gives the number as 218,669. N. Deerr, *History of Sugar* (2 vols. London, 1849–50), 2, p. 00 gives 218,456.
vols. London, 1849–50), 2, 306, gives 218,456.

slave. Not only his entire labour for the estate but also part of his labour for himself on the provision grounds had been directed to that end.

The major effects of emancipation were, first, to increase the necessary money expenditures of the ex-slaves, as rents had to be paid and the previous essential goods provided by the masters, such as working clothes and imported foodstuffs, had to be bought; and, secondly, to give the ex-slaves freedom of choice in the way in which the extra money could be earned. For those remaining in agriculture there were three main sources from which a money income could be derived: estate labour, sales of produce in local markets, or independent production of crops for export.[2]

The post-emancipation movement away from the estates upset the normal tendency towards a combination of estate labour and provisions-growing as a source of money income and gave greater emphasis to the third source, namely freehold farming of crops for export as well as for local markets. In dealing with the agricultural population after slavery, therefore, we can distinguish between three general groups of people: there were those who owned and worked freeholds but did not give any labour on the estates (these people were often the employers of labour, and we shall describe them as small farmers); secondly, there were those who, although they owned small freeholds, depended to some extent on occasional money earnings from estate labour (we shall call these peasants); and thirdly, there were those who continued to labour on estates while renting cottages and provision grounds from estate owners (these will be referred to as labourers).[3] With regard to this last group especially, one important point must be established. Emancipation did not create any group of landless agricultural labourers who were entirely dependent on wage labour for a living. Those who remained on estates, renting land from their employers or neighbouring proprietors,

2. Ex-slaves who migrated to towns or who earned a living as tradesmen, mechanics, shopkeepers, and so on, will be discussed in Ch. 7.

3. In the case of general reference to all small-scale agriculturalists the term "small settlers" will be used.

suffered under no compulsion to do so; they were the victors of the wage and rent disputes. In some cases it was a temporary expedient until they had saved enough money to buy land of their own. In no case did it imply any power of employers to extort rents from a dependent labour force. The situation cannot be put any more clearly than it was by the governor, Sir Charles Metcalfe, who after discussing the scarcity of labour, in a dispatch to the secretary of state, went on to explain:

> the two professions of Day Labourer and Market Gardener seem rather inconsistent; and as long as they remain united, as they now are in most parts of the Island, continuous labour cannot be expected, and all labour must be at the option of the peasant to give or withhold. There is not the same degree of necessity pressing on him as there is on the same Class in other Countries. Or rather there is scarcely such a class in this Island as that of Agricultural Labourers exclusively. The Labourer here goes out to labour for such time only as he can spare from the cultivation of his own grounds: and if the desires of the Negroes were limited to what Labourers in other Countries are forced to be content with: if they were not fond of Luxuries, and Smart Clothes, and good Furniture, and riding Horses, or had not the better motives of educating their Children or supporting their Church, they would hardly have any inducement to labour.[4]

Metcalfe's remarks applied, obviously, to the people we have conveniently classed under the headings of peasants and labourers. The people whom we have described as small farmers gave no estate labour, and because they tended to form a distinct group of middle-class planters, we shall reserve special discussion of them for the next chapter.

Table 19, compiled from estate lists given in the respective Jamaica almanacs, indicates the broad patterns of the chang-

4. C.O. 137/248, Metcalfe to Russell, No. 50, 30 March 1840.

Table 19. *Growth of Freehold Settlement and Redistribution of Landownership*

A. COUNTY OF SURREY

Parishes	Years	Under						Size of Freehold (Acres)				
		5	5–9	10–19	20–49	50–99	100–249	250–499	500–749	750–999	1,000–2,499	2,500 & over
St. Andrew	1840	45	47	111	91	51	60	47	18	9	17	—
	1845	794		128	90	47	35	24	8	10	19	—
Port Royal	1840	4	1	4	11	4	12	22	8	7	7	—
	1845	190		26	17	8	19	13	10	3	7	3
St. David	1840	37	11	16	11	12	23	19	9	6	12	3
	1845	505		23	19	16	24	22	14	9	10	2
St. Thomas in the East	1840	17	17	18	24	10	20	23	16	18	44	7
	1845	751		40	29	12	23	25	11	21	43	4
Portland	1840	?	?	?	?	?	?	?	?	?	?	?
	1845	230		38	22	16	21	7	6	2	4	3
St. George	1840	25	15	43	69	48	35	34	15	14	25	3
	1845	420		63	49	24	29	39	12	10	16	1
TOTALS Surrey	1840	128	91	192	206	125	150	145	66	54	105	13
(1840 totals exclude Portland)	1845	2,890		318	226	123	151	130	55	55	99	7

Parishes	Years	Under 5	5-9	10-19	20-49	50-99	100-249	250-499	500-749	750-999	1,000-2,499	2,500 & over
Metcalfe	1840	—	—	—	—	—	—	—	—	—	—	—
	1845	692		104	67	31	23	13	12	8	23	2
St. Mary	1840	13	12	33	43	33	33	21	22	26	41	—
	1845	1,312		57	30	24	14	12	11	10	19	1
St. Thomas in the Vale	1840	13	20	54	72	55	34	26	11	10	22	4
	1845	1,604		166	100	34	25	20	7	10	18	2
St. John	1840	12	28	31	53	48	46	27	14	1	11	6
	1845	935		175	102	36	48	21	7	2	7	5
St. Catherine	1840	11	6	11	27	18	33	31	12	7	17	4
	1845	450		41	30	28	43	26	9	8	15	3
St. Dorothy	1840	29	23	24	20	8	11	13	3	1	13	2
	1845	380		39	34	16	11	10	6	1	11	2
Vere	1840	30	18	25	15	7	8	7	6	6	19	6
	1845	958		40	24	10	5	4	9	3	21	3
Clarendon	1840	16	31	43	72	49	45	29	18	5	31	23
	1845	1,597		97	65	24	22	23	17	9	25	16
Manchester	1840	12	20	39	48	57	42	61	49	16	48	8
	1845	2,161		167	94	36	50	70	40	16	40	7
St. Ann	1840	28	42	49	84	80	106	67	42	28	75	11
	1845	2,722		131	121	64	89	75	37	28	65	7
TOTALS		164	200	309	434	355	358	282	177	100	277	64
Middlesex (1840 totals exclude Metcalfe)		12,811		1,017	667	303	330	274	155	95	244	48

TABLE 19. *Growth of Freehold Settlement and Redistribution of Landownership* (contd.)

C. COUNTY OF CORNWALL

Size of Freehold (Acres)

Parishes	Years	Under 5 & 5–9	10–19	20–49	50–99	100 249	250 499	500 749	750 999	1,000 2,499	2,500 & over
Trelawny	1840	91 *	27	33	22	16	22	12	13	47	11
	1845	468	34	32	27	18	21	11	19	44	8
St. James	1840	89 *	32	56	36	26	18	12	22	47	6
	1845	1,039	115	93	37	33	19	19	25	42	4
Hanover	1840	435 *	73	64	41	23	16	23	17	31	7
	1845	929	81	74	28	16	14	23	18	30	3
Westmoreland	1840	315 *	60	99	66	40	40	21	10	54	14
	1845	1,169	165	85	51	34	30	9	12	49	14
St. Elizabeth	1840	83 *	45	117	89	122	56	34	21	56	23
	1845	1,418	382	255	121	107	50	28	19	42	17
TOTALS	1840	1,013 *	237	369	254	227	152	102	83	235	61
Cornwall	1845	5,023	777	539	264	208	134	90	93	207	46
ISLAND	1840	883	938	1,009	734	735	579	345	237	617	138
TOTALS	1845	20,724	2,112	1,432	690	689	538	300	243	550	101

* These figures represent the number of acres owned by freeholders in these groups. In the Island totals it has been assumed that a total of 1,013 acres in 1840 were owned by 300 freeholders.

NOTE. All figures have been compiled as carefully as possible, but, especially in the case of the 1845 Almanac, several (about 50) estate acreages were illegible.

ing distribution of landownership between 1840 and 1845.[5] In studying it, the essential point to remember is that no Crown lands were involved in these changes. Because the figures include only those properties which were registered in their owners' names at the Island secretary's office it is obvious that the table does not tell the whole story—especially with regard to the rapid formation of small freeholds which, often, were not immediately recorded.[6]

In all parishes the increase of freeholds under ten acres was noticeable. In many of the central and western parishes it was remarkable. Broadly, the table indicates not only the sale of lands by very large owners, but also the collapse of many of the middle proprietors of a hundred acres or so. For the majority of these people the high wage rates would have been ruinous because they could hardly compete with the wealthier owners of large estates in the attempts to attract workers.

5. Unfortunately all my attempts in England and in Jamaica to find the figures for a later year have been fruitless.

6. The eagerness of the people to obtain land, and their failure, in many cases through ignorance, to secure proper titles and to register them in the Island Secretary's Office was to lead, in the future, to much dispute over title. In 1840 the custos of St. Elizabeth proposed that the Island Legislature should establish villages, complete with schoolhouses and chapels, situated conveniently to the estates, and with cottages and garden lots to be rented by Government to the labouring population. The suggestion was not taken up, nor did the Legislature take any active steps to prevent what the custos referred to as "the impositions which have been so extensively practised on the labouring population in many parts of the island by designing individuals, who have purchased at a low rate large tracts of land, and resold the same in small lots to the peasantry at a shamefully exorbitant profit, the lands being at the same time very poor and unproductive" (C.O. 137/250, report of Custos Robertson, 21 Sept. 1840). In some instances of free village settlement, especially those sponsored by the Baptist and other Missionary groups, care was taken to protect the rights and ensure the claims of the new purchasers, for example at Maldon in St. James (see Ch. 1), or at Sligoville in St. Catherine, founded by Reverend Phillippo; but where the ex-slave negotiated on his own behalf and without advice, he was often taken advantage of (C.O. 137/250, report of S.M. Grant, Manchester, 20 Oct. 1840) or failed to secure his proprietorship by duly recording it.

It is a pity that the figures for Portland in 1840 are not available, for although that most mountainous, and wettest, of Jamaica parishes shows only a relatively small number of properties, there is much evidence that the Portland and St. George people raised provisions which they carried by boat as far west as Falmouth.[7] The Hanover cultivators also took part in this coastal supply of foodstuffs to the Trelawny population, whose parish was very largely unsuitable in soil conditions for provisions-growing.[8]

From the new settlements the sellers of foodstuffs set out each Friday night or Saturday morning to the markets in the towns or on the sugar estates. The scene has not changed a great deal since a hundred years ago: "Saturday is market day; and many of the black and coloured people resort on that day to the towns from the country, some on horseback, some on foot carrying their own loads, others driving donkeys, and others by sea in canoes, with provisions for sale."[9] In the days when roads were few and expensive to the traveller because of toll-gates, passage along the coast by row-boat or canoe was advantageous. In Westmoreland, for example, there was a large market at Morgan's Bridge, near Grange Hill, but at Savanna-la-Mar the canoe traffic was thick from across Bluefields Bay.

The point has already been made that the Jamaica labourer, whether slave or free, has never fitted into the simple pattern of a subsistence enonomy. Quite apart from imports of building materials, metal goods, clothing, and various items of household use, there had always been imports of food, primarily from the American mainland and British North America. Leaving the more durable commodities aside for the moment, the essential goods for immediate consumption can be arranged in three categories: those produced and sold in the

---

7. C.O. 137/322, report of S.M. Lake, Jan. 1854. See also Select Committee of 1842, Minutes of Evidence, Rev. Wm. Knibb, 6183–6191.

8. E. B. Underhill, *The West Indies: Their Social and Religious Condition* (London, 1862), p. 415.

9. P. H. Gosse, *A Naturalist's Sojourn in Jamaica* (London, 1851), p. 57.

Island; those imported as substitutes for the first group; and those imports which were not or were not considered to be, substitutes for the first group.

Among the first were the ordinary vegetable and animal produce of the freeholds and rented provision grounds; yams, "cocoes" (taroes or tannia, an edible root crop), sweet potatoes, cassava, plantains, breadfruit, callaloo (a type of spinach), corn on the cob, fruit, and so on, as well as some small live stock such as pigs and poultry. The supply of these varied with the state of small-scale agriculture and was much dependent on local weather conditions. In time of drought prices rose. In the second group, the imported substitutes included flour, corn-meal, bread, and salted or pickled beef and pork. In times of drought the quantities of these goods increased, and prices tended to rise if importation did not eliminate scarcity. The third group consisted of such goods as salt fish, pickled fish, oil, soap, and candles. The last three of these were not substitutes for local produce and salt and pickled fish, part of the staple diet during slavery, were not thought of as substitutes for local supplies of fish and meat. In prolonged dry weather, when earnings were reduced, prices and the quantities imported tended to decline.[10] The weather was a very important factor.

10. C.O. 137/287, report of Richard Hill, Dec. 1845. These are Hill's classifications of commodities. The point is that during slavery the labourers had been supplied with imported salt fish, and less frequently salt pork and salt beef. These had thus become customary items of diet among the poor. Fresh fish and meats, locally supplied, were less relished. Apart from the established preference for salt provisions it must be remembered that fresh fish and meats do not long remain fresh in the tropics, and no mention has been found of any general knowledge and practice of curing meats. On the contrary, one report in 1865 tells that the fishermen of Spanish Town had little idea of how to preserve fish, and in 1860 another remarked that bacon was seldom cured. The claim by Richard Hill, reproduced here, that salt and pickled fish were not substitutes for local meat supplies is therefore supportable. It would appear that, in fact, local supplies were substitutes for imported salt or pickled fish (that is, the first choice of the consumer would have been given to the latter). The fact that salt beef and salt pork are listed among the substitutes is explainable in terms of prices. They

Adam Smith, in eighteenth-century England, had remarked that when food was cheap wages were high, and when food was dear wages were low. He was discussing the movements of workers between wage-labour and self-employment.[11] In Jamaica during our period the same sort of thing was evident. In time of drought provision grounds became less productive, so labourers and peasants tried to maintain their incomes by finding wage-labour on the estates. But the drought affected canes as well as provisions, and estate managers needed less labour in the fields. The combined effect of increased demand for, and reduced opportunity of, estate employment was a depression of wages. Conversely, when the seasons were good, peasants and labourers became less dependent on earnings from wage-labour, while the labour requirements of the estate managers increased; thus wages tended to rise.

In times of drought, therefore, complaints came from the labourers and peasants of a shortage of estate employment, whereas in good seasons it was generally the estate planters who complained of a shortage of labour. In any sort of weather, moreover, the situation was complicated by the fact that the months of crop season on the sugar estates clashed with the period in which small-settlers were busiest with their own cultivations.[12]

---

were too expensive for everyday consumption. Between 1858 and 1864 (the only period of years for which retail prices have been found for all these items) the prices were roughly as follows: fresh pork, 4½d.–7½d. per lb.; fresh beef, 4½d.–6d. per lb.; salt pork, 6d.–1/– per lb.; salt beef, 6d.–10½d. per lb.; salt fish, 3d.–6d. per lb. By comparison, prices in 1844 were said to be fresh pork, 9d.; fresh beef, 4d.–1/–; salt pork, 6d; salt beef, not stated; salt fish 2d. Finally, the following quotation from James Anderson's report in 1842 (C.O. 137/266) is useful: "The Negro principally lives on Roots, Vegetables and Fruits, but he has also his pigs, poultry and Goats. Salt animal provisions are held in great estimation, and frequently in the evening he uses for a relish Salt animal food such as Beef or Pork, but Salt fish is generally in use as Salmon, Mackerel, Herring and Whitefish, and he occasionally purchases a Barrel of American flour of which he makes puddings and bakes bread."

11. *Wealth of Nations* (New York, 1937), p. 83.

12. See evidence of S. G. Barrett before Select Committee of 1842,

Nor was this the only difficulty. As Metcalfe pointed out, the peasants and labourers generally regarded estate labour as a sort of side-line or part-time employment which provided the money for extra comforts and luxuries. Their demand for estate employment was therefore highly variable, depending on fluctuations in the prices of the extra goods they wished to buy and on their particular and immediate wants. It is easy to see, for example, that a man who wanted to buy land, or a horse, or a boat, might be willing to give good and steady estate labour until he had earned the amount he needed. Then, having made his purchase, he would spend less time working for wages and more time digging on his own behalf, or riding, or boating. On the other hand, just as labour was irregularly offered, so too was estate employment. Quite apart from the seasonal nature of the estates' demand for labour there was the fact that even the ordinary processes of field cultivation did not require the steady employment of a fixed body of men.[13] Cane-trashing and weeding, for example, or ditch-digging, were made more or less necessary by the behaviour of the weather. Manuring called for different numbers of workers according to the types of manure used and the methods and frequency of application. Planting depended upon the nature of the soil, and the age, quality, and extent of the ratoon fields. Fencing and road-mending were only occasionally undertaken when the need arose—and sometimes not even then. When the estate had indentured labour, which had to be paid, the immigrants would not be idle, for there was always some more or less useful work which could be found for them. But if the estate depended on local wage-

---

5278–5279. Also H. A. Alford Nichols, *An Elementary Text-Book of Tropical Agriculture,* Jamaica Govt. Printing Establishment, 1891. Cassava: planted Sept. to May, gathered 8 to 12 months later. Yams: best planted about January to April. Cocoes: as for yams, but second and following crops were gathered about every 5 months after the first harvest. Compare with these *The Farmers' Guide,* Jamaica Agricultural Society publication (Glasgow Univ. Press, 1954), pp. 15–24, for present-day practice.

13. Especially after the general introduction of the job and task systems.

labour many jobs which could have been done were left undone to save money, though the saving might well prove to
have been false.

It would have been miraculous if, with all these compli-
cations, any firm and mutually satisfactory balance had been
struck between the demand for and the supply of estate labour. In fact, there was a basic incompatibility which was
frequently advertised by complaints from both sides; and
between what the planters called "labour shortage" and the
people called "no work to be had," contradiction was more
apparent than real.

Besides its usefulness to the peasant as a source of extra
income in time of emergency or special need, the sugar industry was of indirect but nonetheless great importance to
him in his role of producer of foodstuffs for the local markets.
The greater the number of people regularly employed in
sugar production, whether locals or immigrants, the greater
would be the market for provisions. The more profitable the
sugar industry, the greater the level of employment around
the port towns and on the roads, both in transport and in the
maintenance of roadways, wharves, and so on.

The years between emancipation and the Sugar Duties Act
were a period of high prosperity for the ex-slaves. Giving
evidence before the Select Committee of 1842, the Baptist
missionary William Knibb was justly proud of their material
condition. His questioner enumerated the advantages:

> "What with the four-post bedsteads, the side-boards, the
> mahogany chairs, the riding horses, the brood-mares, the
> provision-grounds, and other advantages whether arising
> during slavery, or during apprenticeship, or during free-
> dom, you consider the labourers in Jamaica at present
> better off than the labourers in this country?" — "Decid-
> edly; I should be very sorry to see them as badly off as
> the labourers here; half of them starving." [14]

The explanation is simple. Estate wages were at a high
level. Provisions sold readily at good prices because supplies

14. Minutes of Evidence, 6275.

were not over-abundant during this early period when freeholds were just being established, and because markets were
good, both on the estates, where immigrants were being
introduced, and in the towns and villages, where trade
was increasing and building and construction work was going
on.[15]

But, as we have seen, estate wages declined after 1846, and
so, too, did the number of estates remaining in production.
Thus, estate employment became harder to find and less remunerative when it was available. The bare figures in Tables
10 and 3 do not tell the whole story. Employment for local
people became even scarcer in those parishes in which a
large failure of estates was accompanied by a significant settlement of immigrant labour on those remaining in production.
A prime example of this was in St. Thomas in the East. As
for the advertised wage rates, they do not indicate the effects
of the introduction of machinery, and especially of field implements, on the earning power of the most efficient labourers.
Not only did implements reduce the demand for people, they
also made some types of work, such as digging and planting,
much easier, so that second-gang people, whose wages were
lower, were employed to do what had formerly been first-
gang work. Thus the wages offered for first-gang work came
to have little more than paper significance, and the strongest
labourers were often forced by circumstance to accept second-
gang wages, or to do longer tasks than before for their usual
wage, or to remain unemployed.[16] The ex-slaves had at first
shown no opposition either to labour-saving machinery or to
immigrant labour. This was because estate employment had
been thought of only as part-time and supplementary to pro-

15. In rural districts, the building of cottages, schools, chapels; in
Kingston, reconstruction after the fire of 1843, the building of a new
lunatic asylum, the laying down of the Jamaica Railway to Spanish
Town; and other projects in various parts of the Island, including new
building and installations on the estates.

16. C.O. 137/391, report of Baptist ministers on Island conditions.
See also Underhill, *The West Indies: Their Social and Religious Con-
dition*, p. 416, giving details of a report by the Hanover Society of
Industry.

visions-growing. But as the 1840's progressed, the prices obtainable for provisions tended to decline (see Table 20).
The reasons for these price falls have already been implied.
As the numerous freeholds were settled and established in

TABLE 20. *Some Provisions Prices in Various Years, 1840–65*

Year	Yams	Plantains	Cocoes
1842	6/9 to 9/– a cwt.	—	—
1844	5/ to 6/– a cwt.	4/– to 5/– a cwt.	4/– to 5/ cwt.
1851	3/4 to 13/5 cwt.	—	—
1858	4/– to 5/– cwt.	2/– to 3/– per 100	3/– to 4/ cwt.
1865	6/8 to 11/3 cwt.	3/– to 4/– per 100	5/7 to 9/ cwt.

Source: C.O. 137/263, report of Stipendiary Magistrate Bell, May 1842; C.O. 137/280, Elgin to Stanley, No. 130, 21 Nov. 1844 (enclosures); R. M. Martin, *The English Colonies* (London, 1852), 4, 105, 71; E. B. Underhill, 'A Letter Addressed to the Rt. Hon. E. Cardwell . . .' London, 1865; C.O. 137/390, Eyre to Cardwell, No. 90 (enclosures), 19 April 1865.

NOTE. 1865 was a year of drought.

production, the output for the local markets tended to increase. But the market was not expanding. Indeed after 1846, when industrial activity slumped and the sugar industry sank into a period of distress, the local market contracted.

We began this chapter by showing that a money income was necessary and by listing the three possible sources from which it might be derived by the agricultural population: estate labour, local sales of produce, or sales of crops for export. There is no doubt that both estate wages and provisions prices tended to decline after 1846. Vague and irregular as they are, the records bear out the argument. Nonetheless, it is not until the 1860's that we begin to find reports of economic distress among labourers and peasants as well as the larger-scale planters. Partly, the general lack of any kind of detailed information followed from the temporary cessation and subsequent limited re-introduction of regular reports by the stipendiary magistrates. Partly, it followed from the priority given by governors, in their dispatches, to the important political crises that followed the Sugar Duties Act of 1846.

In part, also, it very probably followed from a state of affairs in which, though conditions were slowly worsening, there were no signs of general destitution.

The fact is, the peasant or labourer who had some land to cultivate as he wished was, from the economic point of view, a remarkably buoyant individual. He needed money, but he could get by with very little of it. Moreover, it was not difficult for him to vary his crops. If the price of yam proved unrewarding it cost him very little to switch over to cassava or coco, and there was no long waiting period before the new crop yielded. In the meantime he could depend on the cabbages, green beans, and other vegetables which were usually planted between the main crop, to bring him a few pence or shillings.[17] More drastically, it was possible, when provisions prices as a whole were in decline, for the peasant, and the labourer who had enough time off from estate work, to plant minor export crops—such as ginger and arrowroot, and even, perhaps, coffee; or to plant canes with the intention of making crude sugar for sale in the local market. During the 1850's this last was apparently a considerably profitable enterprise.[18]

There are a few available estimates of the returns to be expected from an acre of provision grounds. In 1840 John Candler, the missionary, wrote of an acre and a third in Hanover that yielded a net profit to the owner of £70 sterling, the equivalent of £52 10s. per acre. But this, by Candler's own account, was "an isolated and very rare case." [19]

In 1842 S. G. Barrett of Hanover presented to the Select Committee on the West Indies certain statements intended to show the high profitability of provisions-growing.[20] His estimates of annual net profits are also too high to be taken as representative. He ignored the costs of rent of land, young plants or roots, and transportation to market, and he assumed

17. No record has been found of the prices of green vegetables, and it is therefore impossible to be more precise.

18. See below, Ch. 6.

19. J. Candler, *Extracts from the Journal of John Candler whilst travelling in Jamaica* (London, 1840), p. 32. Conditions of soil and weather were all extremely favourable, and prices had been good.

20. Minutes of Evidence, 5728.

fair weather and good firm prices over a series of years when calculating his annual averages. His accounts are interesting for the facts they contain about the cultivation of provisions (for example that about 2,700 yam hills were planted per acre, each hill yielding from 5 to 10 pounds of yam) but they are less satisfactory in the measurement of financial returns.

For information of the early 1840's we must therefore resort to a more general statement made by John Candler about the people of the Seville district in St. Ann: "Almost all the labourers have provision-grounds of about an acre; and these grounds, if the produce be all sold, will CLEAR to each of these £20 per annum, currency, in this quarter. In the coffee mountains, and on some sugar-properties, the provision-grounds clear more than double this sum." [21]

Assuming that Candler meant that sales of surplus provisions from an acre of land about St. Ann's Bay gave a net yield of £20 currency per year, we can draw the rough conclusion that, depending on advantages of soil and other conditions, the provisions grower in the 1840's could make a net profit of £12 to £25 sterling per annum. [22]

Finally, there is a burst of general information available for the late 1850's and early 1860's. About 1860 a St. Ann overseer told E. B. Underhill, another missionary visitor, that one acre of provisions yielded about £12 to £17 a year. [23] This was apparently the gross yield, and allowance must be made when comparing it with the earlier St. Ann estimate. At the same time, more general statements put the average value of produce from an acre of provisions at £12 to £25—again, it would seem, gross figures.

Other gross estimates, quoted by Underhill, were made with less particular reference to provisions-growing. In 1857 Richard Hill of Spanish Town, in a lecture delivered to an audience which included the governor, reckoned the income of the average family in Jamaica at £26 a year. This figure,

21. Candler, p. 31. This was written on 11 March 1840.
22. Currency was 3/5 sterling. On 1 Jan. 1841 they were assimilated.
23. For this and the following figures see Underhill, *The West Indies: Their Social and Religious Conditions*, pp. 335, 417, 421.

of course, represented more than the earnings from a single acre of provisions. In the early 1860's the Hanover Society of Industry calculated the yearly value of each acre cultivated by settlers at £30. Hanover, it must be mentioned, is one of the finest provisions-growing areas in the Island, and even today is famous among Jamaicans for its yams. The same figure was given, however, by the Jamaica Society of Arts, which presumably based its opinion on conditions throughout the Island, and it is extremely important that these calculations definitely included the yields from other crops, such as sugar, arrowroot, and ginger, as well as from provisions.

It seems clear that though the profits to be made from provisions-growing tended to decline during the 1850's, the small cultivator could improve his position by including other crops in his cultivation, such as the minor export staples or crude sugar for the local market.

It was said by one of the clergy in 1860 that

> The people generally are becoming poorer, unless in a few instances where they have acquired land and enlarged their cultivation—become in short little farmers—raising alongst with the common food of the country, sugar, coffee, cotton, corn, peese, &c. A sort of better class is thus gradually emerging from the masses. Their numbers might be enormously and advantageously increased, had the people any resident instructors in letters, and directors of their industrial and social life.[24]

In all this we have not taken into account the fact that many of the peasants and labourers kept live stock, particularly pigs and poultry, on their small-holdings. Sales of fresh pork, eggs, milk, chickens, and, occasionally, fresh beef, often supplemented the settlers' income from strictly agricultural produce. There was no great expense attached to this sort of production. Pigs and fowls were left to find their own subsistence, their owners providing little more than household food remnants and a few handfuls of corn. In some cases the peasants and

24. C.O. 137/390, Reverend Magnan and W. M. Anderson to the Bishop of Jamaica, 1865.

labourers also owned a cow or two, but beef cattle, it would appear, were raised chiefly on the pens of about twenty acres and upwards rather than on smaller freeholds or rented land.[25] Horses, mules, and donkeys were used primarily for travelling and transportation of produce, but as the prices of provisions declined and, as we shall show, taxes on peasant live stock increased, the services of these animals became more expensive.

The earning from animal produce, though supplemental to earning from cultivation, did not maintain total annual income in the face of falling profits from provisions-growing. Milk apparently sold fairly regularly at 6d. a quart. Fresh beef and fresh pork remained fairly steady at about 6d. to 7½d. per pound throughout our period, with the latter tending to swing regularly between the two figures.[26] The prices of poultry and eggs are unfortunately not available. Insofar as peasants and labourers began to indulge in the cultivation of crops other than provisions, they tended to improve not only their financial condition but also, very probably, their agricultural methods. During slavery Jamaican slaves had seldom been limited in their use of estate back-lands for the growth of provisions. Evidence abounds to show that with wide areas of land at their disposal they had practised an exploitative and shifting cultivation. The method was to clear out an acre or so by burning, cultivate it until it was exhausted and yields declined, and then move on to a new spot.[27] When freedom came, those whom we have classed as labourers remained on the estates as renters of provision grounds, and their method of cultiva-

25. See, for example, Underhill, p. 416, and C.O. 137/323, Barkly's report on his tour round the Island. The best customer for cattle was no longer the planter but the butcher, who paid £9–10 for three-year-old steers.

26. Prices for most years are quoted in the Blue Books. The swing of the pork prices was probably a Jamaican version of the Canadian "hog cycle."

27. See, for example, the evidence of Thomas McCornock (4542–46), and Alexander Geddes (6677–91), before the Select Committee of 1842. These two men between them were closely connected with estates in nine parishes.

tion remained exactly the same as it had been in slavery, with the estate owners generally showing the same disinclination to measure out precise areas of rented land.[28] Those who, by our definition, became peasants purchased their freeholds and, if they cultivated provisions, presumably set about it in exactly the same way as they had customarily done on the estates. Of a freehold of five acres, one or two would be under cultivation at any given time.

The argument that the system of land tenure influences the methods of agriculture used by the farmer is valid only up to a point. Land insecurely held offers little inducement to the farmer to cultivate it well, or to invest much capital in it, since he may at any moment be turned off. But even granted security of tenure, the farmer can cultivate better only if in fact he knows how to do so. A change of the system of tenure, when unaccompanied by a change in the crop cultivated, may lead to no greater efficiency in cultivation. If, however, a change in the system of tenure is accompanied by a change in the type of crop planted, it is possible that the farmer who has had no experience of the new crop may set about to learn how to cultivate it well. At least he must imitate the methods of others who are already engaged in that cultivation. Those who planted crops such as sugar, or coffee and other minor exports, tended to imitate the agricultural methods of the established small farmers and the estates. Moreover, the fact that these were longer-term crops meant that the cultivator was compelled to remain on his freehold, and thus was encouraged to practise a wiser, less exploitative method of agriculture.[29]

In Jamaica, therefore, it was the type of crop planted rather than the nature of the land tenure which influenced the methods of cultivation. Indirectly, security of tenure, by encouraging the cultivation of longer-term crops, influenced agricultural

28. C.O. 137/248, Metcalfe to Russell, No. 50, 30 March 1840. Gosse, *A Naturalist's Sojourn in Jamaica*, p. 151.

29. Cf. W. Arthur Lewis, *Evolution of the Peasantry in the British West Indies*, pamphlet, No. 656 (1936), at the Colonial Office Library; it deals with a later period of development.

method, but this double connection was not always established, because the cultivator's choice of crop was influenced as much by the profits he hoped to make from it as by the system of tenure by which he occupied his land.

Real income depended however, on the prices of the goods which the peasant or labourer bought, as much as on the prices he could obtain for the goods and services which he offered for sale. In Table 21, which includes certain commod-

TABLE 21. *Prices of Certain Imported Commodities, 1844–65*

Year	Flour (per 196 lbs.)	Cornmeal (per qt.)	Salt Pork (per lb.)	Salt Cod (per lb.)	Osna-burgh (per yd.)	Cotton Prints (per yd.)
1844	32/–	—	6d	2d	4½d–6d	—
1858	36/–	3d	9d–1/–	3d	—	—
1860	36/–	4½d	9d	3d–4½d	4½d–6d	4½d–9d
1862	40/–	—	9d	3d–4½d	4½d–9d	6d–7½d
1865	—	4½d–6d	9d–1/–	4d–6d	7½d–9d	9d–1/3d

Sources: Jamaica Blue Books, various years; C.O. 137/280, Elgin to Stanley, No. 130, 21 Nov. 1844, enclosing letter from the agent general for immigration; E. B. Underhill, *A Letter Addressed to the Right Hon. E. Cardwell, with Illustrative Documents on the Condition of Jamaica,* London 1865; *Facts and Documents Relating to the Alleged Rebellion in Jamaica,* published by the Jamaica Committee, London 1866; C.O. 137/391, Eyre to Cardwell, No. 128, May 1865, enclosing Baptists' reports on Island conditions.

ities that were substitutes for local produce in time of drought and certain others that were essential imports at all times, we shall see that apparently in the 1850's, and certainly in the 1860's, the prices of imports tended to rise. Unfortunately, records of prices are few and far between, and the gap between 1844 and 1858 is a wide one. The assumption that prices tended to rise during the 1850's is based very largely on the fact that during that period import duties were considerably increased, and it is necessary to introduce a short discussion of the policy of the Legislature in respect to taxation generally.

There is little evidence to show that the majority of Jamaicans were much concerned with political events as such. This was not extraordinary, for as long as a man could earn enough to provide for himself and his dependents there was little motive for him to engage in politics. It could hardly have mattered to the small freeholder whether the Town or the Country party was in the ascendant, or whether the governor was in difficulty. The important things were the weather, the state of the roads, and other immediate circumstances that clearly influenced the balance between his income and his expenditure. By March 1854, despite the enormous growth of freehold settlement during the 1840's, the total Island electorate—that is, the registered voters—numbered only 2,235, of whom 1,565 were freehold voters, the remainder being rent-paying or tax-paying voters.[30]

There was, however, one broad aspect of government policy of prime interest to the humblest peasant or labourer. This was the incidence of taxation, and the way in which the revenues were spent; for these were matters which plainly affected a man's pocket and his work.

The ending of slavery had been accompanied by a revision of fiscal policy. The old poll tax of five shillings per slave per annum, for example, had been replaced by taxes on live stock, carriages, and trades. In 1840 the Legislature introduced four tax laws: British manufactures entering Jamaica had been taxed one per cent ad valorem, whether for Island consumption or for re-export. This was now changed to 5 per cent ad valorem, with a full rebate on re-exports. A second law introduced excise duties on sugar and coffee consumed in the Island. A third increased various stamp duties. The fourth imposed a tax on "hereditaments," or fixed capital assets.[31]

30. C.O. 137/322, Barkly to Newcastle, No. 37, 22 March 1854. There had, however, been a slight increase since 1838, when the total number entitled to vote had been 2,199, and the number of actual voters had been 1,796. See Burn, *Emancipation and Apprenticeship,* p. 152 and n. The increasing number of Town party members in the Assembly would therefore seem to indicate a change in the type of candidate offering himself for election, rather than any significant addition of new voters to the lists.

31. C.O. 137/250, Metcalfe to Russell, No. 154, 29 Dec. 1840; and C.O. 137/251, Burge to Russell, 17 Feb. 1841.

In addition to the Island Government's taxes and levies, of which the above together with export duties on Island produce were the chief, there were the impositions of the local vestries. These, which varied considerably from parish to parish, were generally direct taxes, were more burdensome, and more obviously so, than the Island taxes.[32]

In 1842 the Legislature, under pressure from Britain, reduced certain import duties from 5 to 3 per cent ad valorem, and considerably lessened the duties on exports. At the same time, new import duties were put on wines and spirits, tea, and coal.[33]

The hereditaments tax was calculated in an arbitrary manner. Paid assessors valued all lands and buildings and 6 per cent of the gross valuation was declared to be the taxable income of the proprietor. But the tax was not equally applied to merchants and traders. In their case the assessors were to estimate the probable net proceeds of their businesses, and these sums would be liable to a rate of one-quarter per cent for Island purposes, and one-quarter per cent for parish purposes. Even so, they were not the best off. Estate attorneys (if they were not themselves proprietors), lawyers, doctors, and all salaried, professional, and other people without real estate but with incomes varying from a few hundred to a few thousand a year were apparently liable to taxation on their horses and carriages, and nothing more.[34]

In 1843 the Island tax on hereditaments was not levied. Lord Elgin explained that it had been a great burden and that larger revenues from duties on imports, as consumption increased, enabled the Legislature to do away with it.[35] In the same year a "capitation" tax of four shillings per head per year was introduced by the vestries and was supposed to be entirely appropriated to road maintenance. The unenclosed state of the Island made an efficient turnpike system impracticable, and both peasantry and planters would benefit from

32. C.O. 137/257, Metcalfe to Stanley, No. 32, 27 Dec. 1841.
33. C.O. 137/261, Metcalfe to Stanley, No. 72, 9 Feb. 1842.
34. C.O. 137/264, report of S.M. Fyfe, Oct. 1842, in which he discusses the incidence of taxation on planters, merchants, and others.
35. C.O. 137/273, Elgin to Stanley, No. 72, 10 Jan. 1843.

improved roadways. Elgin went to great pains to justify this new imposition. The Colonial Office was quick to challenge any laws which seemed to bear heavily on the newly emancipated. The governor concluded his dispatch by saying that he would "oppose at all hazards" any legislation which was "prompted by hostility to the independence of the Labourer, and designed to produce artificial poverty." [36]

It has been shown how by 1854 altered political conditions in the Island and new opinions and policies in England and at the Colonial Office had removed this early concern with the protection of the ex-slaves. In the Jamaica legislative session of 1854–55 the ad valorem import duties were increased to 12.5 per cent on most imports of British manufactured goods, though certain listed commodities were charged at 4 and 10.5 per cent.[37] These higher duties applied to clothing but not to imported foodstuffs, most of which came from the United States and were not charged on an ad valorem basis. The duties on certain items of foodstuffs were, however, separately increased. In 1856 the parochial vestries were made financially dependent on the Island Government, which took over control of local revenues and expenditures.[38] Instead of making their own appropriations, the vestries now had to submit estimates to the governor and Executive Committee for approval. Two years later the parochial hereditaments were abolished, and the measure was said to please the small farmers and peasants as much as it pleased the estate planters. The assessors of these taxes had often been incompetent or dishonest, and sometimes both. Besides, from the revenue aspect falling property values meant that where the assessments were revised and honestly collected the revenues derived were smaller and hardly covered the costs of collection. In the 1850's the total annual yield from hereditaments had been about £24,000. Of this, the small settlers and householders paying taxes of under £2 each had usually contributed about £7,600. The loss to the revenue was made up by increases on import and export duties and on breeding stock, and

36. C.O. 137/274, Elgin to Stanley, No. 124, 20 May 1843.
37. C.O. 137/324, Barkly to Sir George Grey, No. 130, 30 Dec. 1854.
38. C.O. 137/331, Barkly to Labouchere, No. 52, 9 April 1856.

by a tax on town houses according to their declared value.[39]

These changes can be briefly summarized. Taxation at the parochial level had been discontinued and the Island Government had substituted increases on import and export duties for the unsatisfactory hereditaments levies. The going of the last-named displeased hardly anyone, and it is not at all clear that the new import and export duty schedules excited general protest.

The local merchants who dealt in minor export crops might have passed the new export duties back to the producers, by reducing the prices offered for goods received, or they might have tried to pass them on to the consumers, by increasing the prices asked for goods exported; but although the former course was probably taken, there is no available series of prices of minor export crops from which we might try to establish the case one way or the other. The immediate effects of the increases on import duties on prices in the Island have been, as far as possible, illustrated in Table 21.

The fact is, however, the 1850's were, generally speaking, years of good seasons—years in which plentiful crops might reduce prices in the local markets, but at the same time years in which money income was less important to the small settler who grew provisions and vegetables.

Referring to English workers, Ashton has said: "In the early and middle decades of the eighteenth century only a narrow range of commodities competed for the surplus income of the workers. That is why (to the distress of the well-to-do observer) any easement of the position of the poor was taken out in the form of more drink and more leisure—or in "debauchery and idleness," as the sedate and leisured observer usually put it." [40]

In Jamaica in the 1850's the situation was much the same. In the 1840's, surplus income had for the most part been used in the purchase of land and the establishment of small set-

39. C.O. 137/336, Darling to Labouchere, No. 33, 26 Feb. 1858.

40. T. S. Ashton, "The Standard of Life of the Workers in England, 1790–1830," *Journal of Economic History*, Supplement 9 (1949), reprinted in *Capitalism and the Historians*, ed. F. A. Hayek, London, 1954.

tlements and villages. By the 1850's this great post-emancipation movement had largely subsided, and the demand for more land came chiefly from those small settlers who wanted to increase their acreages and cultivate additional crops or to plant crops such as coffee which require wider spacing than root provisions.

Taking James Anderson's account of the common workingman's diet,[41] the food purchases of the provisions-grower were generally limited to salt or pickled fish or meat and an occasional barrel of flour (or perhaps corn-meal). In 1858, according to Table 21, ninepence a day would provide enough meat and corn-meal for a family of, say, two adults and two children. In 1844, according to the agent general for immigration, a workingman's shirt and trousers had cost about four shillings.[42] In the 1850's (again see Table 21) they apparently cost nothing more, if we judge by the price per yard of osnaburgh, the material commonly used. These were the essential purchases of the mid-nineteenth century Jamaican who had, in the 1840's, established himself as small producer cultivating at least some of his own food.

Finally, in the 1860's, when disaster came, we hear much from "sedate and leisured" observers of the past laziness of the people who, by failing to save in good times had made no provision for future bad times.[43] From all this, it seems a safe conclusion that although in the 1850's the money incomes of most peasants and labourers were declining, there was no general poverty or destitution. Estate labour was harder to find exactly when it was wanted, and wage rates were lower, as also were the prices obtainable for provisions. But at the same time the land hunt was no longer in full fever and the incentive to earn more than was necessary for ordinary day to day existence had largely subsided for all except those who were striving to move upwards into the ranks of the small farmers.

41. See above, n. 10.
42. C.O. 137/280, Elgin to Stanley, No. 130, 21 Nov. 1844 (enclosures).
43. C.O. 137/390, reports of the clergy, custodes, and others.

CHAPTER 6

The Small Farmers

IT IS IMPOSSIBLE to distinguish definitely between the three groups of labourers, peasants, and small farmers on the basis of the kinds of crops they grew, but the general impression given by contemporary accounts is that the peasants and especially the labourers grew provisions rather than export crops, whereas those who moved into the category of small farmers carried on a more varied agriculture, including one or other of the minor export crops. In 1843 it was stated that:

> the high prices charged for manufactured goods and provisions, *not necessaries*, have gradually thrown the labourers on the resources within their reach, which give a progressive and profitable employment to many now unconnected with Estates or other plantations. These resources have so much increased lately that they naturally become a subject of attention. I may enumerate Farinaceous Roots, Fruit, poultry, pigs, fish, honey, and wax, sugar, starch, tobacco, ginger, allspice, and Dyewoods. The manufacture of uncured sugar with rude hand mills has become very general. One labourer in the Nassau District has a cultivation of five acres of the best description of cane. Another individual realises upwards of £200 stg. per annum by the cultivation of tobacco. A proprietor of great respectability assures me that he bought last year, ginger in his immediate neighbourhood, to the amount of £2000 Stg., the produce of free settlers . . .[1]

1. C.O. 137/274, report of S.M. Ricketts, May 1843.

Nor is it possible to distinguish between the groups on the basis of the size of their landholdings. It is true that in provisions-growing three or four acres were the most that the cultivator could manage without outside assistance, whereas, in other crops such as cocoa ("cacao") or coffee, wider spacing between plants made it possible for the cultivator to manage 12–15 acres by himself.[2] But the problem is that the size of the landholding was in itself no indication of the area actually under cultivation at any given time. Underhill, for example, mentioned that: "One smallholder owned 10 acres and got £12 p.a. from each acre cultivated, but he always left a part to lie fallow. He had not worked on an estate since he became free."[3] By our definition, based on the amount of estate labour given and the difference between proprietors and renters, this man was a small farmer. He gave no estate labour himself, and was probably, on occasion, an employer of labour. By the end of the 1850's, certainly, the small farmers were recognized as a labour-employing group.

In 1860, Governor Darling wrote of the rapid growth of middle-class small-holders: "who are to a limited extent, themselves the Employers of hired labour, paid for either in money or in kind,"[4] and in the same year Stipendiary Magistrate Crewe, in Clarendon, reported that: "From no class of people do I hear more complaints of want of labour than from small Farmers (coloured and black people for the most part) who endeavour to Cultivate a few acres more than their families can manage."[5] But Darling thought that as a body these small farmers were "not sufficiently imbued with a sense of their moral obligations" to allow the assignment to them of imported indentured labourers.[6] Through the export duties on some of their produce, these people had for several years helped to finance immigration; but they themselves were al-

2. Lewis, *Evolution of the Peasantry in the British West Indies*, p. 18.

3. *The West Indies*, p. 403.

4. C.O. 137/349, Darling to Newcastle, No. 49, 28 March 1860, and Crewe's report enclosed.

5. Ibid.

6. C.O. 137/350, Darling to Newcastle, No. 109, 6 Aug. 1860.

lotted no immigrant labour until 1862,[7] when a new inflow of Indians coincided with a fall in the price of sugar which made estate owners reluctant to employ the newcomers.

Some attempt has been made to indicate the areas most favourable for peasant cultivation, and it was in these parts that the small farmers also flourished. Undoubtedly the thickest concentration of them was in the County of Middlesex, especially in St. Ann, the parish of diversity, the garden parish of which Richard Hill wrote so lyrically:

> Earth has nothing more lovely than the pastures and pimento groves of Saint Ann's; nothing more enchanting than its hills and vales delicious in verdure, and redolent with the fragrance of spices. Embellished with wood and water, from the deep forests, from whence the streams descend to the ocean in falls the blue haze of the air blends and harmonises all into beauty.[8]

From St. Ann over the great hump of Mount Diablo the settlements of the small farmers flanked the ancient Spanish road southwards through St. Thomas in the Vale, where Linstead, the now famous market, thrived on their produce. Near Linstead, the roads from St. John, St. Ann, St. Mary, and St. Catherine converged. It was an obvious centre of trade, both retail and wholesale, and it was in an area from which sugar cultivation had long been retreating.

In parishes such as St. Andrew, St. John, Manchester, and Metcalfe, small settlers moved into the abandoned coffee estates. In 1844, two years before the Sugar Duties Act, the duties on foreign and colonial coffees entering Britain had been equalized, and the abandonment of coffee estates had been even more rapid than that of sugar. The Committee of the Assembly which enquired into agricultural conditions in 1847 reported that since emancipation 465 coffee plantations containing 188,400 acres, and having 26,830 slaves in 1832, had been abandoned and the works broken up.[9]

7. C.O. 137/374, Eyre to Newcastle, No. 193, 17 Aug. 1863.
8. Hill, *Lights and Shadows of Jamaica History*, p. 33.
9. J. Maxwell, *Remarks on the Present State of Jamaica* (London, 1848), p. 9.

Equalization of the coffee duties had not raised such a storm of protest as the Sugar Duties Act was to do. There were several reasons for this: coffee was a far less important staple than sugar. In the 1840's the value of coffee exported was about 11 per cent of the total value of exports; the value of sugar was over 50 per cent of the total.[10] Secondly, the coffee planters sold their produce in other markets besides the United Kingdom. The American market, particularly, had been important since the mid-eighteenth century.[11] Thirdly, the coffee planters had less capital invested in buildings and machinery than the sugar planters had; and as their estates were less encumbered with claims and joint-proprietorships, they were more willing and more able to cut their losses by selling out, or by switching over to the cultivation of other minor exports.[12] Before emancipation, coffee had been grown on a large scale, not only in the mountains of Manchester, Clarendon, and Port Royal, but in the hill country of many other parishes as well. The planter had simply looked for a good, fairly light soil on a well-drained slope.

The export figures reflect not only the decrease in estate production but also a very significant and slowly counterbalancing increase in production after the mid-1850's, as the new small-farmer and peasant classes entered production. These people sold most of their produce, which was of inferior quality, to merchants engaged in the American trade, receiving, in Kingston, prices which ranged from 28/– to 37/– per 100 pounds.[13]

The entry of small producers into coffee-planting reflected one of the most important distinctions between sugar and coffee production for export in this period, namely that whereas the mechanization of sugar production made heavier

10. Jamaica Blue Books.

11. Edwards, *History of the British West Indies*, 2, 337–53; *1*, 304, 315.

12. Sometimes when the land was unsuitable for ginger, arrowroot, and other crops, the owner could still reap a profit from the harvesting of pimento from the groves on his land. Pimento was not cultivated; it sprang up from seeds indiscriminately scattered by wind and birds.

13. C.O. 137/250, reports of S.M.'s Grant and Crewe, and Darling to Bulwer Lytton, No. 160, 27 Dec. 1858.

demands on capital than ever before, new and improved coffee machinery cost far less to make and install than had the
old less efficient plant. A general account of the cultivation
and preparation of the coffee berry for market will illustrate
the point.

As coffee is a high altitude crop and as there are no elevated
plains in Jamaica the cultivation took place on mountain slopes.

Millions of lbs.

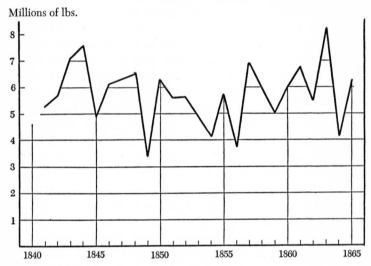

Chart 3. Jamaican exports of coffee, 1841–65.

Thus the agricultural mechanization which had followed
emancipation in the cane-fields could not be adopted on the
coffee estates. But coffee cultivation required less in the way
of regular field labour than cane. The trees, once planted and
matured, needed little more than an annual pruning, and, of
course, picking in harvest. We find, therefore, that after emancipation the coffee planters tended to introduce the systems
of job and task work almost immediately. There was no basic
incompatibility here, as on the sugar estates, between the
need for steady, continuous field labour and the method of
employment by task or job.

Unlike sugar, which had a generally fixed planting period,

coffee was planted at any time of the year. The plants were put in at eight feet intervals and were treated to occasional selective pruning. They did not reach maturity until the third year, when a small crop might be yielded. Not until the fifth year, however, could a full crop of about 750 pounds of marketable coffee per acre be expected. From then on, regular annual yields might be obtained until either the soil was exhausted or the tree rotted.[14] Because the plough and the harrow did not replace the hoe, planting methods continued the same as they had been during slavery.[15]

In the preparation of the crop for market there was a significant change. The procedure had been as follows: when the berries were ripe they were hand-picked, about seventy-five bushels being gathered from each acre in a good season. They were then passed through a pulping mill which separated the outer pulp from the beans. This mill was usually turned by hand, and if vigorously worked could pulp about a bushel of berries in a minute. The beans were then spread out on a flat barbecue built to catch the sunlight, and left for four or five days to dry. In the second phase, the dried beans were passed through a grinding-mill, which did not, as the name implies, grind the beans but only removed the fine parchment-like skin in which they were still encased. This skin was blown away, in a third process, by a winnowing machine. The coffee was then hand-picked to remove broken or discoloured beans, packed in tierces, and sent to market. The grinding-mill was driven by water, or by about six horses or mules, and could peel about 3 tierces per day of nine hours. The winnowing machine could be operated by one or two men. The capital cost of buildings and machinery was about £1,000 to £1,200 sterling. The grinding-mill and its roofing cost about £400.[16]

Clearly, this sort of production was not within the reach

14. Edwards, 2, 337–53.

15. From the Jamaica Assembly's investigation in 1857 it appears that there had been an increase of the number of trees planted per acre, but the actual methods of planting remained the same.

16. Edwards, 2, 351. *Jamaica Almanac*, 1841.

of the peasant or even the small farmer. But there was another way. When coffee estates were abandoned and sold in small parcels, say of up to ten acres, a peasant might buy. There could be standing trees, which, if thoroughly pruned, would continue to yield. Also, more by accident than by design, the peasant might act to arrest the process of soil erosion which was rapid on these hillside estates. Because the pruned trees would take about three years to give another full crop, the peasant often planted provisions between the coffee, thus raising catch-crops and at the same time binding the soil against further deterioration.[17]

Labour, under peasant cultivation, was a family concern if the holding was small. In 1840 it was estimated that twenty-five men employed for eight days every three months could keep 100 acres of coffee in cultivation. In other words, eight man-days per acre per year.[18] A man and his family might therefore manage up to twenty acres quite easily, and still have time to grow provisions.

The real drawback, even on a small holding, had been the harvesting and preparation of coffee for market. Without the capital for the various machines used by the plantation owner, a cheaper, less efficient, and far slower method had to be used. The coffee berries, when gathered, were put, still in the pulp, to dry in the sun. This took up to three weeks. Then, when pulp and all was dry, the berries were pounded in mortars until the beans were separated from both pulp and inner skin. The whole product was then allowed to fall through a current of air which blew away the chaff and left the beans, often damaged by pounding, to be packed for sale. This slow and laborious method tended to restrict the acreage which a family might expect to cultivate profitably. Nonetheless, the

17. No direct description of this sort of cultivation has been found, but various evidence is highly suggestive that it was common. See, for example, C.O. 137/263, report of S.M. Kent, May 1842; C.O. 137/250, report of S.M. Gurley, Oct. 1840. Nicholas, *An Elementary Text-Book of Tropical Agriculture*, p. 73, lists crops which might be so grown.

18. C.O. 137/250, report of S.M. Gurley, Oct. 1840.

far less capitalized scale of production explains why it could be carried on at all on land which had been abandoned by plantation owners as unprofitable.

In 1840 an inventor, John Humble of St. Ann, came to the rescue. He constructed a machine which, worked by one horse, not only combined the peeling and winnowing processes but also prepared about 8 tierces of marketable coffee beans per day. All this, moreover, could be had for the sum of £80, and it was said that: "The simplicity of the machine puts it in the power of the rudest artisan to construct it for himself." [19] The way was now open for the industrious peasant to enter coffee-planting in earnest. Unlike the experience of the sugar planters, therefore, improvement cost so little that it probably saved a few who thought that only failure lay ahead, and it certainly encouraged the entry into coffee-planting of the little man who had some money and the desire to escape the fluctuations of the local provisions market. In 1855 a stipendiary magistrate wrote:

> A considerable quantity of sugar and coffee is now manufactured by small settlers some of whom make as much as 3 and 4 tons. Their sugar being however in general soft grained from using bad temper and defective apparatus is not fit for shipment and is all taken for island consumption at about 10/– per 100 lbs. Their coffee is also inferior and brings about 28/– per 100 lbs. for the American market. The trade with this latter country has much increased of late years.[20]

This report came from Clarendon, but it was corroborated by the report of the Hanover Society of Industry in 1860. In the six districts surveyed, small settlers had about 1,000 acres in ground-provisions, sugar, arrowroot, ginger, and other minor crops. There were 143 small cane mills which, complete with coppers, cost about £10 each, and in 1859 they had

19. C.O. 137/250, report of S.M. Grant, Oct. 1840. *Jamaica Almanac,* 1841.

20. C.O. 137/326, report of S.M. Crewe, March 1855.

produced 455.5 barrels of crude sugar valued at £2 per barrel.[21]

In 1870 the governor estimated the Island consumption of sugar at nearly 6,000 tons,[22] and it was this demand for cheap sugar that encouraged small settlers to go into production. Unfortunately, there are no records to illustrate the growth of consumption since emancipation, or to show the extent to which the large estates did in fact supply the local market. The latter, of course, would have depended in part on the level of prices in Britain.[23] If sugar prices in Britain were at all remunerative, the estate planter would not hesitate to export his entire crop. The Island market was too small to absorb any significant proportion of the total output of the estates. In any case, the local market for estate sugar would have tended to decline as the small settlers moved into production.

It is interesting that in Jamaica attempts to introduce metairie [24] or variations of the crop-sharing system failed. In certain other islands, especially in the Windwards,[25] metairie was rather more successful. The first notice in Jamaica is of a plan by a man named John King. King's scheme was a straight-forward small cane-farmers' system rather than metairie, for it involved no arrangements between himself and the cultivators in respect of land tenure. The idea simply was that King would establish a sugar mill, collect canes grown by small settlers, manufacture sugar, sell it locally, and share the

21. C.O. 137/351, Darling to Newcastle, No. 170, 26 Dec. 1860.

22. C.O. 137/457, Grant's report on the Blue Book, 1870.

23. According to Blue Book prices, estate sugar sold locally at about 9*d.* per lb. of loaf sugar; raw sugars (as the settlers produced) sold at 16/– to 22/– per 100 lbs., retailing at 3*d.* per lb.

24. Whereby the proprietor gives a certain acreage, called a "metairie," to a competent person, called a "metayer," for a number of years under conditions by which the proprietor provides capital equipment and the metayer gives labour and supervision of cultivation. Profits on the crop, after deducting expenses and providing essentials such as seed or plants for the following year, are divided between proprietor and metayer. See Richard Hill's Memorandum in C.O. 137/262.

25. See Davy, *The West Indies before and since Emancipation.*

proceeds with the settlers. At first, the arrangement seems to have worked well, for King established his small factory at Stony Hill, near the Kingston markets and in an area where small settlers were numerous.[26] But it is not clear that the scheme survived, unless King was the person to whom brief reference was made in 1865 as "an American" who manufactured small settlers' canes for a share of the proceeds.[27]

In 1843 there came the only other notable attempt at a crop-sharing system of production. This, an example of metairie, was on Windsor Castle Estate in St. David. The overseer, John McLean, signed contracts with the estate headmen [28] by which he bound himself to put estate buildings and equipment in good order, to pay half the costs of maintaining them in repair, to pay half the costs of hogsheads for curing and packing, and to give half the sugar made to the other contractors. In return, the headmen pledged themselves to bear their share of costs, and to provide all necessary labour until the canes were manufactured into sugar.[29] This attempt failed within a few years.

The explanation of these failures and of the lack of other attempts along these lines rests on various factors. In the first place we must distinguish between King's scheme, which was intended to provide sugar for local sale, and McLean's, which apparently was to produce for the overseas market. King's venture could succeed only if the small settlers thought it more profitable to devote their time and labour exclusively to cultivation. The fact that the local market for cheap sugar was good would clearly have tempted them to try to secure even greater returns by undertaking their own manufacture, especially when a small mill and copper could be erected on a freehold for about £10. This was not a great outlay for the

26. C.O. 137/262, Elgin to Stanley. No. 120, 26 April 1842 (enclosure).

27. C.O. 137/390, Bowerbank to Eyre, April 1865. Bowerbank was custos of Kingston, so it is possible that the "American" was Mr. King.

28. Foremen in charge of groups of labourers.

29. C.O. 137/275, Elgin to Stanley, No. 158, 23 Sept. 1843 (enclosure).

small farmer or peasant, and in return the whole proceeds of the crop would be his own. The essential point is that the local demand was for cheap sugar. Cheap sugar of relatively good quality could only be produced on a very large scale, for which King had neither the motive nor the resources. Cheap sugar of very inferior quality could be produced by the individual small settler just as well as by King, who therefore became a generally unnecessary link in the chain.

The Windsor Castle sugar would have been of a better quality, and here, surely, the most discouraging factor was the fall of prices in Britain. In the Island market the effective demand for better quality raw sugar, such as that produced by the estate factory, was limited by the fact that supplies of cheaper and of poorer quality raw sugar were becoming increasingly available.

Insofar as they grew crops for export, the small farmers were, like the big sugar planters, subject to fluctuations in overseas markets. Unfortunately, no series of prices for minor exports have been found, and therefore that side of the small-farmer's accounts must pass without proper illustration. The Blue Books for the period give annual figures of total exports and the value of produce, but the value columns are of little use as guides to price movements.

Primarily, however, the small farmers seem to have concentrated during the 1850's and 1860's on coffee and crude sugar as the most dependable sources of profit. By the 1870's, for example, their cultivation of arrowroot had declined, partly because the London market preferred Bermuda arrowroot, which was of a better colour.[30]

Because they had little capital fixed in machinery and specific equipment, they enjoyed a certain flexibility of operation. The years which brought a decline of arrowroot also brought an increase in the production of lime juice, and a new development in the growth of bananas and other fruit for the American trade.[31] At the same time, coffee and crude sugar

30. C.O. 137/457, Grant's report on the Blue Book, 1870.
31. Ibid. By this time also the profits to be made from provisions-growing were said to be attractive. This is in agreement with the argu-

remained profitable. It is worth stressing that although the development of the banana trade in the late 1860's and the 1870's has generally been associated with the rise of the Jamaican small farmers, the real establishment of these people as a recognizable and significant group began much earlier and was based not on bananas but on coffee and sugar.

It is very difficult to come to any dependable conclusion about the number of small farmers in the Island in the 1850's. The censuses of 1844 and 1861 provide no comparative data.[32] In 1861 one visitor claimed that there were 50,000 small proprietors owning an average of three acres each.[33] But these would not all have been small farmers according to the definition used here. In any case, that estimate differs from another made in 1865 by one of the Island's largest planters, who estimated nearly 70,000 giving labour on sugar estates; 6,000 cultivating pens and tending cattle; 4,000 in road work; and fully 30,000 engaged in the production of coffee, pimento, logwood, arrowroot, and other minor products.[34] It seems, moreover, that the 30,000 would include people who worked on but did not necessarily own coffee, pimento, and other properties.

Going by the previous table of small freehold establishments between 1840 and 1845, we see that the number of registered freeholds, of areas from ten to forty-nine acres each, increased from 1,647 in the former year to 2,122 in the latter, an increase of 475 in five years. Ten to fifty acres was probably the range into which the majority of small farmers would fall, but it must be considered that these were registered freeholds only, and also that a small farmer might not have held all his land in a single plot. Freehold establishment slowed down after the mid-century, but a rate of growth only half

---

ment that during the 1850's and 1860's there was a tendency for small settlers to move from provisions-growing into the cultivation of cane and minor exports. The former would presumably have become scarcer and dearer in consequence.

32. See Appendix 1.
33. Sewell, *Ordeal of Free Labour in the British West Indies*, p. 247.
34. C.O. 137/390, Westmorland to Eyre, April 1865.

as rapid as that given for 1840 to 1845 would have established over 3,000 proprietors of ten to forty-nine acre lots by 1865. Taking all these factors into account, it would not be an unreasonable guess that by that year there were at least 4,000 small farmers in Jamaica.

There is less doubt about their relative prosperity. In 1863 a local paper, *The Guardian,* spoke out in praise of the small settlers generally: "Their industry is helping materially to sustain trade, such as it is. The money they make is spent in the country, or re-invested in the soil here. Let them have all the encouragement and help which Legislation can give. For instance, they require good roads to take their produce to market. They must have them." [35] In 1865 the Rector of St. Thomas in the Vale wrote of conditions in his parish:

> In this, and the surrounding districts, I think that the number of poor persons has been becoming greater for the last few years; but the aggregate wealth of the labouring class has been, and still is, increasing. This is to be inferred from the progressive growth which has been taking place in the central village of Linstead, of trade in products brought to market by small cultivators, particularly in coffee. That trade of this kind had been advancing, I conclude, not only from my own observation, but from information given in Linstead.[36]

Generally speaking, there are distinctions made in the numerous reports submitted to the governor in 1865 between a suffering estate proprietory, a destitute labouring population, and a middle group of comparatively well-off middle-class agriculturalists.[37]

Whatever their advantages, however, these people had their problems. Some of the more important were stated by the small farmers and peasants of St. David in an address to Governor Eyre when he toured that parish in 1864:

35. C.O. 137/375, Eyre to Newcastle, No. 260, 4 Nov. 1863 (enclosure).
36. C.O. 137/390, Reverend J. Campbell to the bishop, April 1865.
37. C.O. 137/390, and C.O. 137/391.

Most of us, through much difficulties, have purchased land, and portions of these are in canes, others in coffee, cotton, and provisions; and we hope by these means to subscribe for the education of our children, and support the Public Institutions, as we hitherto have done. But there are some who lurk in secret places to plunder, when good men have gone to take their rest—too lazy to work for themselves. The law punishes them, however, when they are overtaken. We are lacking a continuous and remunerative labour, and hence we have to pick out for ourselves such employment as will pay us best, looking for better days when our clothing and food will be reduced, as the present prices are intolerable. Your Excellency, the difficulties to obtain land to cultivate extensively, and the overrunning by cattle, our provision fields —the owner having no fences to keep them from trespassing—fill the country with abandoned fields, and thereby want and destitution. The state of the by-roads which lead to the main trunks by which produce is taken to market, and those roads which lead to the small freeholders' and taxpayers' cottages, are uncared for, and in the most deplorable condition—some resembling goat-tracks, and not ways for human beings. We speak out now, because we know Your Excellency will do all in your power . . .[38]

During slavery the theft of growing crops, especially cane, had been a common practice. Slaves had considered it no crime to rob their masters: "What I take from my master, being for my use, who am his slave, or property, he loses nothing by its transfer."[39] The masters, however, had not accepted this argument, and theft had been punished, though seldom by recourse to processes of law. The master often had been

38. C.O. 137/384, Eyre to Cardwell, No. 234, 6 Aug. 1864 (enclosure).

39. J. Stewart, *A New View of Jamaica* (Edinburgh, 1823), p. 249, quoted by M. G. Smith, "Some Aspects of Social Structure in the British Caribbean about 1820," *Social and Economic Studies, 1*, No. 4, U.C.W.I., 1953.

judge and jury in the decision of cases occurring on the estates.

In the 1840's the reports of custodes and stipendiary magistrates in the rural districts tell of a decrease of all crime, including larceny, and it is not until the later 1850's and, especially, the 1860's that the general outcry is raised against those "who lurk in secret places to plunder, when good men have gone to take their rest—too lazy to work for themselves."

This explanation, laziness, was commonly offered for the phenomenon. It was the Jamaican counterpart of the picture drawn by Carlyle of the negro lying under a tree, stupefied from a surfeit of rum and pumpkin. But there were a few observers who pointed to other reasons. Some, like Benjamin Vickers, custos of Westmoreland, referred back to the great cholera epidemic of 1851: "When numbers of orphans were left destitute, without parents or advisers—left entirely to their own resources they drifted, little by little, into crime, until they became habitual thieves." [40] It is possible that some of the children orphaned in 1851 had become criminals, but they alone could hardly have accounted for the great increase of larceny complained of ten or twelve years subsequently.

Others blamed a religious revival organized by the Baptists in 1861, when thousands had abandoned work and flocked to the chapels, going from one district to another in procession. Eventually, according to Richard Carter, a coloured man and a justice of the peace in St. Ann, hunger had forced them to steal, and: "I find an opinion still prevalent among the people that it is no crime for the poor man to help himself of the property of the rich . . ." [41] This too, was of possible importance, though complaints of larceny had become prevalent before 1861. Carter's most important comment was that which has been quoted.

Richard Hill of Spanish Town, the senior resident magistrate of St. Catherine, put forward other explanations. He referred to the fact that it was not until the 1850's that thefts

40. C.O. 137/390, Vickers to Eyre, April 1865.
41. C.O. 137/390, Carter's letter is with Royes' letter to Eyre, April 1865.

of cane and growing provisions had been classed as larcenies punishable by imprisonment, and that the recent appointment of rural constables, paid for each summary conviction they obtained, had brought about: "a very diligent multiplication of small offences into what are now registered as larcenies." [42] In short, the increase was not so much of acts committed as of convictions recorded. And yet, during the 1840's and even in the early 1850's there was little said about any theft of growing crops, not even a request, as we might expect if it had been prevalent, that the punishment for it should be made more severe.

Finally, there were those who coupled destitution and moral depravity, giving the greater emphasis to one or the other, and occasionally—like the Reverend H. Clarke of Grange Hill, untypical of the Anglican clergy, who stated it bluntly in 1865—declaring that the increase of larceny was without doubt due to lack of food. [43]

It is only when we assemble these various explanations together with some additional comment that the real picture emerges. Apart from those few with inherent tendencies towards kleptomania, people who steal do so from a combination of two factors: need and opportunity. We shall see that in the 1860's economic conditions in the Island rapidly deteriorated. At the same time, as the small cultivations filled the more accessible areas and moved farther away from parts settled after emancipation, it became easier for passers-by to steal without being detected. Thus the number of thefts increased.

The institution of the rural constabulary, moreover, tended to increase the number of apprehensions and accusations, so that greater publicity was given to the increase of crime; the small settlers, and especially the better-off small farmers who had crops worth stealing, grew louder in complaint; and so the circle went round.

The matter of trespass by cattle was not nearly so complicated. It followed, quite simply, from the existing legal posi-

42. C.O. 137/390, Hill to Eyre, April 1865.
43. C.O. 137/390, Reverend Clarke to the bishop, April 1865.

tion. Until 1860 the law had allowed the complainant assessment of damages by immediate survey. It had then been repealed, and the new law required the complainant to bring an action in the petty debt court. This meant delay, during which the signs of damage might disappear, and also the costs of bringing witnesses, perhaps from long distances. As Richard Hill commented: "The proper redress for this evil so grievous to the small settler should be immediate reference under the provision and guarantee of a special Act." [44] The St. David settlers implied that there should be a law compelling cattle owners to fence in their pastures. The question was apparently debated in the legislative session of 1864–65, but no new action was decided. Two of the Island's largest graziers [45] had in fact argued the responsibility of the cattle owner to erect proper fencing, but a law to this effect would clearly have had to make provision for possible complicated cases, such as the existence side by side of a large cattle pen and a small freehold whose proprietor owned a few live stock. There was also the fact that not all cattle pens were adjacent to cultivated land.

Complaints about the state of the Island's roads was no new thing. At last, in 1859, it seemed that something would be done to improve matters. In that year, a main-road commissioner and a civil engineer were appointed to each county,[46] the Middlesex engineer also holding the office of colonial engineer and architect.[47] But, as their titles suggest, the attention of these people was almost entirely devoted to maintenance of existing main highways, and the smaller parochial and branch roads and by-paths were left in their original condition.[48] To the small settlers, like those of St. David, who

44. C.O. 137/390, Hill to Eyre, April 1865.

45. McKinnon and Moncriefe. See Hill's report of April 1865.

46. West of St. Ann and Manchester was the County of Cornwall; east of St. Catherine and Metcalfe was the County of Surrey; and the centre parishes comprised the County of Middlesex.

47. C.O. 137/343, 345, Darling to Bulwer Lytton, Nos. 28, 70, 4 Feb. and 23 May 1859.

48. C.O. 137/384, Eyre to Cardwell, No. 256, 10 Sept. 1864.

were very much aware of their contribution to the Island revenues, the neglect appeared unjust.

The St. David settlers referred also to the difficulty of obtaining land "to cultivate extensively." Presumably this meant that it was becoming harder for the established small farmer to expand his production and for the new small farmer to get land on which to start the cultivation of crops other than provisions. It is possible that the St. David people were referring to their declining money incomes, but reports available in the following year, 1865, indicate that there were other factors. There are comments, for example, to the effect that estate owners were becoming reluctant to sell land to small settlers.[49]

The details given in these reports of land rents and prices are at first glance confusing. In the 1860's land sold at £3–5 an acre in most parts of the Island (nearly 50 per cent cheaper than in the 1840's); but rents were disproportionately high, ranging from 15/– to £2 per acre per year. The explanation seems to be that two quite different types of land were involved. The settlers, obviously, wanted good, fertile land, if possible, within easy access of roads and markets. Large proprietors, however, may have been unwilling to part with land of this quality, and it is possible that the lots they offered for sale were either of poor quality or were still uncleared estate backlands, distant from roads and existing settlements. If that were the case, then the apparent discrepancy in reports which speak of great demand for land by settlers and low land prices is removed. The point would seem to be that the type of land being offered for sale was not what the settlers wanted to buy, hence low prices.

But though the large proprietor might have been unwilling to sell any of his quality land, he might have been prepared to rent parts of it which were temporarily idle. The demand by settlers for these lots would, presumably, have been strong, hence high rents. On the other hand, the large proprietor would probably have been unwilling to part with particular

49. C.O. 137/390, 391, esp. the reports of the Baptist clergy.

areas of good land for long periods, depending on the system of planting on his estate—thus complaints by settlers that proprietors were generally unwilling to contract to rent land for periods longer than one year. It is possible also that in some cases the high rents charged followed from the usual failure of the proprietor to restrict the tenant to the agreed acreage; but the explanation based on the different qualities of land is probably the more applicable, for it is not clear that the purchasers of estate backlands could have been effectively restricted to the exact acreage purchased.

Finally, in this brief survey of some of the difficulties which faced the small farmers and other producers of minor crops, there was the matter of marketing their produce. Apart from retail selling in the market-places, the small settlers dealt with local merchants. Obviously, those who produced export crops were most closely connected with the mercantile groups in the port towns, or with middlemen buyers who passed on the produce from the cultivator to the merchant. The difficulties of transportation encouraged the growth of this middleman group, and to the extent to which their services became essential to the producers, so the power of the latter to bargain over prices became weaker.[50]

On several occasions the small cultivators tried to organize their own marketing organizations, and in one instance to persuade the Legislature to establish a government marketing agency. But without exception their attempts failed. They lacked capital, credit, leadership and good management, and, above all, official encouragement.

In October 1865, while the civil disturbance which came at the end of our period was going on in Morant Bay, John Salmon, the custos of St. Elizabeth, informed the governor of meetings of black and coloured small settlers in that parish at which it had been decided to form a commercial and agricultural association. Each member was to subscribe £5, and the money was to be taken to England by a local magis-

---

50. There are several mentions of advantage being taken of small producers. See, for example, Custos Georges of St. David to Eyre, April 1865.

trate named Brydson. There he would purchase a vessel, load it with goods wanted by the small settlers, and return to Jamaica to pick up a cargo of settlers' produce for return to England. Obviously either Brydson was sincere and very naïve or else, and very probably, he was trying to exploit the naïveté of the small settlers. The important point is, however, that the settlers were enthusiastic for the launching of the organization. Salmon, quite rightly, suggested that the proposal was unsound: either Brydson and the subscribed capital would disappear or the enterprise would fail from sheer lack of commercial intelligence on the part of its members and their agents.

Mr. Eyre submitted Salmon's outline of the scheme to Attorney General Heslop for his opinion. Heslop's reply was indicative of the temper of the time. There was, he said, no legal objection to the proposed association, and he saw no need for "legal preventive measures" even though it was a foolhardy business, for

> as by foolish or wicked Counsels the small producers seem to have lost confidence in the Mercantile Capitalists I know no better way of enabling *them to find out their own blunders* than that they should try their experiment. . . . And no time better than the present . . . when there is a strong Force in the Country to preserve the peace against any attempt against it which should arise from the dissatisfaction of the Industrious producers as the result of their own folly.[51]

Nothing more was heard of the scheme. Perhaps Custos Salmon talked the small settlers out of it; perhaps Brydson talked himself out of it; perhaps the small settlers refused to hand over their £5 each to a man who was going 4,000 miles away; but obviously, the people got neither advice nor assistance from their government. The same can be said of a few other commercial associations which were actually operating in St. James during this period,[52] and of the "Mercantile

51. C.O. 137/394, John Salmon to Eyre, Malvern, 31 Oct. 1865.
52. C.O. 137/391, the Baptist's report on island conditions, 1865.

Agency Association" formed at Black River to facilitate export of freeholders' produce.[53] One or two struggled on beyond 1865, but they did so only by their own effort and tenacity of purpose.

One other actual association of small settlers which had previously been formed may be given passing mention. In 1857 "The St. David's Joint-Stock Company and Society of Arts" had been formed by small farmers in the Yallahs valley district. The plan was to raise £1,000 in 200 shares of £5 each, but in this case it was to finance production and not marketing. The enterprise was intended "to regulate by means of co-operative labour, certain schemes of cultivation upon such lands as the Company might be able to purchase." By early 1858 the association had bought about 450 acres, but what was done with the land and what happened to the Company remain a mystery.[54] There is simply no further official mention of the project. It is possible that after a struggling start it fell victim to the troubles of 1865.

In the remaining paragraphs of this Chapter we shall take a look at the attitude of the Legislature towards small-scale agriculture during the 1850's and up to 1865. Barkly's governorship, from the end of 1853 to the middle of 1857, coincided with a period of rising prices for sugar, broken only in 1854 when complete equalization brought a short decline. This improvement, together with a more stable political administration following the 1854 reforms, was temporarily productive of renewed confidence and a restoration of credit to the planters. It was a period of new immigration plans and the time in which planters once more began to import equipment and machinery in significant quantities. Nevertheless, it was the prelude to both economic and political disaster.

One of the latent political problems concerned the status of the new Executive Committee. The situation was ambiguous, for although the Committee was assumed to be directly re-

53. T. Harvey and W. Brewin, *Jamaica in 1866* (London, 1867), p. 40.

54. C.O. 137/336, S. M. Ewart's report of early 1858.

sponsible to the governor, it was also the governor's duty to call for the resignation of the Committee if it could not obtain the support of the Assembly and if there were others who could.[55] This seemed to imply that the Executive Committee should be chosen from the majority party in the Assembly. The question of responsible party government was raised by Governor Darling in 1860,[56] and the ensuing controversy revived the former political unrest in an even more disturbing form.

The fact that economic conditions rapidly deteriorated at a time when there was acute political crisis is of fundamental importance. Before leaping to pin accusations on the planters for the non-production of this or that measure of reform or improvement, we shall have to know a great deal more about the politics of the time and the relationships between the governor, the Executive Committee, the two parties in the Assembly, the Legislative Council, and the Colonial Office. A Government whose chief characteristic appears to have been discord and internal strife was hardly capable of any sort of legislation.

But even if there had been political calm, it is not likely that positive measures would have been taken to meet all the requirements of people such as the St. David settlers. Steps were taken to reduce predial larceny, and harsh penalties were introduced for offenders. The matter of cattle trespass, debated in Assembly, was a complicated one if compulsory fencing were to be introduced. The plea by Richard Hill for a new law relating to the assessment of damages might have won attention in a more peaceful session; at any rate there is no reason to be sure that it would not. In the matter of road repair it is certainly reasonable that where all roads are bad, as they were in Jamaica, first attention should be given to the main highways. The regulation of rents and prices of land, and the establishment of a government marketing agency were not in the mid-nineteenth century considered to be within

55. Wrong, *Government of the West Indies*, p. 67.
56. C.O. 137/351, Darling to Newcastle, confidential, 24 Nov. 1860.

the proper limits of government action. It was from Britain that colonial governors received their directions and colonial politicians their philosophies.

At the beginning of Barkly's governorship there had been changes in fiscal policy which were designed to increase the revenues by taxing the general population more heavily. The secretary of state for the colonies had advised Barkly that there were sources of revenue "capable of being drawn upon without deranging trade or discouraging industrious habits." [57] The justification was that the sugar industry, which was the main prop of the Island's economy, was in distress while the small settlers were, to all appearances, thriving. It is to be noticed, however, that the settlers seem to have made no complaint of high taxes until the 1860's, when during a period of high prices of imports (as a consequence of the American Civil War), flood, drought, and crop disease greatly reduced purchasing power in the Island.

There is no doubt that in the 1860's certain taxes were scheduled to fall more heavily upon the small producers than upon the big planters.[58] It is possible that this was an aspect of planter tyranny; but until a political survey has established what seems doubtful—namely, that the planters were in fact sufficiently agreed and powerful in the Legislature to put such a scheme into effect, we must assess them as the occasional and unfortunate measures of a Government which was too much torn by dissension to give careful thought either to what was desirable or to what was proposed.

The Assembly was not a body of cultured, intelligent people combined in sincere desire and effort to legislate for the benefit of the whole community, without favour to any particular group. No legislature has ever attained that apparent perfection. But this does not mean that there were no well-intentioned men among them.

Awareness of the need for corrective legislation and the passing of the desired legislative act are not one and the same thing. There were many who realized the need for fiscal re-

57. C.O. 137/319.
58. See Appendix 4.

form: there had been successive attempts since 1840 to remove or lighten the hereditaments taxes and the duties on imports, exports, and tonnage—replacing them by taxes on incomes over £40 or £50 a year, and by increased taxes on land.[59] There were many who would have supported a measure for the disestablishment of the Church of England, which was a heavy burden on the revenues. The Baptists were foremost among them, but other non-conformist bodies would certainly have given support, and the Jews were said to have little liking for the heavy appropriations for ecclesiastical purposes.[60]

It is reasonable to attach blame to the Legislature on two broad charges: for the failure to give careful consideration to Government expenditures with a view to possible reduction of revenues; and secondly, for the failure in 1864–65 to introduce any form of assistance to the public either in a temporary reduction of taxes or, alternatively, in an increase of expenditures for poor relief.[61] At the same time the degree of blame must be qualified by two influential facts: the po-

59. See Phillippo, *Jamaica: Its Past and Present State*, p. 112; also G. Scotland, *A Letter Addressed to the Public of Jamaica on the Political and Financial State of the Colony* (Jamaica, 1847), in which a tax of 5 per cent on all incomes of £50 a year and over, and an increase of the tax on cultivated land to 1/– per acre are proposed; also C.O. 137/314, Grey to Pakington, No. 84, 24 Sept. 1852, in which the governor proposed an income tax and an increased tax on all land, whether cultivated or not. The income tax proposals would not have pleased the merchants and others who were so lightly touched by taxes on hereditaments, live stock, etc.; and the increased land tax would not have pleased the planters. It is possible, therefore, that any proposed bill which contained both these items would have been solidly opposed by the Assembly as a whole, while it is understandable, political conditions being what they were, that the executive was unable to introduce either of them with success.

60. C.O. 137/316, Grey to Newcastle, No. 40, 10 May 1865.

61. Any consequent excess of expenditure over revenue would almost certainly have been made good by the British Government (or at least a loan could have been obtained to cover it) if the true circumstances of distress had been admitted. That they were not was less the fault of the planters or any other economic or political group than of the governor, Mr. Eyre.

litical turmoil of the time, which was not conducive to considered policy, and the sudden outbreak of civil disturbance in Morant Bay in October 1865, after which the Legislature appears entirely to have lost its head.

CHAPTER 7

Towns, Villages, and the Non-Agricultural

Occupations

THE PERIOD of comparative political quiet and economic recovery during the second half of the 1850's was too short. Generally speaking, the circumstances of that decade and the five years following operated to restrict the expansion of employment in agriculture, and gave rise to Richard Hill's comment in 1865 that the population, totalling about 441,500,[1] was "not exactly pressing on subsistence, but on employment. Capital and new sources of productive industry and trade, are the only cure for this state of evil." [2]

Agriculture could not provide the answer, especially with the conditions then prevailing. Major attempts to diversify the economy had been unsuccessful, and the towns and villages, themselves built upon and continuing dependent upon agricultural prosperity, could provide no balance in the economy. Their main function was to fulfil the need for ports and market-places.

In the days of slavery the coastal towns had been the gateways through which sugar, coffee, rum, and other export crops had passed on the way overseas, primarily to Britain; and through which imports of foodstuffs, estate supplies, and manufactured goods had entered the Island. But with a slave population tied to the estates and largely dependent on slave owners for supplies of imported food and clothing, the trade routes had generally followed this pattern: estates to coastal towns to markets in Britain; and, in the other direction, from

1. According to the 1861 Census it was 441,264.
2. C.O. 137/390, Hill to Eyre, April 1865.

Britain through Jamaican sea ports to the estates. The inland towns of the Island were small centres of a limited internal trade in provisions, handicraft goods, and other commodities produced by slaves in their spare time, or as posting-places where travellers could put up overnight in a local boarding-house or tavern. Indeed, it is hardly an exaggeration to say that the large estates were themselves villages.

> The stranger is apt to ask what village it is? —for every completed sugar works is no less, the various and many buildings bespeaking as much at first sight; for besides the large mansion-house, with its offices, the works, such as the well contrived mill, the spacious boiling house, the large receptive curing houses, still house, commodious stables for the grinding cattle, lodging for the overseer, the white servants, working shops for the necessary smiths, others for the framing carpenters and coopers; to all of which, when we add the streets of negro houses, no one will question to call such complicated sugar works a small town or village.[3]

Some estates also contained market-places to which slaves, free coloured people, and itinerant traders resorted on Sundays which, until emancipation, were the accustomed market days. After slavery we find some of the larger inland markets, still in existence today, keeping the names of the estates on which they originated.[4]

In freedom, too, it became quite common for estate owners or attorneys to establish estate shops in which imported goods were sold to the labourers. Some of these, such as one run by Thomas McCornock on Golden Grove in St. Thomas in the

3. This is an account by a visitor to Jamaica in the late seventeenth century, quoted by Gardner in his *History of Jamaica,* and reproduced in F. M. Henriques, *Family and Colour in Jamaica* (London, 1953), p. 18.

4. For example: Golden Grove in St. Thomas in the East; Papine and Constant Spring in St. Andrew; Porus in Manchester; and Darliston in Westmoreland. In some cases, and it would be hard to distinguish, the market-place was itself a post-emancipation development along with the establishment of the village or freeholders' settlements.

East, were strictly non-profit enterprises. McCornock merely acted as an importer for his workers, charging them cost plus freight and other shipping charges for the goods they ordered. On other properties, such as the neighbouring Hordley Estate, owned by the heirs of Matthew ("Monk") Lewis and managed by Robert Kirkland, the attorney allowed an outsider to open a shop on the estate. In these latter instances the outsider, quite obviously, intended to make a financial profit. In Kirkland's case the Hordley labourers complained of high prices and asked him to follow McCornock's example. Kirkland claimed, however, that he had nothing to do with the shopkeeper or his prices, and "all the advantage I get is that he is bound to supply me with silver at par for notes, that I may always have change to pay the people."[5] Small silver for wage bills was scarce and sold at a premium, so Kirkland apparently made no personal profit, provided that Mr. Lewis' heirs knew that he was getting his small silver at par.

After emancipation the decline of many estates, and the volume of exports from and imports to them, was matched by the rapid rise of the inland towns and villages. Not only did internal trade vastly increase but, as the small farmers and others entered into the production of export crops and as labourers earned money wages and demanded goods to buy with their earnings, the villages gradually joined the remaining estates in the trade-routes pattern. By the middle of the nineteenth century, therefore, we get something like this: inland towns, villages, and estates to coastal towns, to overseas buyers; and, in return, overseas sellers to coastal towns, to inland towns, villages, and estates. The general picture of change would therefore be as follows: in the coastal or old port towns there was an expansion of trading, as distinct from

5. Candler, *Extracts from the Journal*, Pt. II, p. 6. There is no suggestion, in early reports, that these shops were operated on the "truck" system, and indeed as long as the labourer was not entirely dependent on estate employment it would have been impossible for the planters to introduce such a system. In the 1860's, however, when drought and high food prices increased the importance of estate employment, there were occasional reports (C.O. 137/391) of "truck-shopping" on individual estates.

shipping, business; [6] on the estates there was a general process of disintegration as estate populations tended to disperse; [7] those old, established interior towns that lay on or near to main roads or new settlements tended to develop as trading centres; [8] and fourthly, there was the building of new towns, villages, and settlements throughout the Island by the emancipated population.[9]

It is extremely difficult to draw clear distinctions between towns, villages, and settlements. Population data are hardly available, are in fact almost entirely limited to the figures shown in Table 22. Many of the places built after 1838 were given the name of a town—for example, Sturge Town, Phoenix Town, and Clark's Town—but in the 1861 Census, "Towns and Villages" were classed together and there are some surprising omissions, such as Claremont in St. Ann, Ewarton in St. Thomas in the Vale, Lacovia in St. Elizabeth, and Alley in Vere. By 1861 these were all well-established centres.

We are therefore compelled to use incomplete information and to assume that mid-nineteenth-century Jamaicans distinguished only between the agglomerate collection of buildings into "Town or Village" and the more diffuse "settlement" or group of adjacent small freeholds.[10]

From these available figures we can draw only one dependable conclusion, namely that the port and coastal towns were generally more thickly populated than the interior ones. It is noticeable, however, that the planned, or mass-settled, centres (for example, Seaford Town, Clark's Town, and Stewart

6. For example, at Savanna-la-Mar, Port Antonio, Falmouth, and Kingston.

7. Especially in those areas where estates were abandoned or greatly reduced in size.

8. For example, Old Harbour Market, Four Paths, Duncans, Mandeville, and Chapelton.

9. As described above, Chs. 1, 6.

10. In other words, a contiguous string of small freeholds along both sides of a section of main road (such as the road from Spanish Town through St. Dorothy, Vere, and Lower Clarendon) would be termed a "settlement" rather than a "town or village."

TABLE 22. *Town and Village Populations (1861 Census)*

PARISHES	PORTS		INLAND MARKETS		OTHER TOWNS AND VILLAGES	
	Name	Popn.	Name	Popn.	Name	Popn.
Kingston	Kingston	27,359	—	—	—	—
Port Royal	Port Royal	1,553	—	—	—	—
St. Catherine	Spanish Town	5,362	—	—	—	—
St. Thomas in the East	Manchioneal	732	—	—	Bath	233
	Morant Bay	1,133	—	—	—	—
	Port Morant	138	—	—	—	—
Portland	Port Antonio *	941	—	—	—	—
St. Thomas in the Vale	—	—	Linstead	554	—	—
St. George	Buff Bay	364	—	—	—	—
Metcalfe	Annotto Bay	963	—	—	—	—
St. Mary	Port Maria *	944	—	—	—	—
St. Ann	Ocho Rios *	449	Moneague	117	Browns Town	605
	St. Ann's Bay *	1,276	—	—		
	Dry Harbour *	346	—	—	—	—
St. Dorothy	Old Harbour Bay	454	Old Harbour Market	375	—	—
Clarendon	—	—	Four Paths	125	Chapelton	583
Manchester	—	—	Porus	388	Mandeville	312
	—	—	—	—	Wigton	172
St. Elizabeth	Black River	970	—	—	—	—
Westmoreland	Savanna-la-Mar	2,064	Grange Hill	560	Seaford Town	1,568
	—	—	—	—	Petersfield	661
Hanover	Lucea	1,426	—	—	—	—
St. James	Montego Bay	4,553	—	—	—	—
Trelawny	Falmouth	3,127	Duncans & Crawle	784	Clarke's Town	540
	Rio Bueno	280	—	—	Martha Brae	372
	—	—	—	—	Stewart Town	800

* Including "environs."

NOTE. Kingston, though included in the "Towns or Villages" in the 1861 Census, was regarded as a city.

Town) were generally among the more heavily populated of the interior places.

Post-emancipation changes in the town and village pattern had been accompanied by, and very greatly influenced by, population movement. There had been both a geographical and a functional spilling-over from estate employment. The fact that the coastal towns had existed before emancipation explains their relatively greater population subsequently. Not only did they contain those people who had been town dwellers during slavery; they also attracted those who wanted to become town dwellers after slavery. No new ports were established after 1838.[11] On the other hand, the people who remained in the interior were more concerned with the establishment of new centres than desirous to flock into the few that already existed.

Those who preferred not to continue in any type of agricultural work found that the alternatives were strictly limited. Broadly, there were four outlets: the skilled crafts, petty trade, general unskilled town labour, and various other ancillary occupations or "services." By examining each of these, we shall be able to build up a picture of the post-emancipation changes.

The range of skilled trades and crafts demanded in an agricultural community was limited, not only in rural villages but also in the larger towns. In Kingston in the 1860's it was said that large numbers of people "eke out a miserable existence . . . as tailors, shoemakers, straw hat platters, cigar makers &c; and who in the country would do much better for themselves, did they not look down upon agricultural labour with contempt."[12] How much better they would have done in the country in a time of drought and low wages is questionable, but the point is that they probably would not have been willing to work the land in the most favourable of seasons.

Suggestions were made about the possibilities of creating jobs for the urban unemployed. In 1865 the Baptists' report[13]

11. There were some new fishing villages, but no town or port centres.
12. C.O. 137/390, Dr. Bowerbank to Eyre, April 1865.
13. C.O. 137/391.

contained a detailed picture of conditions in Spanish Town and suggested remedial measures. There were at that time in the capital 33 bakers, 91 shoemakers, and 127 tailors, all of whom worked mainly in the town. Other skilled workers were 38 bricklayers, 63 masons, and 228 carpenters, whose work was done largely throughout the parish; and 33 black-smiths, 21 builders, and 20 wheelrights, who also probably found work on the estates. All these, as the report pointed out, had "a very precarious existence" because of their large numbers. Other Spanish Town residents included nearly 1,000 domestics, not half of whom were employed; 772 seamstresses, who got only occasional work before the August and Christmas holidays; 422 laundresses, who were nearly all out of work; and 163 fishermen and fisherwomen, "who on the whole do very well, but would do much better if fish curing were properly understood." [14] The town was pauper-stricken, with large numbers seeking relief. These unemployed people, the report continued, "could be profitably employed in a paper-manufactory, dye-works, or something of the kind, but who must otherwise continue to lead a life of poverty and almost necessary immorality." Conditions in Spanish Town mirrored those in other large towns. They had been much the same ever since emancipation, certainly since 1846. In his report on the Blue Books for 1847 and 1848, Sir Charles Grey had described the Island as having no manufactures except sugar and rum "and I believe a little tanning and dressing of leather. It would be a mercy to find some easy and healthy employment for the women and children who are or who consider themselves to be just above the necessity of assisting in field labour; but they do not even make straw hats." There was, he said, a large

14. In Table 22 the total Spanish Town population in 1861 is given as 5,362. The sum of occupations listed here is 3,011, and as it does not include retailers, government servants, unskilled labourers, and people in other occupations, it seems much too large a proportion of the total. The explanation may well be that among those listed as "domestics," "seam-stresses," and "laundresses" (total 2,194) there were included many who were housewives offering part-time labour in these occupations, and children who were put out to work as domestics, or who assisted older women as laundresses.

"unemployed fund of latent labour of this sort," and he recommended the hand-picking of cotton as a possible source of employment.[15]

In 1855, about the middle of our period of twenty-five years, George Willis, the stipendiary magistrate in Kingston, wrote that "Except some few industrial institutions, of which notices appear in the public prints, the only pursuits of industry coming within my observation are the mere handicrafts, as Carpenters, Masons, Shoemakers, Tailors, Tinmen, Cigar Makers, and such like; most of which, as carried on, hardly deserve the name of industrial pursuits." [16] In the town, Willis continued, the labour supply exceeded the demand. The "few industrial institutions" which Willis saw advertised in the newspapers could not have employed very many. The most important were probably the various foundry-yards, such as that of Messrs. W. James and Company, which earned double notoriety in 1843: on August 10th the "Anglesey" an iron steam-boat owned by the Kingston merchant firm of Thomas Lundis put to sea on the coastal run from Kingston to Port Henderson; it had been "put together at, and launched from" William James's foundry. On August 26th the great fire which destroyed nearly half of Kingston broke out; its source was discovered to be the foundry of this same company.[17] Other "industrial institutions" no doubt included such small ventures as that of Edward Aarons, who manufactured perfumes and cosmetics; his competitor W. A'Cort; and John Abrahams, who specialized in engravings on visitors' cards and such like.[18]

In the rural areas, and especially where soil conditions made peasant agriculture difficult, the people often attempted to supplement estate wages by the sale of domestic handicraft goods. At Goodwill village, seven miles from Falmouth in Trelawny, for example, there were handicraft shops where

15. C.O. 137/304.

16. C.O. 137/326, Willis' report of 17 Jan. 1855.

17. *Jamaica Almanac*, 1845.

18. C.O. 137/364, catalogue of exhibits sent by Jamaica Society of Arts to the Industrial International Exhibition in 1861.

articles such as mats, fans, baskets, and calabash ornaments could be purchased. In Falmouth itself there was a small handicrafts establishment run by a Mr. J. O'Halloron; and in Mandeville, in Manchester, a Mrs. James Nash produced similar goods. The extent to which these two people and others like them depended on hired labour is uncertain, but it is not unlikely that they followed the domestic industry system, providing the raw materials to cottage workers and paying by the piece for goods made.[19]

In the rural towns and villages and on the estates, according to Richard Hill, few trades were practised: "We enumerate them when we say they are the Blacksmith, the Carpenter, and the Tailor: they seldom have the addition of the Shoe-maker and the Tinsmith. The Sugar Estates give occasion for the mill and wheelright, the copper and the mason." [20]

Since 1838, however, there had been a scarcity of good skilled labour. There were hundreds of people calling themselves skilled tradesmen and mechanics, but in fact the number of reliable and expert master craftsmen was small. This is an important point because it explains several apparent incompatibilities, such as a superfluity of skilled labour, shown in the statistics for Spanish Town, together with complaints of scarcity; or the cry of lack of employment for skilled workers and the entry of such people into the retail trade, together with the relatively high wages of skilled labourers. An explanation of this division of the skilled worker population into one small efficient group and another, much larger, less competent group is essential.

During slavery, both in the towns and on the estates, master craftsmen, many of whom were white or free coloured people, had handicraft slave gangs under their direction. These slaves, by their long apprenticeships, gradually acquired the master's skill and sometimes themselves became the instructors of

19. See the following: Select Committee of 1842, Minutes of Evidence, W. Knibb, 6437–9439; C.O. 137/287, report of Richard Hill, 23 Dec. 1845; C.O. 137/364, catalogue of exhibits to 1861 Exhibition.

20. C.O. 137/324, report of Richard Hill, July 1854.

new recruits. In 1834, however, after the Emancipation Act, master craftsmen on the estates generally ceased to be provided with recruits intended to undergo a proper apprenticeship. There was little economic incentive to train a youngster whose services would soon be lost. During the years of the transition into absolute freedom, therefore, the usual arrangements were not made for a succeeding generation of master craftsmen.

After 1838 subordinate workmen, who had picked up the rudiments of the various trades, set themselves up as master craftsmen, while the old qualified masters searched around for new apprentices. But apprenticeship meant a contract of labour and a willingness to accept the instruction and disciplinary measures of the masters, and neither of these conditions was popular with people who had just been freed from slavery. Such apprentices as did come forward proved intractable, and the masters' control over them was generally feeble. As a result their training suffered, and at the end of the accepted period of apprenticeship these "half-taught journeymen" also established themselves as skilled workers, much to the disgust of the small band of pre-emancipation master craftsmen. The master carpenter who supplied this information to Richard Hill finished by saying that not a single one of these men in his craft could cut wood economically for any specific piece of work, and that they were incompetent to do many of the more precise or delicate jobs. These remarks, he said, applied particularly to such everyday crafts as carpenters, cabinet-makers, bricklayers and masons, shipwrights, millwrights, chaisemakers, smiths, shoemakers, and saddlers.[21]

Thus emancipation brought a lowering of the standards of skilled craftsmenship in Jamaica. In addition, it tended to alter the distribution of skilled workers over the island. During the eighteenth-century prosperity of sugar each estate had carried its full complement of skilled workers. As profitability declined and estates went out of production, the master craftsmen also left the abandoned areas. In the towns them-

21. C.O. 137/287, report of Richard Hill, Dec. 1845.

selves, parents who were willing that their children should learn a trade were often unwilling that they should go out into the country to practise it.[22] During our period, therefore, there is, combined with a deterioration of standards a withdrawal of skilled and semi-skilled labour from the rural districts into the towns.

These concentrations of the skilled and the not so skilled emphasized the already noticeable rift in the ranks between the qualified masters and their former employees who now posed as masters. The situation is illustrated in Table 23 by figures showing the wages paid for various types of skilled

TABLE 23. *Wages of Skilled and Other Non-Agricultural Labour in Various Years*

Description	Wages in 1841	Wages in 1848	Wages in 1865
Blacksmiths	up to 6/– a day	18/ to 20/ weekly	—
Bricklayers	—	16/ to 20/ "	up to 3/– a day
Cabinet-Makers	up to 6/– a day	—	2/6 to 3/4 a day
Carpenters	up to 6/– a day	16/ to 20/– "	2/6 to 3/4 a day
Glaziers	—	16/ to 20/– "	2/6 a day
Masons	up to 4/– a day	18/ to 20/– "	about 3/ a day
Painters	—	16/ to 20/– "	3/ to 3/6 a day
Paper-Hangers	—	—	5/– a day
Plasterers	—	18/ to 20/ "	—
Plumbers	—	18/ to 20/ "	4/– a day
Shipwrights	up to 6/– a day	—	—
Slaters	—	18/ to 20/ "	—
Domestics *	about 8/ weekly	—	3/ to 8/ weekly
General Labour	1/6 to 2/6 a day	9/– to 10/– wkly.	9*d.* to 1/6 a day

* Excluding butlers, cooks, and grooms, who generally got more, according to ability.

Sources: C.O. 137/257, report of H. Moresby, Kgn., Dec. 1841; C.O. 137/263, report of S. Pryce, Kgn. May 1842; C.O. 137/297, Sir C. Grey to Earl Grey, separate, 7 July 1848, with enclosures, etc.; C.O. 137/391, Mr. Clarke and Mr. Bicknell to Governor Eyre, April 1865.

NOTE. The figures for 1841 and 1848 refer to Kingston, those for 1865 were paid in Spanish Town for work done to the governor's residence there. The likelihood of much variation between Kingston and Spanish Town rates is small.

22. C.O. 137/390, Dr. Bowerbank to Mr. Eyre, April 1865.

labour in 1841, 1848, and 1865. The general decline which followed from competition for employment is noticeable.

The resistance of the qualified masters to any lowering of their customary wage rates, either as a result of competition or of depression after 1846, was strong. In 1848 the governor, Sir Charles Grey, was asked by the Colonial Office about "the terms on which coloured Mechanics can be obtained in Jamaica for employment in Sierra Leone." In his reply he enclosed a letter from David Soares, the principal builder in Spanish Town, respecting the terms on which the "better class of coloured Mechanics" would be available for emigration. Soares gave the rates of wages of these "better class" craftsmen as follows (and his statement is worth comparison with the figures in Table 23). Blacksmiths, according to him, were paid from 32/– a week; cabinet-makers and carpenters, 30/– to 40/– a week; masons and painters from 24/– a week; upholsterers and paper-hangers 30/– to 40/– a week; and of the other craftsmen he mentioned—saddlers, turners and carvers, printers, tailors, shoemakers, and chaise-builders—none accepted less than 24/– a week, while the turners and carvers asked as much as 40/– to 60/– weekly. A master builder, presumably like himself, would earn £300–500 a year. These, he said, had long been the accepted rates, and even during the present distress and under-employment (perhaps only nine months work in twelve) of many of these people "still wherever their services are required, the prices have been uniformly as above stated." [23]

The interesting point about all this is that the rates given by Soares coincided with the maximum rates for 1841 rather than with the general rates of 1848: the conclusion must be that the "better class of coloured Mechanics" had always been paid at higher rates than the semi-skilled or half-trained and in 1848 could still command more than the current general rates in return for better work done. The state of under-employment indicates, however, that the competition of the less skilled was in some measure effective. It is also of interest

23. C.O. 137/297, Sir C. Grey to Earl Grey, separate, 7 July 1848, with enclosures and Colonial Office minutes.

to observe that in 1848 the wages paid to European craftsmen were higher than the general rates and equalled the rates obtained by the "better class of coloured Mechanics." [24]

The enquiry of the Colonial Office elicited a few letters of application, but the actual emigration was negligible, partly because wage rates in Sierra Leone were lower than those in Jamaica, partly because the Colonial Office eventually limited its request to four master craftsmen.[25]

Nonetheless, the letters of application are worth further mention for the general information they contain. They came in answer to circulars sent out by the governor to six craftsmen, as a sort of sample investigation, and they are extremely interesting because they indicate the emergence from the main group of Jamaican craftsmen of a smaller body of masters whose greater proficiency and business ability gave them the stature of small businessmen or master builders rather than skilled wage earners.

One letter came from Richard Cowan of Spanish Town. He was 41 years old and his household included his wife, his mother, his mother-in-law, his sister-in-law, and a maid. He was a stonemason, bricklayer, plasterer, paver, and brick-maker. He was a master craftsman and had taught many apprentices. He claimed to be well informed in his trades, having read Nicholson on masonry, Nicholson's *Mechanical Exercise,* Tredgold and Guilt's *Encyclopaedia;* and, he said, he generally adopted the principles used by government engineers in Jamaica. His present income was £350–400 a year. He would go to Sierra Leone for five or seven years if he could earn more money there and if the passages of himself and his family were paid there and back.

Another applicant was L. A. Price of Kingston, a house carpenter and joiner. He was 33 years old and lived with his wife, mother, brother, and sister. At the time of writing he had five apprentices under him. His reading had included Nicholson's *Carpenter's Assistant,* Smeaton's *Builder's Manual,*

24. Ibid.
25. C.O. 137/297, Colonial Office draft reply to Sir Charles Grey, dated 30 Sept. 1848.

"the Cyclopaedias," the *Builder*, and other books and periodicals. His income, he said, fluctuated widely. During the last four years it had varied between £480 and £300. He would emigrate for five, seven or nine years if his passage were paid both ways.

A third letter came from John Nash, whose home was in Spanish Town but who at the time of application was a work superintendent on Worthy Park Estate in St. John. He had been to England to learn the trades of millwright and engineer, and since his return to Jamaica had done various other work as carpenter, smith, and mason. He, too, had taught apprentices, and kept up to date on all improvements, although "as regards to Machinery in this Country, I very often have to adopt my own invention to suit the emergency required." His present income was small and he was accustomed to better things, having "lately enjoyed £600 a year." He had a wife, a son, and two daughters. He would go to Sierra Leone for £800 a year, and his son would go for £150. If they enjoyed good health there, he would be willing to remain permanently.

There is no need to summarize all the letters. In conclusion, here is an extract from the application of James Smythe of Morant Bay, whose letter was endorsed by nine prominent people:

> I beg respectfuly to inform your Excellency of my willingness to engage myself in the service if the remuneration are any way adequate to my station of life. My occupation is Upholstering a business I have been Master of and carrying on for the last 13 years, Eight years of which in the City and parish of Kingston four years in the Parish of Portland, and now is resident at Morant Bay during these term of years I has Taught several apprentices under me   I have &c.[26]

26. C.O. 137/297. These and the other two applications from W. M. Meigham of Kingston and J. Waldron of Spanish Town are all enclosed with Sir C. Grey to Earl Grey, separate, 7 July 1848.

The figures in Table 23 show a slight recovery in the ordinary wages paid to skilled workers in 1865. Unfortunately, there are no available figures of the wages demanded, in that year, by the bona fide master craftsmen. It is possible, of course, that many of them had died and that the distinction no longer existed, but if some of them were still active it is probable that they continued to ask and obtain rates somewhat higher than the ordinary. The slight rise in the ordinary rates was due partly, no doubt, to the effects of the cholera epidemic, and also in part to a large emigration of workers, especially from Kingston, in 1853 and 1854. In July of the latter year Governor Barkly informed the Colonial Office that 2,000 to 3,000 adult males had already left Kingston for Panama, where the railway across the isthmus was under construction. He had been forced to intervene to regulate the emigration because ship captains, who were getting £1 a head bounty on immigrants in Panama, were overcrowding their vessels. Although Jamaica employers were alarmed by the size of the exodus, the governor said he would do nothing to stop it, although the Legislature might reasonably want to ensure that families left behind would be provided for. Wages of 2/6 a day and rations were being offered on the railway, but the work was hard and conditions difficult and unhealthy.[27]

By March 1855, the railway having in the meantime been completed, many of the emigrants had returned to Jamaica. Their going, said the governor, had given proof of great enterprise and initiative when inducement offered. He was interested to see what they would now do in Jamaica.[28] In time, many of them returned to their old occupations; some, apparently, used their savings to buy land and establish themselves as freeholders.[29] But large numbers of the emi-

27. C.O. 137/323, Barkly to Sir George Grey, No. 87, 10 July 1854.
28. C.O. 137/326, Barkly to the secretary of state for the colonies, No. 32, 20 March 1855.
29. C.O. 137/327, Barkly to Molesworth, No. 97, 2 Oct. 1855 (Hill's report).

grants did not return to Jamaica, and—since many skilled
workers, especially carpenters and masons were among them
—the competition among such people, in Kingston at any
rate, was modified. In 1865 it was said to be difficult to find
skilled people of this sort even at 3/– a day.[30]

The fortunes of the skilled workers during 1840 to 1865 may
thus be summed up as follows: after emancipation the ranks
of the master craftsmen were swollen by the entry of large
numbers of less qualified people into the trades. The ensuing
competition, though resisted by the masters who apparently
demanded and received higher wages than were paid to the
less skilled, led to a measure of unemployment or under-
employment among them. After 1850 the numbers of tradesmen, particularly in Kingston and Spanish Town, were reduced
by cholera and, more obviously, by a large emigration to
Panama, whence many of the emigrants did not return. Wage
rates thus tended to rise slightly during the later 1850's and
early 1860's, but they did not again reach the high levels
of the immediate post-emancipation period.

It is quite clear that among those who turned to petty
or retail trading to make a living were many who had failed
to prosper as craftsmen.

> A carpenter or other handicraftsman, for instance, finding
> himself restricted by his trade to two or three shillings
> a day, obtains credit from one or more store-keepers in
> a neighbouring town for a barrel of flour and pork, and
> a few pieces of cloth, and thus commences as a country
> shopkeeper. A short period having elapsed, by the sale
> of these goods he has contrived to amass fifty pounds.
> With this money, and an introductory letter, he travels
> to Kingston, and obtains goods to the extent of several
> hundred pounds. By the exercise of much dexterity, the
> various creditors are assured and cajoled, until the bubble
> bursts; writs are issued for a thousand or more pounds,
> and the goods sold by VEDITIONI EXPONAS for less than
> one-third their original cost. Thus the community loses

30. C.O. 137/390, Bowerbank to Eyre, April 1865.

a valuable mechanic, or other producing member, and the legitimate trader is seriously injured by the sales of bankrupt property.[31]

Thomas Jelly, to whom we are indebted for the quotation, was obviously overstating his case, which was to show that a "mania for trucking and shopkeeping pervades all ranks" and that large numbers of unqualified men were seeking "this dubious road to wealth."

But he was not the only observer to remark on the effects of an expanding number of new dealers on the established group of retailers: "the regular retailers complain that they are greatly hampered by numerous petty dealers in the country who were formerly labourers and mechanics . . . being compelled by the petty dealers to reduce their prices to very low rates in order to obtain a livelihood, the chances of failure are increased and the Merchant may thus be ultimately affected." [32]

There is no doubt, however, that the old organization of retail and wholesale commerce was quite inadequate to satisfy the new conditions of wage-labour and freehold production. As we have shown, retail commerce during slavery had been confined almost exclusively to the local markets for island-grown provisions.

In the country districts, where development of retail commerce was most rapid, the small local market-places were soon surrounded by the shops of people entering the trade. The reports of the stipendiary magistrates in the 1840's are full of comment concerning the establishment of small dealers in imported goods and the increasing number of itinerant traders. The shops were being opened not only by those labourers and craftsmen who left their former occupations but also by the merchants in the large towns who seized the opportunity to spread their businesses, and by the managers of sugar estates.[33]

31. Jelly, *A Brief Enquiry into the Condition of Jamaica*, p. viii.

32. C.O. 137/275, report of G. M. Lawson, senior magistrate of St. James, 13 Nov. 1843.

33. For example, those on Golden Grove and Hordley, to which we

Throughout the Island both the business of the shopkeepers and the pockets of the purchasers were seriously affected by an obvious inadequacy in the system of currency. Until 1839 there had been no banks in Jamaica; coins in circulation had been, for the most part, Spanish and Portuguese gold and silver pieces; and the paper currency consisted entirely of unconvertible notes issued by the receiver general upon the security of the revenues.[34]

During slavery the need for an Island currency had been small because labour was not commonly paid for in money wages and because of the agency system, by which sugar planters sold their crops and bought much of what they required in Britain. Money transactions with Britain, we are told "were carried on by means of bills of exchange, usually bearing a rate of premium in proportion to their demand in the market, besides the nominal par of exchange. Sometimes the premiums have been as high as 25 per cent." [35]

The ending of slavery had brought an immediate demand for small coin to be used in the payment of wages.[36] This was met by imports of British silver coins, but for some time the supply of small silver remained insufficient to fulfil the planters' requirements.[37] At the same time the circulation of British coin, in company with the confusing mixture of Spanish and Portuguese which were also current, brought the need for regulation. In 1839 an act was passed for the assimilation of the Island currency to British sterling. By the end of 1841 the use of Jamaica currency in ordinary business

---

have already referred. See also C.O. 137/255, report of S. M. Finlayson, Feb. 1841.

34. Phillippo, *Jamaica: Its Past and Present State,* p. 118. The gold and silver coin were doubloons, pistoles, dollars, half dollars, macaronies, tenpences, and fivepences. The last-named was the equivalent of 3*d.* sterling.

35. Ibid.

36. C.O. 137/192, Forbes to Norcott, May 1834; C.O. 137/228, Smith to Glenelg, 25 June 1838.

37. For example, on Hordley Estate, mentioned above.

and in the public accounts appears to have been entirely abolished.[38]

Since the Island expenditures of the big planters had increased, however (at least by the amounts they had to pay out in wages), it became necessary for them either to earn more money in the island or to organize a system of credit whereby they could obtain supplies such as foodstuffs and lumber products, which they purchased locally rather than in Britain. To this end certain planters and merchants associated to form two local credit institutions, the Jamaica Bank and the Planter's Bank.[39] Eventually their functions spread, though they were both refused charters, to include the issue of notes which, though not even redeemable in Island notes or silver, gained wide acceptance among all but the labourers. In the meantime the Island notes continued in circulation, still unconvertible into coin on demand but still backed by the Island revenues.

Apart from the two mentioned above, a third bank commenced operations in Jamaica about the time of emancipation. This was the Colonial Bank, operating under charter and with its head offices in London and branches in the West Indies. The notes of this bank were convertible into sterling; and although it at first seemed rather unsuccessful in Jamaica one would suppose that after 1846 when the Planter's Bank failed and the Island revenues were threatened, its notes would have been much in demand.[40]

The increasing use of bank notes, however, did not solve one of the main difficulties in the existing currency situation. Throughout our period, copper coins, though issued as subsidiaries to silver, were not legal tender in Jamaica and

38. C.O. 137/257, Metcalfe to Stanley, No. 15, 24 Nov. 1841.

39. The latter has already been discussed. Less is known of the former, though it probably lasted longer, as there is no mention of its failure in 1846–48.

40. For details of the Colonial Bank see C.O. 137/216, 217, 237, 245, and other volumes. The Jamaica branch opened about the end of 1836. Early lack of success probably followed from a comparatively restricted credit policy on the part of the Colonial Bank.

were freely acceptable only at the post office. Workers, for
the obvious reason, refused to take copper in their pay
packets. The smallest available silver coin was worth $1\frac{1}{2}d$.
and this led to hardship and confusion which were not
conducive to trade. In April 1865 the manager of the Colonial
Bank advised the governor:

> It would be a boon, I think, to the labouring class if the
> payment of this coin (copper) was made a legal and
> compulsory tender to a certain *small* amount. Now, they
> cannot buy anything for a penny. . . . a man can buy
> for 2d. (a silver coin) but if he tenders 3d. in payment
> (another silver coin) he cannot effect the purchase as
> there is not any change.[41]

It is surprising that no one had suggested this before. It is
the sort of thing which Richard Hill of Spanish Town, for
example, was always quick to bring to the governor's attention, but no record has been found of any previous mention
of the subject. It is certainly not surprising that nothing was
done to remedy the situation in the few remaining months
before the catastrophe at Morant Bay.

In short, just as the Island Legislature had for one reason
or another neglected to provide, or to encourage the provision
of, assistance to small cultivators in the form of roads, credit,
and marketing facilities, so it neglected the needs of a
rapidly expanding internal commerce for regulation and
encouragement. But it is also clear that lack of capital or
credit was not by any means the only reason for failure. The
small settlers had their other problems; the "skilled" worker
was often deficient in his skill; and the retailer who had no
head for business and the keeping of accounts could hardly
have prospered, no matter how much capital he could lay
out in goods.

His larger brothers, the established merchants and storekeepers in a port or inland town, were generally more ex-

41. C.O. 137/390, Theodore Gordon, manager of the Colonial Bank
(not to be confused with George W. Gordon) to Mr. Eyre, April 1865.

perienced in business matters and were prospering. It has already been pointed out that the local Jamaica merchants were originally connected with the American rather than the British trade, and that the enormous increase of local buying and selling which followed the emancipation had been largely to their advantage. It was the local merchant who dealt in minor exports, such as the small settlers produced, and who supplied these people with the various imports which they needed.

A good picture of the merchants' establishments in Savanna-la-Mar about 1850 was given by P. H. Gosse:

> The lower parts of most of the houses are used as shops, or stores as they are called in American fashion, each one, whatever the character of its merchandise,—drapery, "dry goods", "hardware", provisions, spirits, or tobacco, are all fitted up in the same manner, with an open piazza in front, three or four yards wide, where the various goods are exposed, and in which the proprietor, and a friend or customer, may commonly be seen, seated on chairs, their feet often on another chair (also in the American fashion), smoking a cigar, and sipping some cooling syrup, or inbibing the more enticing and dangerous beverage known as "sangaree". Behind the piazza is the shop, with unglazed windows, through which comcunication is frequently held with the clerks and assistants inside; this is fitted up with counters and shelves in the English style. Above, the ceiling of the piazza being supported, on the street line, by one or two slender pillars, are the rooms of the dwelling-house, or else balconies; in either case furnished with jalousies, or strong Venetian blinds. Towards the upper end of the long street the shops cease, the houses become more elegant, each enclosed in a court or garden, often adorned with beautiful or fragrant blossoming trees and plants of the island, or such as unite fruit with beauty and shade.[42]

42. *A Naturalist's Sojourn in Jamaica*, p. 37.

This description of comfortable prosperity was given after the 1846 act had so violently upset the sugar industry. Indirectly, it emphasizes the fact that the majority of local merchants and storekeepers had no straight forward and obvious connection with the sugar trade with Britain. In the long run, of course, the decline of the sugar estates would clearly affect the purchasing power of many of their working-class customers.

It has also been shown that the merchants were among those members of the community least burdened by taxation. In 1847 George Scotland, of Portland and Metcalfe, put forward proposals for fiscal reform suggesting the abolition of all duties on imports, and all tonnage dues. These were to be replaced by a land tax and a tax of 5 per cent on all incomes of £50 a year and upwards. In calculating how much the income tax would yield, he used the occupational classifications of the 1844 Census, putting against each group his estimate of the annual income of each member of it (see Table 24).

TABLE 24. *Average Annual Incomes Attached to Various Occupations in Jamaica, 1847*

Occupation	Income	Occupation	Income
Ministers of religion	£400	Merchants	£700
Schoolmasters	70	Storekeepers	300
Planting attorneys	600	Retailers	100
Planters (all grades)	80	Clerks	120
Bankers	500	Master tradesmen	150
Public servants	500	Journeymen	50
Professional persons	500	Tavernkeepers	300
Surveyors	300	Lodging-house keepers	150
Artists	150	Master mariners	80
Architects	200	Pilots	70
1,000 persons (unclassified)	50 *	Miners	70

* £50 and over.

Source: G. Scotland, *A Letter Addressed to the Public of Jamaica on the Political and Financial State of the Colony,* Jamaica, 1847.

Now it is possible that Scotland, in order to carry his point about income tax, pitched his averages as high as he could. His estimates for master tradesmen and journeymen suggest that this might be the case. Nonetheless, it is interesting to see his implication that the merchants were the people who enjoyed the highest annual incomes.

That their prosperity continued, though perhaps slightly checked, during the 1850's seems to be borne out by their apparently increasing association after 1846 with the estate planters as creditors, and by the fact that in the main the condition of the mass of the population deteriorated only at a slow rate during that decade. Without doubt, it can be said that of estate planters and local merchants the latter were, as a group, the far better off during our period.[43]

The first important sign of the merchants' anxiety over trade within the island came only in 1863, when civil war in the United States and the system of charging ad valorem duties on goods entering the Island combined to push the local prices of certain imports very high. Then they complained to the governor, who put the problem to the Colonial Office, who passed it on to the Treasury. Inflation in the United States had meant that buyers of American goods, who paid in gold or desirable foreign bills, had an advantage. This was so for Jamaica merchants. But when the goods arrived in Jamaica, customs duties were levied ad valorem on the sterling value of the goods, translated at the ordinary legal rate of exchange between American dollars and sterling.

The answer from the Treasury was that in Britain ad

43. Some import figures, especially of goods such as foodstuffs brought from North America for general consumption in the Island, would be useful here, but the Blue Books do not sufficiently distinguish between goods imported for immediate use, for warehousing for later supply within the Island, and for warehousing for re-export, to make a useful table practicable. In certain years from 1857, for example, quantities of goods entered for "home consumption" are sometimes greater than the quantities entered under "total imported." One must assume, therefore, that home consumption included releases from the warehouses, without being able to say exactly when the amounts released were actually brought into the island. See Appendix 5, below.

valorem duties were based on the declared marketable value of the goods imported, not on the foreign currency price in the country of origin. To prevent undervaluation by importers, the Crown reserved the right to take the goods imported at the declared value plus 5 per cent and sell them on behalf of the Revenue.[44]

Finally, before passing on to discuss the position of general unskilled labourers and others, brief reference should be made to the members of another of Scotland's groups—the "Professional Persons." Of these, the most important subgroups were the medical men and the lawyers.[45] Generally speaking, the incomes of these people tended to decline after emancipation, and this it would seem was particularly true of the doctors. During slavery many of them had lived in rural areas and enjoyed fairly lucrative employment by planters in estate hospitals and clinics. Emancipation put an end to this, and by the 1860's there are occasional reports of a shortage of doctors, especially in the country districts.[46] More frequently, also, the reports speak of the unwillingness of the people to seek medical aid. Attempts in the mid-1840's to establish district dispensaries to which people might resort for advice and medicines were not successful for the simple reason that these centres were to be financed by annual contributions from families.[47]

People who were in good health showed no desire to pay out money in advance against a time of illness which might never occur. In any case, as the doctors decreased in number and withdrew into the towns it became more difficult for people in rural areas to obtain attendance even when they wanted and could afford it.

The lawyers were less unfortunately affected by emancipation. The decline of many great estates possibly brought the lose of some of their important clients, but on the other hand

44. C.O. 137/377, Treasury to Colonial Office, 11 Nov. 1863.
45. The clergy and teachers will be mentioned in Ch. 8.
46. C.O. 137/391, the Baptists' report of 1865. Also Dr. Milroy's report on the cholera epidemic, 1850–51.
47. *Jamaica Almanac*, 1846, and Milroy's report.

freehold settlement and the redistribution of landed property would have ensured new business. To the extent, moreover, that the new small settlers indulged in litigation over titles to land, debts, and other matters of dispute (and they were, and still are, described as a litigious group) the lawyers would have profited. Scotland's figures, placing the professional people fairly high in the income scale, seem to give a reasonable idea of their comparative financial condition during our period.

The decline of wages paid to general unskilled labourers in the towns (see Table 23) followed from the decline of urban industrial and construction projects after 1846 and also from the continuous immigration, particularly into Kingston, of those who had abandoned agriculture or skilled work or retail trading in the country districts.

In May 1842 Stipendiary Magistrate Pryce complained that within the past seven months nearly 1,000 cases had been brought before the Kingston magistrates in Petty Sessions. The large number was due, partly at any rate, to the inflow of "idle and disorderly persons from all the out Parishes." [48]

At the end of our period Dr. Bowerbank, custos of Kingston, referred to the town as the meeting-ground of soldiers, sailors, immigrant labourers who had deserted or whose indentures had expired, criminals, lepers, the disease-ridden, and the unemployed. More than 500 people got a small weekly relief of a shilling or two, and as many more again qualified for assistance without getting any.[49] William Sewell cannot have been exaggerating when he wrote of the Kingston population in 1860: "The Kingstonians remind me much of the Bahama wreckers. Having little or nothing themselves, they look upon a steamer-load of California passengers, cast away in their harbour for a night or a day, as very Egyptians whom it is not only their privilege but their duty to despoil." [50]

In the optimistic and industrious period of the 1840's before

48. C.O. 137/263, Pryce's report of 1 May 1842. See also C.O. 137/289, his report of 1 June 1846.

49. C.O. 137/390, Bowerbank to Eyre, April 1865.

50. *Ordeal of Free Labour in the British West Indies*, p. 174.

the Sugar Duties Act, the townspeople had been better off. At almost any given time there had been some project afoot which offered employment to unskilled workers. The Spanish Town Railway, for example, during its construction had provided regular employment for about 500 labourers every day for about a year.[51] But the very nature of most of these occupations, which were not founded on any permanent and basic industrial growth, suggests the weakness of the nonagricultural economy. Except for occasional enterprises, more numerous in years of prosperity and optimism, the town labourers were uncertain of employment. The decline of sugar prices reduced the number of other undertakings which were indirectly encouraged by sugar prosperity, and, more directly, reduced the level of town and port employment in the handling of estate produce and supplies.

Under the heading of services we shall consider three types of employment: domestic service, needlework, and innkeeping. Of the first it is necessary only to refer to the decline of wages for domestic labour shown in Table 23. The explanation is implied in all that has been previously said. People were becoming poorer: there was less demand for domestics. At the same time the reduced demand for other labour increased the number of those willing to enter domestic service.

Among those who had been important employers of household servants were the urban middle-class families who had once owned slaves whom they "jobbed out," or whose incomes were fixed,[52] so that they became poorer as prices increased in the 1860's. Others found their chief sources of income undermined by industrial progress or other economic change. Such were the seamstresses and needleworkers, of whom there were hundreds in Kingston and Spanish Town, and large numbers scattered throughout all the large towns.

51. C.O. 137/287, Elgin to Stanley, No. 9, 13 Jan. 1846.
52. For example, those holding military or civil offices with fixed salaries, those receiving pensions, those dependent on inheritances or investments yielding fixed annual amounts, and those Anglican clergy who lived on their stipends.

These women belonged to the "respectable" lower middle class. In their social status and increasing poverty they might be classed with those whose husbands had left them with little financial provision for the future, and of whom one commentator said, "work they cannot, to beg they are ashamed." [53] They suffered from the general depression of the 1860's that reduced the incomes and the purchases of their customers. They also suffered from the increased importation of ready-made clothing and from the introduction of the sewing-machine [54] (see Table 25).

TABLE 25. *Number of Sewing-Machines Imported*

Year	No.	Other Designation	Total Value in £
1860	13	—	146
1861	—	29 packages	224
1862	23	2 cases	195
1863	23	25 cases	451
1864	17	16 packages	191
1865	—	13 cases	70

Source: Jamaica Blue Books.

Such, too, were the lodging-house keepers of Spanish Town, who found their guests fewer in number after the railway to Kingston simplified and quickened the journey between the commercial and political capitals. And the inn-keepers in the rural districts, who, unless they were fortunate enough to be situated in a strategic position, often found themselves handicapped by the rapid growth of new towns and market-places. Where necessary journeys were shortened, they found themselves and their services less in demand. Where new towns arose, they had to face competition. In 1854 Governor Barkly remarked of Moneague, in St. Ann, where several roads converged: "Here there is the best Inn in the Island,

53. See the reports contained in C.O. 137/390. The quotation is from the report by H. B. Shaw, inspector of prisons, in Vol. 390 (1865).

54. C.O. 137/390, Reports of the custodes, Church of England clergy, and others on the state of the Island. Also C.O. 137/391, report of the Baptists on conditions in the larger towns.

several good stores, a public Market, and a Police Station, but a Church has still to be erected." [55]

In view of the fact that the resident population of Moneague seven years later was only 117 (see Table 22), this is a highly suggestive comment which illustrates an essential characteristic of the rural town in an agricultural country, or even more peculiarly, a characteristic of such a town in a district of small-scale farming.

Towns of this sort do not usually contain a large permanent population. They are essentially shopping and marketing centres, and the number of people required to maintain shops and markets is small compared with the market-day inflow of neighbouring but scattered farmers. Moneague, by the governor's description, was a fairly important centre. It is about half-way along the old trans-island road from Spanish Town to St. Ann's Bay, an ideal stopping point for travellers —hence the good inn. But it was primarily a business and resting-place which provided for a non-resident population —hence the lack of a church or chapel and the small population. It could be compared with many contemporary English towns which fulfilled similar functions, though on a larger scale.[56] In these places the striking features are the market-places, the retail trading establishments, and the public houses. In Jamaica there were the markets and traders and the rum shops.[57]

We began, immediately after emancipation, with a town and a village pattern in which only the port towns or shipping places were really significant, although the larger estates— to the extent to which they maintained their own craft and trading centres, their hospitals, and occasionally their own schoolrooms and chapels—might also claim a degree of urbanization.

After emancipation a minority of estates remained pros-

55. C.O. 137/323, Barkly to Newcastle, No. 73, 26 May 1854.

56. For example, Thame in Oxfordshire or Chelmsford in Essex.

57. The reports of the custodes and stipendiaries contain numerous references to the establishment of rum shops. See, for example, reports in C.O. 137/250 (Oct.–Dec. 1840) and subsequent volumes.

perous and kept up their old establishment. From the majority, however, the estate populations spilled over; some to establish themselves, entirely or in part, as independent agriculturalists; others, having no wish to continue in agriculture, attracted towards the larger coastal towns. Among them were many skilled workers and members of professions, especially doctors who had been employed by estate owners to supervise or visit estate hospitals. These people and the many unskilled agricultural labourers who also moved towards the coast were to discover that the post-1846 decline of sugar and the non-emergence of other industrial development would limit the capacity of the towns to offer them employment.

In the interior, besides the surviving estates and the few small pre-emancipation villages, three general types of new town or village appeared. There was the "planned" or ag-glomerate centre, which generally housed an agricultural pop-ulation whose freeholds were either limited to garden size or else situated beyond the borders of the township. There was the "market" town, which emerged in answer to the needs of an increasing internal retail trade, both in local produce and in imported goods. These were generally places of concentrated trading facilities, but small resident popula-tion. Thirdly, there was the diffuse "settlement" stretched out along a section of main highway, lacking the social con-centration of the "planned" townships and the business fa-cilities of the "market" town. In all these types of interior growth the decline of the late 1840's and after resulted in varying measures of underemployment rather than in outright unemployment. It was only when both small-scale and estate agriculture declined or were simultaneously handicapped that complete destitution appeared.

CHAPTER 8

Crisis and Assessment

DURING 1855 to 1860 sugar prices were better than they had been for several years previously and estate abandonment was no longer taking place on the scale of previous years. The various mining enterprises had been busy during 1854 to 1857, even though little copper had been produced, and there was, especially after the appointment of the Main Roads Commission in 1859, a certain amount of work available on highway maintenance.

In November 1858 Governor Darling, opening the Legislative Session, remarked: "The spirit of public enterprise is not, I have been rejoiced to find, altogether dormant among us." He went on to speak of proposals for a slip-dock in Kingston harbour, of new projects for railway expansion, and of the need for "tramways in agricultural districts." But the most interesting part of his speech concerned the financing of these various works. He understood the prevailing hesitancy of capitalists to embark on new and especially such long-term enterprises, and had heard that there would be requests for government guarantees and assistance:

> Should they assume a substantial form, and reach me,
> supported by your approval, which I am confident will
> not be granted without the fullest enquiry and delibera-
> tion, you will find me disposed, and ready to act in hearty
> co-operation with you, believing as I do, that there is
> scarcely a limit to the extent to which a government may,
> under the requisite precautions, wisely and safely promote

the initiation of public works, whose reproductive character may be relied upon with reasonable certainty.[1]

The governor, apparently, was willing to introduce a policy of deficit financing, or, to use the more attractive American term, "pump-priming," by which Government would deliberately overspend the amount received in revenue so as to boost production, employment, and purchasing power and thus stimulate the demand for goods and services.

From the improved political and economic state, after the harder days of 1846–54, there was a sudden plunge in the early 1860's into deep depression, culminating in 1865–66 in bloodshed and drastic constitutional change.

In order to understand the tragedy of 1865 it is first necessary to realize that in the period of five years after 1860 a rapid succession of economic and political catastrophes, each of which by itself would have raised serious problems, had hit the island. Behind these, moreover, and enhanced by them, was a gradual worsening of relations between employers and labourers, and also between the people as a whole and the Island Legislature and governor.

In November 1860 a great religious revival began, quite suddenly, among Moravian churches in Manchester, and soon spread throughout the Island to include the members of other sects.[2] It became known, subsequently, as the Baptist Revival. It is difficult to explain why the movement began where it did. Manchester contained no sugar estates. It was a relatively prosperous parish of small settlers. It is unlikely that the religious feeling arose as a reaction to any peculiar economic distress. In part, it may be ascribed to a desire to break away from the rather hum-drum routine of daily labour. Social amenities and recreational facilities were limited. The chapel was usually the social centre. An intense emotional appeal by the local preacher might well sway a congregation, and the response, as well as the appeal, might prove infectious.

1. C.O. 137/340, Darling to Bulwer Lytton, No. 141, 10 Nov. 1858 (enclosure).

2. W. Carlile, *Thirty-Eight Years' Mission Life in Jamaica*, London, 1884.

There is less need to fumble for explanation of the spread of the Revival to other sects and other parts of the Island. The Baptists, for example, had encouraged it. In the early post-emancipation period they had been given strong voluntary financial support by their members, and, as a result had arranged that financial aid from the parent society in England should be withdrawn. Then, as freehold settlement took the people away from established centres of influence, as the people became poorer, and as the old ministers and the old ex-slaves died out and were replaced by others who were not bound by such close memories and associations, the Baptists had lost both numerical and financial support.[3] There had been a small recovery of membership in the 1850's, which possibly reflected the slightly improved conditions of those years, but membership and funds were still well below the good days of the early 1840's. A recruiting campaign had been decided upon in February 1860, and Revival meetings had been held in the western part of the Island in that year. Until November, however, the response had not been encouraging, and when the great movement actually began in Manchester in that month, it was joyously hailed by the missionary bodies: "the revival for which we as ministers and churches here have been so long praying and labouring has at length been realised in the numerous districts of the island." [4]

As the first revivalists took to the road they were joined by others along the way, and the emotional appeal gained

3. Underhill, *The West Indies,* pp. 429, 430, gives the following data:

Year	No. of Baptist Members	Year	Average Annual Contribution Each
1839	21,337	1844	11s. 11¼d.
1843–44	31,000	1849	7s. 4¼d.
1845–55	steady decline	1854	7s. 7½d.
1855–60	slight increase	1859	3s. 2½d.

See also C.O. 137/390, report of Archdeacon W. Rowe to Eyre (1865).

4. E. B. Underhill, *Life of James M. Phillippo, Missionary in Jamaica* (London 1881), ch. 34. See letters between Phillippo and Underhill, June–Dec. 1860.

strength. From the point of view of the planters and their supporters, who wanted an abundance of cheap labour, the cross-country processions were proof that the workers were content to fiddle while Rome burned. From the point of view of the Anglican clergy, who had never been closely allied with the people, it was an "awful profanation of religion" which led the people to forsake work and thus to starve, and later perhaps to steal.[5] The more "respectable" citizens were prone to condemn it on the grounds that the revivalists were behaving immorally as they went "in thousands from one District to the other, sleeping in Chapels and Houses promiscuously for many months." [6] The movement, it was said, encouraged "sensuality and reckless vagaries." [7] But the sponsoring missionaries and preachers reacted quite differently:

> I have engaged Darliston house, in which there is a good room for the meeting and we shall, all well, remove up there in a few days. I am just returned and have only time to save the mail to add a mere line or two. On Lord's day, in the evening, many were brought to the Lord, falling down while I was speaking. At the end thirteen were found prostrated in different stages of their new birth. Before they left about eleven p.m., they were full of joy, with one or two exceptions.

And again, by the same writer, "One of the Kingston newspapers complains that 'the people cannot be induced to come to work, even if you offer them one pound per day.' The fact is, the people have a more important business to attend to for the present!" [8]

The Revival ended in 1861, and its economic effects might

5. C.O. 137/390. See references to the Revival in the reports of the clergy and custodes in April 1865. The quoted words are from the letter of Rev. C. R. Chandler of Guy's Hill in St. Ann, to the bishop.

6. C.O. 137/390, Richard Carter to Charles Royes.

7. C.O. 137/391, Mr. Harrison, (successor to Robert Kirkland as attorney for Hordley Estate, St. Thomas in the East) to Custos Baron von Ketelhodt.

8. W.W.T., *A Letter from Jamaica on the Subject of Religious Revivals,* London, 1860.

have been so short-lived as to be negligible, but in the same year the American Civil War began. The Revivalists had neglected not only the estates but their provision grounds as well, and thus, at a time when the prices of imported foodstuffs were increasing, local produce was scarce in the markets. There was probably, therefore, subsequent to the dying down of religious fervour, a return to labour on provision grounds rather than on the estates. The planters would have continued their tirades against the unwillingness of the creole to labour.

Early in 1862 there was an incident involving the seizure of two Americans from the Southern States who were on board one of the Royal Mail steamers. Both Darling and the Colonial Office feared that the occurrence might lead to an outbreak of war with Britain and the threat of invasion of Jamaica. The Island was therefore to be prepared to meet attack.[9] Plans were immediately entered into to strengthen the force of Island volunteers. Membership in this body was open to all who had an annual income of £40 a year or more.[10] Thus at a time when agricultural employer-employee relations were somewhat strained, the policy was adopted, for a very good reason, to put weapons into the hands of the comparatively well-to-do.

In the meantime the sugar industry had suffered from another price fall in Britain. American Civil War affected the North American market and supplies of Cuban, and other foreign sugars were diverted to the United Kingdom.[11] Prices, excluding duty, fell from 26/10 per hundredweight in 1860 to 23/5 in 1861, with further decreases in the next two years. The price fall was followed, as usual, by attempts of the planters to lower wages, by reducing the rate per day or task, or by increasing the amount of work to be done for a given sum of money. The power of the peasant or labourer to earn was reduced, and at the same time there was a renewed inflow of indentured labour which reduced the number of estate jobs offered to local people. It is only fair to remark that the arrangements for these immigrants had been entered into before the outbreak of the American Civil War and the fall of sugar

9. C.O. 137/364, Darling to Newcastle, No. 9, 8 Jan. 1862.
10. C.O. 137/367, Eyre to Newcastle, No. 37, 20 June 1862.
11. Reed, *The History of Sugar and Sugar Yielding Plants*, ch. 8.

prices. Their arrival was another accidental addition to the sources of ill-feeling.

By the spring of 1862 it must have been abundantly clear that the Island was in a period of economic crisis that demanded action by the Legislature. At that time Governor Darling went to England on leave, which eventually ended in transfer to another colony, and the administration was taken over by Edward Eyre.

The change of governors at a time of crisis was made worse by the fact that for the first two years Eyre held appointment only as acting lieutenant governor in expectation of Darling's return, or the definite appointment of a successor to him. In short, as Eyre often pointed out in his dispatches, the executive was in an embarrassing position. In matters of dispute he was unwilling to take up a position unacceptable to Darling, even when he did not support the absent governor's point of view.[12] Yet the fact that Eyre continued to accept this situation for two years, during which he sank into irreconcilable disagreement with the Town party, suggests that despite its inconveniences conventional deference to the absent governor had its advantages for an incompetent lieutenant.

To begin with, Eyre was not considered by the Colonial Office to be competent for the governorship of Jamaica.[13] Secondly, he was a "correct" and abstemious son of a Victorian clergyman, and he disliked those whose social behaviour exceeded the limits of his own narrow code. He was the sort of man least likely to seek or to find friends in a colony where alcoholic drinks were habitually consumed in large quantities, and where one of the crying needs was for a bastardy law to ensure the financial support by fathers of their illegitimate offspring. Moreover, and this probably from his own awareness of his unpopularity and the need to prove himself in the

12. C.O. 137/371, Eyre to Newcastle, Nos. 59 and 76, 9 March and 7 April 1863, dealing with the Jamaica Tramway, are a good illustration.
13. C.O. 137/371, Darling to Newcastle, No. 173, 9 Dec. 1861. See Taylor's minute. Eyre's past record as a colonial governor was not satisfactory, but he was unemployed, he had a family to support, and applicants for the stormy post of Governor of Jamaica were few in number.

eyes of the Colonial Office, he resented all criticism and would go to great lengths to prove that his critics were either liars or nobodies.[14]

Almost from his moment of landing in the Island, Eyre became involved in political troubles. Incident succeeded incident, and in 1864, commenting on a recent fracas in the Assembly, the *Morning Journal* of 15 January remarked: "Whether it comes about now or hereafter, it seems inevitable that his Excellency will fall into difficulties from which, perhaps, it will not be possible to extricate him without serious embarassment both to himself and the colony. His Excellency is not responsible so much as the Colonial Secretary, who has been remarkably indifferent about Jamaica affairs." [15]

Already it was clear that serious trouble lay ahead, arising out of political disagreements alone and without even considering the economic problems which were, in the same year, to be still further increased.

In May and June 1864 the annual spring rains were heavier than usual. They resulted in floods which damaged crops, roads, and bridges.[16] Later in the year the governor reported that school attendance had fallen off considerably during past months: "from the Poverty and distress which existed amongst the labourers, owing to the failure of the provision crops." [17]

The floods were succeeded by drought.[18] Prices of provisions rose in almost every parish of the island.

14. On occasion this earned him a rebuke. C.O. 137/367, the secretary of state to Eyre in the case of George W. Gordon, a J.P. whom Eyre dismissed: "I take this opportunity of observing to you that I feel sure you will find it most conducive to the public interests you have at heart, to occupy yourself rather with the substance of acts & proceedings with which you have to deal than with the private characters of the persons who may assail or defend them."

15. This was perhaps the most balanced of the local papers of the day. It was owned and produced by Edward Jordon and Robert Osborn, and the quoted editorial was probably written by the former. It is enclosed in C.O. 137/378, Eyre to Newcastle, No. 14, 18 Jan. 1864.

16. C.O. 137/383, Eyre to Cardwell, No. 167, 6 June 1864.

17. C.O. 137/384, Eyre to Cardwell, No. 256, 10 Sept. 1864.

18. And in certain areas by a disease which attacked root crops, though this does not appear to have been widespread (C.O. 137/391, reports of the Baptists, 1865).

In January 1865 E. B. Underhill, honorary secretary of the Baptist Missionary Society who had a few years previously visited Jamaica, wrote to Mr. Cardwell, the secretary of state for the colonies. He referred to letters he had received from Jamaica and set about to describe conditions in the Island. The drought, he said, had aggravated previous distresses. The people were starving because they were too heavily taxed and because there was not sufficient employment for them. He accused the Legislature of unjust taxation of the coloured population, of refusing just tribunals, and of denying political rights. He recommended a searching enquiry into the Island's political and economic affairs, formation of marketing associations, and institution of other encouragements to small-settler cultivators of all minor crops, but not of sugar, which could best be done by the estates.[19]

The secretary of state forwarded Underhill's letter to Governor Eyre and asked for his comments. Eyre in turn asked the custodes, the Anglican clergy, the Baptists, and other missionary bodies to give him their views on "the various allegations" made by Underhill. The reports of these people have been extensively quoted in previous pages. It would be impossible to present a summary of every argument advanced and every point made, but one clear fact is this: in view of the evidence contained in many of the reports it was without the shadow of doubt the duty of Governor Eyre to have invited a thorough official enquiry into Island affairs. Underhill's letter had been vague and in some respects ill-informed, but there was no reason why a Baptist minister in England should have been accurate in a survey of current economic conditions in a colony several thousand miles away.

Where Eyre failed, the Colonial Office failed also, for the reports were duly forwarded to the secretary of state for the colonies. But there—under the persuasion of the governor's covering dispatches—drought, prices, taxation, and all else were forgotten while the theme of the lazy negro was drummed home. The propaganda had its effect. A Colonial Office minute

19. *A Letter Addressed to the Rt. Honourable Cardwell, with Illustrative Documents on the Condition of Jamaica and an Explanatory Statement,* London, 1865.

of June 1865 remarked: "I am not sure that this distress is a bad thing. The idleness of the peasantry needs an exemplary punishment. It may do something to open their eyes." [20]

News of the Underhill letter and the allegations it contained leaked out—not surprisingly, since Eyre had communicated it to so many people without any request for secrecy. Throughout the Island mass meetings were held at which the governor and Legislature were asked to take some action to alleviate the distress. Some of these meetings appear to have been sponsored by people who were attempting to make political capital out of the situation, but the fact remains that conditions were favourable to their attempts. One of the petitions came from certain poor people of St. Ann, and "The Queen's Advice" sent in reply to it, deserves quotation in full as a supreme example of administrative failure:

> I request that you will inform the Petitioners that their Petition has been laid before the Queen, and that I have received Her Majesty's command to inform them that the prosperity of the Labouring Classes, as well as of all other Classes, depends, in Jamaica, and in other Countries, upon their working for Wages, not uncertainly or capriciously, but steadily and continuously, at the times when their labour is wanted, and for so long as it is wanted; and that if they would use this industry, and thereby render the Plantations productive, they would enable the Planters to pay them higher Wages for the same hours of work than are received by the best Field Laborers in this Country; and as the cost of the necessaries of life is much less in Jamaica than it is here, they would be enabled, by adding prudence to industry, to lay by an amble provision for seasons of drought and dearth; and they may be assured that it is from their own industry and prudence, in availing themselves of the means of prospering that are before them, and not from any such schemes as have been suggested to them, that they must

20. C.O. 137/391, Sir Frederic Rogers, minute on Eyre to Cardwell, No. 135, 23 May 1865.

look for an improvement in their condition; and that Her Majesty will regard with interest and satisfaction their advancement through their own merits and efforts.[21]

This supercilious message contains little for us to dwell upon. The contradiction implied in the comment that the people should give labour "steadily and continuously, at the times when their labour is wanted, and for so long as it is wanted" hints at the seasonal nature of the estates' demand for labour but pays no attention to its importance. The completely baseless assumption that labour would make the estates more productive and thus enable planters to pay higher wages than were given to English field workers simply drew rings around the high labour cost of sugar production and the influence of prices in Britain on wage rates in Jamaica. The planter's aim was to reduce the cost of labour. This could be done by lowering wage rates still further or by reducing the number of workers employed by the introduction of implements and machinery. In the latter case, any slight wage increase which might be awarded to those remaining in employment would be offset by an increase of the number of unemployed workers, who would be unlikely to find new jobs in a period of economic depression.

The secretary of state [22] either failed or refused to acknowledge the complicated nature of the labour market in Jamaica, and of course the comparison with agricultural wage rates and the cost of necessities in Britain was invalid.

On Saturday, 7 October 1865, a Court of Petty Sessions was in progress at Morant Bay in St. Thomas in the East. There was a case of assault in which the accused was ordered to pay a fine, with costs. A spectator in the court thereupon loudly informed the defendant that he should pay only the fine. The justice ordered the arrest of the man who had interrupted, but he was rescued by a large number of people who attacked and beat the police. According to the governor's

21. Cardwell to Eyre, Jamaica, No. 222, 14 June 1865.
22. "The Queen's Advice" was actually drafted by Henry Taylor, but it was approved by Secretary Cardwell.

subsequent dispatch telling of the outbreak, "No further injury appears to have been done at this time, and the magistrates seem to have thought so little of the occurrence that no steps were taken to communicate with the executive." [23]

On the following Monday, 9 October, the justices were again assembled to hear a case of trespass which involved a long-standing dispute over the ownership of land on Middleton Estate near Morant Bay. The accused was found guilty and ordered to pay a fine, with costs. Again there was an interruption from the crowd in court, telling the man to appeal against the judgment. The appeal was entered.

On the next day warrants were issued for the arrest of a man named Paul Bogle and several others who, with him, had been responsible for the interruptions in the courthouse and for the attack on the police the previous Saturday. Six policemen and two rural constables were sent out to Stony Gut, a settlement bordering Middleton, where Bogle lived. On arrival there, they were surrounded and beaten by a large number of people, and made to take oaths swearing to "join their colour" and "cleave to the black." Bogle and his associates also informed the policemen that on the following day they intended to go to Morant Bay, where a vestry meeting was scheduled to take place, "to kill all the white men and all the black men that would not join them." That evening, Tuesday, 10 October, the custos, Baron von Ketelhodt, who did not live in the parish, arrived at Morant Bay and was told of the previous events. He immediately sent a letter to the governor telling what had happened and asking for troops to be sent.

Eyre received the letter at eight o'clock on Wednesday morning and at once gave orders for 100 troops to be sent to Morant Bay. There was some delay in the embarkation,

---

23. This dispatch and other official documents and records on which the following account is based are to be found in *Facts & Documents Relating to the Alleged Rebellion in Jamaica*, published by the Jamaica Committee in London (1866), and W. F. Finlayson, *A History of the Jamaica Case*, London, 1868. Of these, the former criticized and the latter defended the actions of Governor Eyre.

however, and the warship that eventually took them did not leave Port Royal until the following morning, Thursday, 12 October. The governor, having seen the troops on board on the previous afternoon, went off to Flamstead in the Port Royal Mountains, where he was accustomed to spend the latter part of each week.

At Morant Bay, in the meantime, the vestry had met as planned, and while they were in session, Paul Bogle and a large gathering of armed people approached the courthouse square where the custos had assembled the local militia of about twenty men. The mob was met by the custos, who told them not to enter the square. They did so, and the militia withdrew to the steps of the courthouse. The custos then began to read the riot act and at the same time people in the crowd began to throw stones. The custos ordered the militia to open fire, and some of the people fell to the ground. The mob then rushed the militia who took refuge in the courthouse, and a siege began. Finally, the courthouse was set on fire, and as the inmates ran out, several of them were killed by the attacking people. Among the dead were Baron von Ketelhodt, the Reverend Herschell (curate of Bath, a nearby town), and C. A. Price, a black man who was a local builder. The rioters, in command of the town, set out on the following day, Thursday the 12th, to attack and plunder Bath and sugar estates down the line of the Plantain Garden River. That day the first troops dispatched by Eyre reached Morant Bay.

On Thursday the 12th also news reached the governor at Flamstead of the happenings in Morant Bay on the day before. He returned to Kingston, dispatched another 100 troops by sea, ordered a detachment of white troops to march eastwards along the Blue Mountain range to approach the rioters from the interior, and proclaimed a state of martial law to exist over the whole county of Surrey, except Kingston. On Friday Eyre himself set out by sea with 50 more troops, arriving at Morant Bay at seven o'clock in the evening.

There is no need to enter any further into the detail of military operations. The balance sheet of destruction and retaliation by itself tells a tale. On 11 October the rioters had killed 18 and wounded 31 people. Subsequently, they were responsible for the killing of 4 and the wounding of 3 others. They plundered 20 houses and shops and burnt down five buildings, including the Morant Bay Courthouse. The number of people killed and wounded by the militia on 11 October is not known, but the authorities were later responsible for the execution of 354 people by sentence of courts-martial, the shooting or hanging of 85 others without trial of any kind, the flogging of 600 men and women, and the destruction of nearly 1,000 huts, cottages, houses, and other buildings. Writing to the secretary of state for the colonies on 2 November, Eyre commented: "The retribution has been so prompt and so terrible that it is never likely to be forgotten."

There had been other disturbances in the Island since the emancipation, but in no case had the events been as disastrous, and in no case had the governor in power qualified himself to make such a claim.

In 1851 there had been brief local riots in Spanish Town, between rival Baptist factions; and in St. David, where an attempt was made by a candidate for election to the Assembly to win the contest by force of arms if necessary.[24]

In 1859 two far more serious outbreaks had occurred. The first was the "Toll-gate riots" in Westmoreland in February, when armed mobs demolished the toll-gates in the Parish. In the open countryside the tolls were easily outflanked, but evasion was more difficult on the outskirts of towns, and the approaches to Savanna-la-Mar were heavily taxed. When some of the offenders were arrested and brought to trial, their fellow rioters attacked the police station and according to local officials "were hardly restrained from committing bloodshed." In the following week troops arrived by sea from Port Royal and peace was restored. There were no deaths recorded.[25]

24. C.O. 137/309, Sir Charles Grey to Earl Grey, No. 17, 27 Feb. 1851.
25. C.O. 137/344, Darling to Bulwer Lytton, No. 48, 25 March 1859, with enclosures.

In the following August disputes arose over rights to land on Florence Hall Estate near the town of Falmouth in Trelawny. A man named Theodore Brine and about sixty others were arrested. When the trials began, a mob stormed the courthouse, attacked the magistrates and police, and rescued the prisoners. During the next few days there was general rioting. Buildings were set alight and the town's water supply was cut off. Finally, there was an armed attack on the police station. The riot act was read; the police, greatly outnumbered, opened fire, killing two women and injuring a number of people. The town was soon in the hands of the rioters.

Six days after the first outbreak, troops of the West India Regiment arrived.[26] The rioters were arrested and order was restored. It was emphasized that the military were there to support and not to supersede the civil authority. A special tribunal of non-local magistrates was established,[27] and the arrested people were afforded fair trials. Brine and his associates were all dismissed, and of the Falmouth rioters some were acquitted and the remainder sentenced to imprisonment for periods up to two years.[28]

The circumstances of the Falmouth Riot of 1859 and the Morant Bay Riot of 1865 were not dissimilar, except in the reactions of the governors and the means employed to subdue the rioters.

Apart from a brief disturbance in Kingston during March 1863, when fighting broke out between men of the West India Regiment on the one side and the Kingston police and populace on the other (following an insult offered by a soldier to a woman in the market),[29] there were no other actual uprisings in the Island until October 1865.

26. Men of the same regiment had been used to quell the Westmoreland riots. They were black troops, recruited in Sierra Leone and the West Indies.

27. J. F. Cargill, F. Roper, Richard Hill, Henry Laidlaw, W. H. Cooke.

28. C.O. 137/348, Darling to Newcastle, No. 29, 28 Jan. 1860.

29. C.O. 137/371, 372, Eyre to Newcastle, No. 63, 19 March 1863, and No. 133, 14 May 1863.

These short accounts serve to emphasize the two important aspects of rioting in Jamaica during the twenty-five years under consideration. First, the rioters were not concerned with any new social, political, or economic philosophies. Their objectives were clear-cut, concrete, and limited. In Westmoreland they objected to toll-gates, so they removed them. In Falmouth and in Morant Bay they disputed rights to specific areas of land. Secondly, in all three cases, the riots spread when mobs attacked the police and the magistracy either to force the release of arrested persons or to prevent arrests.

The disaster at Morant Bay was no inevitable outcome of any long previous chain of events. The actual riot was symptomatic of social and economic ills, but the plain fact of local riot is not of itself catastrophic. Catastrophe was created in the manner of dealing with the riot and in the subsequent constitutional change.

It is just possible that a single timely action by the Legislature in acknowledgement of existing distress might have reduced the number of those who followed Paul Bogle.

In the other direction, it is also just possible that if Governor Darling had stamped out the Falmouth riot with equivalent bluster and bloodshed the Jamaica Assembly would have abolished itself in 1859.

Unfortunately, the Morant Bay riot (which arose out of similar circumstances) occurred in a year of unhappier economic and political conditions, when an incompetent governor was in power and when the Colonial Office seemed determined to support the governor even when his action was highly questionable. These were all more or less temporary conditions, but unfortunately they were coincidental, and thus the Morant Bay riot became catastrophic. Upon these unhappy coincidences was based the drastic measure of self-abolition urged upon the Assembly by a governor who had notably failed to work in co-operation with it.

We must not be misled by the emotional shouts of Paul Bogle's followers at Stony Gut. The Morant Bay disturbance was not a colour conflict. That is made clear by the fact that black and coloured people were among those killed, wounded, or assaulted by the rioters; and by the fact that there were black and coloured men in the Volunteers, and in other groups (such as the Maroons) [30] who were employed by the authorities. It is significant, for example, that of sixty-seven Special Constables sworn in in Westmoreland at the end of October 1865, when nerves were frayed by rumour, twenty-two were white German settlers from Seaford Town, eighteen were coloured men, and twenty-seven were black men. The common minimal qualification was that they each possessed property to the value of at least £30.[31] Nor can it be simply described, on the basis of known facts, in terms of a popular reaction against oppression by a white planter oligarchy. The Assembly elected in 1863 to serve for the following seven years consisted of ten coloured members, of whom one was an estate owner, and thirty-seven whites, of whom twenty were owners of estates.[32]

Nor was it a "Jamaica Rebellion," for it was confined almost entirely to a single parish. It may be argued that the confinement was due to prompt action by the authorities, but Eyre himself spoke of general uprising and Island-wide plots

30. This is the only reference to the maroons in this book. They are the descendants of runaway Spanish and British-owned slaves who maintained a long and successful guerilla war against the British in the late seventeenth and eighteenth centuries. In 1738 a peace treaty was signed which gave the maroons territorial rights in certain areas of the Island and upheld the authority of their own administration within those areas. Since then, except for a recurrence of warfare at the end of the eighteenth century, the maroons have lived peaceably as small cultivators. By the Treaty of 1738, however, they undertook to give all aid in their power when called upon by the Island Government. The most detailed study of the Maroons is R. C. Dallas, *History of the Maroons*, 2 vols. London 1803.

31. C.O. 137/394, W. H. Cooke, J.P., to Custos Vickers, 30 Oct., and Vickers to Edward Jordon, governor's secretary, of same date. Most of the 22 Germans, survivals or descendants of the white immigration policy, were small settlers. The coloured men were: 6 carpenters, 4 labourers, 4 settlers, 3 domestics, and 1 blacksmith. The black men were: 17 labourers, 5 settlers, 1 penkeeper, 1 estate headman, 1 carpenter, 1 mason and 1 saddler.

32. G. E. Price, *Jamaica and The Colonial Office: Who Caused the Crisis?* (London, 1866), pp. 118–19.

only after, and not before the beginning of the Morant Bay Riot. Much was said after 11 October 1865 of plans by Paul Bogle and George William Gordon, an ex-justice of the peace who had been dismissed by Eyre in 1862, to promote a general revolt against the Government. But before that day Gordon was only one of many talkative demagogues and the official records do not contain a single mention of Bogle. Even when the governor was informed of the second disturbance on 9 October, there was not, apparently, much general alarm. It would surely have been thought ridiculous to send eight policemen to nip the bud of revolution.

St. Thomas in the East was administered by a custos and vestry who were widely disliked. Most of them had been directly implicated in the dismissal of George William Gordon from the Commission of the Peace, and Gordon was popular with the labourers and small settlers—perhaps more popular than he really deserved to be. Apart from the personal animosities, it would also appear that the St. Thomas vestry was one of the most corrupt and inefficient of the time.[33] Finally, add

33. There is evidence of this in the account by T. Harvey and W. Brewin. Other evidence can be seen in C.O. 137/392, Eyre to Cardwell, No. 220, 4 Sept. 1865 (with enclosures), in which the removal of Stipendiary Jackson from the St. Thomas in the East magistracy is explained; and in Price, *Jamaica and the Colonial Office*. This book is violently anti-Eyre, but the writer had a long experience of Jamaica. He was part owner of Worthy Park Estate in St. John, had lived in the Island since the 1840's and had been custos of St. Catherine and for a time a member of the executive committee. There may be reason, at times, to doubt his opinions and conclusions, but in the light of other information there is no reason to doubt statements such as the following taken from p. 130 of his book: The Church of England Chapel at Bath needed repair, and Custos Ketelhodt, as chairman of the parish building committee, allowed the curate, Mr. Herschell, to become the contractor for extensive repairs. The curate, knowing nothing about building, employed Mr. C. A. Price, a builder, to do the work. Price made a hash of it, and finally, at the request of Ketelhodt, Herschell, and Price, the Island Government provided extra money for additional work. In the Assembly George W. Gordon had put up some opposition to the grant. See also W. F. Livingstone, *Black Jamaica* (London 1899) p. 68, in which the Morant Bay "disturbance" is classed as a "parochial riot" originating in "local circumstances of a special kind."

to all this the presence in the parish of Bogle who, although he certainly does not merit recognition as a leader or lieutenant of organized rebellion, showed himself to be a dangerous man who could command a large body of followers, especially in a time of general hardship in a parish in which the local officials were unpopular.

Abolition of the Assembly was an end which Eyre had long hoped to achieve, and in it he had the approval of the Colonial Office. In March 1864 he had written his opinion that the present "miscalled Representative Institutions" did not reflect public opinion. Somewhat illogically, he recommended not an extension of the franchise or a lowering of the qualifications for candidature for election to the Assembly but the constitution of a single-chamber Government composed of representative and nominated members.[34] In October 1865 he declared that he would like a completely nominated single chamber, but thought that it would be easier to get the Assembly to agree to one with half the members elected and half nominated. He proposed to press the Assembly to take the necessary action.[35]

On December 1 the secretary of state for the colonies wrote Eyre to say that the British Government would willingly consider any plans of the Jamaica Legislature to change the constitution, but that full information about recent events would be required, including notice of what specific measures of general benefit might be expected of a newly constituted government, what expenses these measures would involve, and how these expenses would be met.[36] But by the time the dispatch reached Eyre, he had already sent off to England an act which abolished the Assembly and substituted a single-chamber Government of twenty-four members, half to be elected and half nominated.[37] The governor had moved quickly, and for good reason, as one of his supporters admitted:

34. C.O. 137/380, Eyre to Newcastle, separate, 28 March 1864.
35. C.O. 137/393, Eyre to Cardwell, confidential, 24 Oct. 1865.
36. C.O. 137/394, Cardwell to Eyre, confidential, 1 Dec. 1865 (draft).
37. C.O. 137/396, Eyre to Cardwell, No. 313, 7 Dec. 1865.

> The doing away with the House of Assembly—that "caricature of representative government"—has been an unmitigated blessing, and great praise is due to Mr. Eyre for the promptitude which he displayed in inducing the House of Assembly to act at the moment when men's minds were panic-stricken, and when they were willing to make any sacrifice so that they might escape from the dangers which seemed to be imminent. One week later, and the measure of self-sacrifice, if carried at all, could only have been carried with extreme difficulty.[38]

The abolition of the Assembly did not come out of any lasting conviction on the part of its members of their incompetence to legislate for the community. It was achieved by the subtle persuasiveness and the astute political timing of the governor. Full understanding of his success in these matters cannot be gained by any further discussion of the events of 1865. It must come from a general assessment of the Jamaica scene during the entire period under review, for though the Morant Bay riot was not inevitable, it was, obviously, not unrelated to previous conditions and events.

During the twentieth century increasingly unhappy connotations have become attached to the word "colonialism." Usually, colonial problems have their roots in the relationships which exist between an indigenous subject population and a ruling and administrative group of foreigners. In Jamaica, as in most of the British West Indies, the conditions have been rather different. There has not been an indigenous subject population under British rule. The root difficulty in Jamaica has been one of adjustment between a number of imported races and cultures. For nearly all of the first two centuries of British occupation the practice of slavery apparently simplified but in fact greatly complicated the social structure. There was a sharp line of demarcation between the free people and the slaves, but on each side of this line there developed complex social structures [39] in which race, colour, wealth, position,

38. J. W. Mitchell, "Contrasts in Jamaica," in *The Sugar Cane* (periodical), *1* (London, 1869), 87.

39. M. G. Smith, "Some Aspects of Social Structure in the British Caribbean about 1820," *Social and Economic Studies, 1,* No. 4, 1953.

education, and religion all influenced the standing of the individual in his group hierarchy, whether free or slave.

During slavery, moreover, the free people, with certain exceptions, were subject to the laws of the country and were equally liable to penalties for infringements; [40] but the slaves were subject to the laws and rulings of their masters. For the former, proven civil or criminal misdemeanours merited certain punishments, harshly fixed perhaps but nonetheless roughly based on some accepted code or precedent. For the latter, any action which displeased the master, or even a suspicion of such action, might be met with almost any penalty, depending on the personal character, attitude, and momentary passion of the master involved. Thus there were completely differing concepts of what constituted a misdemeanour and what might be expected in punishment for it.

Nor, of course, was there any common history, tradition, language, or national objective which might have penetrated the barrier between the free and the slave. The former were Europeans by birth, loyalty, or social and intellectual orientation. They were primarily concerned to produce sugar at a profit so that they might have money enough to afford the importation of refinements to a basically crude colonial agricultural society. The slaves were Africans severed from Africa, or Creoles confused by the white-washed mosaic of Africanisms which provided the life-force of estate society. Free immigrants travel with ideas, beliefs, and institutions in their baggage. Slaves were allowed no baggage. In Jamaica their dearest and almost unattainable objectives were leisure—since hard work brought no positive rewards—and freedom. In short, their objectives were, in the eyes of their masters, the ruin of the sugar industry.

All these forces of incohesion would unquestionably con-

40. The exceptions here referred to are not the individuals who, in almost all communities, are able to use their influence to escape penalties. The reference is to the free coloured people, who until the early 1830's were not allowed equal civil rights and liberties with the whites. See my article "The Social and Economic Background to Sugar in Slave Days," *Caribbean Historical Review*, 3–4, 1954.

tinue to affect life and labour in Jamaica after 1 August 1838, when the population of the island was by law transformed into a whole single society of free people equal before authority. But these forces in turn would be affected by other determinants of the conditions of life and labour, such as the prices obtainable for sugar, the desire of the ex-slaves to establish freeholds, and the possibility that the economy of the island might be diversified by the introduction of industries other than those concerned with the production of staple agricultural crops. Finally, the direction and leadership which might help people to make the most of good times and the best of bad times would depend upon the wisdom of governors and legislatures, and the understanding of the Colonial Office.

The Colonial Office have always been aware, or at any rate have always had the information in their files, that Jamaica is mountainous; but in the nineteenth century they never understood the full implications of the fact. To them, Jamaica remained a plantation colony, albeit a temporarily depressed one. The sugar industry and the estates were of chief importance, and the settlement of ex-slaves on mountain freeholds was regrettable insofar as it detracted from the supply of labour for lowland sugar cultivation. The nineteenth century was, in Britain, the century of land enclosures. Official policy favoured the large agricultural establishment, and special Parliamentary enactments facilitated the aggrandizement of private property. It would not have been easy for administrators in Britain to understand, and sympathize with, a fragmentation of estates in Jamaica and the rise of a class of small settlers, particularly when the produce of their land was not entirely measurable in terms of export quantities.

There were other smaller but important points on which comprehension floundered. It was too easily assumed that because Jamaica is small in area, labourers could always move freely and easily in search of employment. In mountain country, where roads are bad and seasonal rainfall heavy, transportation is always difficult and often impossible.

In consequence, when after 1846 the cry that "the people

will not labour on the estates" was by a growing number of spokesmen abbreviated to "the people will not labour," the British official view of mountain settlement was easily clouded over by visions of rum-filled negroes vegetating under shade trees and withdrawing from civilization into the primitive savagery of forest darknesses.

> I conceive that, by the acquisition of its Colonial dominions, the Nation has acquired a responsibility of the highest kind, which it is not at liberty to throw off. The authority of the British Crown is at this moment the most powerful instrument, under Providence, of maintaining peace and order in many extensive regions of the earth, and thereby assists in diffusing amongst millions of the human race, the blessings of Christianity and civilization. . . . No one acquainted with the actual state of society in the West India islands, and the feelings prevalent among the different classes of their inhabitants, can doubt that, if they were left, unaided by us, to settle amongst themselves in whose hands power should be placed, a fearful war of colour would probably soon break out, by which the germs of improvement now existing there would soon be destroyed, and civilization would be thrown back for centuries.[41]

Earl Grey, secretary of state for the colonies, when he wrote those words, was displaying both the complacency which "later generations have found the most unattractive of Victorian characteristics," [42] and his indigestion of Jamaica facts.

He and his staff were, however, dependent on reports from Jamaica for the facts, and after the mid-century the official reports tended to be fewer, less informative of general conditions, and biased. There were two reasons for this: first,

41. Henry George, Earl Grey, "The Colonial Policy of Lord John Russell's Administration (1846–1852)." This extract has been taken from a longer passage quoted by George Bennett in *The Concept of Empire* (London, A. and C. Black, 1953), p. 186.

42. D. Thompson, *England in the Nineteenth Century* (Middlesex, 1950), ch. 5.

the decline of the stipendiary magistracy and their system of
quarterly reports reduced the volume of information submitted to the secretary of state. The magistrates had not all
been competent observers and few had practised verbal economy; but out of the welter of their descriptions, comments,
and opinions, it had been possible to pick out the threads of
the pattern. Secondly, before the mid-century there had been
little real antagonism between estate agriculture and small-
settlers' agriculture. During the first half of the 1840's sugar
prices had been declining from the immediate post-emancipation peak, but the rewards were still worth while and the
labour shortage seemed set for correction by immigration
schemes. But with the fall of prices below thirty shillings a
hundredweight and the collapse of immigration plans, the
competition for labour between estates and small settlements
was emphasized and the strictures against "the lazy negroes"
began.

Not all the voices supported this theme, however, and both
within and without the Legislature there was room for honest
attempts at compromise. It is historically unfruitful but
curiously interesting to wonder what a Metcalfe or an Elgin
would have made of the difficulties of the 1860's, and how
their covering dispatches to the secretary of state would have
presented the Jamaican situation. The skill of compromise
was perhaps the most needed qualification for post-emancipation governors of Jamaica. The diverse origins, practices, and
interests of Jamaicans demanded it; and it was required if
any correct exposition of Island affairs was to be received
with equanimity in Whitehall. Unfortunately, successive post-
emancipation governors seem to have brought less of this skill
to their labours, and in the 1860's Mr. Eyre, who excelled
in misrepresentation, commanded no such power at all.

In consequence, the first lessons in co-operation and inter-
dependence which Metcalfe and Elgin had begun to instill
were rapidly forgotten, and under the pressure of falling sugar
prices, stoppage of immigration, collapse of new capital enterprises, and competition for labour, any significant demolition

of the barriers between those who had always been free and those who had not became increasingly improbable.

In this respect, too, the topographical distinction between mountains and lowlands was important. The mountain settlements, distant from established centres, were beyond the ordinary reach of the established church, the bona fide missionary centres, the schools, the police, the daily news, and the "Europeanizing" influences of Jamaica town life. The separation, let it be clear, was of necessity and not of choice. The country settler's week-end treat is to go to the nearest town or market to do business and to gossip, and in this respect rural Jamaicans are no different from people in other countries. Nor have the epithets been heaped on them alone. Ignorant, superstitious, fatalistic, crude—these descriptions have been applied to peasants everywhere, not always without reason, more often without understanding.

But in the mid-nineteenth century four distinctive marks were upon the Jamaican peasant: he or his parents had been slaves, he or his forbears had come from Africa, his veneer of "European civilization" was either very thin or non-existent, and he displayed a calm indifference to the welfare of the sugar industry. It was on these grounds that the charges were driven home in Jamaica and in Britain.

With leadership of an able governor lacking, there was no chance that the pros and cons of projected legislative policies might be carefully assessed. Discussion became argument and argument reached deadlock. When the crises of the 1860's came, the Legislature was in no state to meet them, and faced with Mr. Eyre's and his supporters' terrible pictures of violent death at the hands of fiendish negroes, the Assembly surrendered. The surrender was born of political despair and personal panic. With such parentage and with the accomplished mid-wifery of Mr. Eyre, it was safely but regrettably delivered.

The Jamaica Assembly was no more. Yet, considering the times and conditions it had faced since the emancipation, it had merited no such fate. There had been corruption in the public business,[43] and bribery at elections was commonplace. But in Britain public officers and politicians were just beginning to conceive the maxim that the holders of public office should not only *be* incorruptible but also *appear* to be so; and it was not long before this period that Charles Dickens wrote his famous description of the "Elections at Eatanswill." [44]

The sugar planting interest in the Assembly was concerned with the protection and furtherance of its own interests. But in Britain slave owners had fought strongly to maintain slavery; landowners had vigorously opposed the abolition of the Corn Laws; industrialists had struggled long to achieve the acceptance of free-trade policy; and in the 1860's the sugar refiners were beginning their long campaign to limit free trade in sugar.

The people of Jamaica, it was said, were ignorant, unschooled, and unfit to vote in the elections. That argument is still offered by people everywhere who are in principle opposed to adult suffrage. Unfortunately, no one has been able to state exactly the criteria by which a person's ability to use his vote intelligently can be measured.

However discriminating an electorate and however enlightened a government, critics are always able, with facility, to compile a catalogue of the things which ought to have been done but were left undone, and the things which were done which ought not to have been done. This is because the policy of any successful government must be shaped largely by compromise: compromise between measures urged by the various spokesmen who address the government, compromise between what is believed to be right in principle and what is thought to be, at the time, most expedient.

In considering the actions of the local administration of a colonial or dependent territory, moreover, it must be taken

43. The outstanding example of this during 1840 to 1865 was the Jamaica Tramway Case of 1863, in which Mr. Leahy, the colonial engineer, was the prime figure.
44. *Pickwick Papers,* ch. 13. See also Thompson, *England in the Nineteenth Century,* pp. 121, 122.

into account that on any important subject there are at least two public opinions, two companies of spokesmen, and two governments to be addressed—the colonial and the metropolitan. The literature on both emancipation and the Morant Bay riot can be analysed in this light. Even on lesser issues which do not excite any wide interest among the metropolitan public—for example, the matter of the geological survey— well-defined, intelligent, and generally acceptable policy is only with considerable difficulty achieved because of differences between metropolitan and colonial official attitudes and motives.

In view of these and all the other conditioning factors, the record of the Jamaica Assembly between the emancipation and 1865 is not simply to be dismissed as unworthy. Indeed, if its record be compared with that of the metropolitan government in important matters of social welfare, it will be seen that conditions in England were not much, if at all, better than those in Jamaica.

In the colony, as in England, education was the acknowledged responsibility of the Church and the formulation of standards was prevented by dispute between the various religious denominations who were engaged in educational work. In Jamaica, the situation was further complicated by a rapid increase in the number of "local" missionaries of unquestionable faith and energy but scarcely possessed of other qualifications either for preaching or teaching. As settlement spread farther up into the mountains, the control of the central missionary bodies was lessened, and the way was opened for the emergence of "break-away" pastors and small independent religious groups such as that to which Paul Bogle belonged.

In the colony, as in England, the Poor Relief system was unsatisfactorily administered. The Jamaica Poor Law in the period after emancipation offered relief to the aged and infirm.[45] It had been designed, during slavery, to do no more and, indeed, little more was required of it until the widespread destitution of the middle 1860's appeared. The system of out-

45. Details of the Jamaica Poor Law are in C.O. 137/385, and in Price, *Jamaica and the Colonial Office*, p. 9 n.

door relief inaugurated by the Berkshire magistrates at Speenhamland in 1795, and Edwin Chadwick's reform of 1834, had no application to Jamaican slave society. Nor was reform of the Jamaica Poor Relief system seen to be necessary until economic conditions rapidly deteriorated in the 1860's. When current political thought in Britain favoured as little social and economic legislation as possible, so that the forces of competition and the open market might exert full play, colonial legislators were not stimulated to much vigorous action.

But in Britain, when official action seemed to lag behind public need, Englishmen, in voluntary associations, acted in their own behalf to initiate desired improvements; whereas, for Jamaicans, newly freed from bondage, the idea of voluntary association was, in the main, repugnant. Moreover, the objectives of such associations would have been less clear in the minds of people who were just beginning to face the basic problem of adjustment to life in a free society.

These points have not been raised in an attempt to absolve the Jamaica Assembly from blame for neglect and mismanagement. They have been stated simply to indicate the harshness of any opinion that the Assembly was unfit to legislate. The wiliest of monarchs could not have persuaded the British House of Commons to abolish itself after Peterloo, for the wiliest of monarchs could not have suggested to the members any acceptable alternative authority. In colonies there is always the ultimate power of the metropolitan government which can be called into play. Moreover, in colonies where party political systems have not developed, control by the metropolitan power is the most obvious alternative to rule by the existing local political group.

The consequences—political, economic, and social—of the institution of Crown Colony Government in 1866 did not positively justify its introduction. We cannot say what a continuation of the previous system would have brought, but the new system did not solve the problem of Town versus Country, or the question of responsible party government, or the question of the relationship between the executive and the legislative branches of the Legislature; it simply evaded them.

Nor did it provide any political tutelage for people who were then thought to be unfit to exercise the vote. The introduction of adult suffrage in Jamaica in 1944 followed not from any growth of political intelligence nor from improved social and economic conditions but rather from new theories of government which hold that poverty and illiteracy should not disqualify a man from having a voice in the selection of those who shall govern him.

Within the Island, with Crown Colony Government after 1865, the Church of England was disestablished, the number of parishes was reduced, and Government revenues and expenditures were affected by other financial and fiscal reforms. More money was spent on social services, but this was countered by a rapidly growing population. Fundamentally, the economic structure remained the same. Jamaicans still prosper or decline according to price fluctuations in overseas markets over which they have no command.

The social consequences of the constitutional change can be gathered from the reported words of a coloured man who had been a member of the Assembly. In 1869 he said to a member of the new Legislative Council: "You and I have been equals, but what will be the respective position of our children? Yours will hardly speak to mine." [46] Under Crown Colony Government high political and administrative positions were fewer and were generally reserved for whites and, even more exclusively, for Europeans. One of the paths which the non-whites had used to attain social acceptance among the whites was now practically closed to them. It is important to remember that by the 1860's black and coloured men had attained positions of prominence, not only as merchants and the owners of landed property, but also as members of Assembly, magistrates, barristers, schoolteachers, newspaper editors, clergymen, and as the occupants of important public offices. Not all these people had been slaves; many had been free coloured people in time of slavery, but they had provided the example which others followed.

Yet, amidst the ashes, certain foundations remained firm.

46. Mitchell, "Contrasts in Jamaica," p. 87, reports this comment.

There were fewer sugar estates, but they were better equipped, better cultivated, and, on the whole, better managed than they had been in slavery. There was a large class of small farmers, grown up for the most part since the emancipation and now an important social and economic group in the Island. The peasants and labourers, with many continuing disadvantages in insecure land tenures, soil deterioration on their holdings, less opportunity for estate employment, and a lack of the most necessary social services could, nevertheless, show their great contribution in the establishment of interior towns, villages, and market-places. Whatever had been lost, these things, and their freedom, remained basically secure.

Appendix 1. Population and Occupational Statistics, 1844–1861

	1844	1861
A. TOTAL POPULATION	377,433	441,264
B. COLOUR GROUPS [1]		
White	15,776	13,819
Negro	293,128	346,377
Coloured	68,529	81,068
C. AGE GROUPS		
Under 5 years	51,707	61,137
5 to under 10	47,221	54,571
10 to under 20	62,733	104,525
20 to under 40	121,309	124,444
40 to under 60	68,499	65,793
60 years and over	25,963	30,546
D. PLACE OF BIRTH [2]	1844	1861
Jamaica	332,922	423,071
Other British Territories	7,960	3,563
Foreign-born	36,551	14,630
E. OCCUPATIONS 1844 [3]	1844	1861
Agriculturalists (apparently estate attorneys)	61	

1. These are the figures given in the Censuses of 1844 and 1861. They may not, however, be accurate. Apart from other possible sources of error or uncertainty (for example the classification of Indians, or the near impossibility of distinction in many cases), there was the likelihood that many coloured people claimed to be white, and many negroes to be coloured.

2. In these figures Africans and Indians have been included among the "foreign-born" because although shipped by British agents from British-controlled ports they were not all recruited from British colonial or other British-administered areas.

3. These are the classifications and figures given in the 1844 Census. The only change has been to break up the original alphabetical presentation of the classifications and to put them into groups which give a clearer picture of the distribution between various types of occupation.

Planters (apparently including small farmers)	3,987
Agricultural labourers (apparently including peasants)	132,192
Labourers	50,653
Domestics	20,571
Journeymen tradesmen	10,097
Master tradesmen	7,399
Lodging-house keepers	157
Tavern-keepers	59
Retail traders	1,672
Storekeepers	544
Merchants	433
Bankers	13
Boatmen	564
Mariners	97
Fishers	1,484
Pilots	26
Clerks	1,555
Artists	108
Architects	29
Surveyors	86
Teachers	649
Ministers	267
Professional persons	453
Miners	41
Military (attached to, and pensioners)	136
Policemen	315
Other various occupations	948
No occupation	142,831

DIFFERENT CLASSIFICATIONS USED

F. OCCUPATIONS, 1861

In this respect the 1861 Census is almost entirely useless. A comparison with conditions in 1844 would have been invaluable to the account of the intervening seventeen years; but to attempt it would require so much guesswork as to invalidate the results. In the first place, different classifications were used. Secondly, the enumerators in 1861 were not properly instructed and each invented his own classifications (C.O. 137/364, Darling to Newcastle, No. 46, 28 Feb. 1862). The following extracts from the occupation returns will illustrate the point:

Gardeners	17	Proprietors	36
Gatemen	3	Proprietors and planters	2
Gentlemen	56	Proprietors and proprie-	
Gentlemen or proprietors	3	tresses	25
Gentlemen, gentlewomen, persons cultivating their own settlements, females calling themselves seam-stresses, and children incapable of labouring	15,764	Provost marshal	1
		Public officers	3
		Purveyors of military stores	2
		Rangers	21
		Rectors	1
Gentlewomen	353	Receiver general	1
Geological surveyors	2	Reporter for the press	1
Gingerbeer sellers	1	Retail traders	24

etc.   etc.

Appendix 2. Sugar Exports and Prices, 1831–1865

THERE is no single record of Jamaica sugar exports for this period which can be counted as reliable. Basically, the available figures are those in the Jamaica Blue Books (showing exports of Jamaica produce), those in various trade returns printed for Parliament (showing imports of sugar into the United Kingdom from Jamaica), and those which are abstracts from the Island Blue Books printed for Parliament. Clearly enough, the information given in groups one and three (of Jamaican produce exported) do not agree with those in group two (of imports from Jamaica into the U.K.). Small quantities of Jamaica sugar were exported, during our period, to places other than Britain—chiefly the United States, British North America, and other Caribbean territories. Small quantities of foreign-produced sugar reached the U.K. via Jamaica and were included in British customs records as Jamaica produce.

As far as records are concerned, the period 1831–65 can be split into three parts: 1831–40, during which the Jamaica Blue Books do not always give the amount of sugar (or any other produce) exported and the only useful source of information is the record of trade returns to Parliament; secondly, 1841–52, for which both Blue Book and trade-return accounts exist; and thirdly, 1853–65, when British records are made up of abstracts from the Blue Books and therefore are in general agreement with the Island records.

In the following table we are compelled by necessity to use the trade returns for 1831 to 1840—thus for this period the statistics are of sugar imported into the U.K. from Jamaica. For the second period, 1841–52, both the Blue Book (prefaced B.B.) and trade-return figures (prefaced T.R.) are quoted. It is impossible to explain the occasional great differences between them, or to claim that the Island records are more reliable than those of the British customs. In the last six of those

268

years there was no export duty on sugar leaving Jamaica, and there is no apparent reason for supposing that the accounts were accurately kept. Nonetheless, the Blue Book figures have been given preference in the text, simply because they were the Island's records and perhaps were of more immediate importance in shaping island policy and production plans than were the British trade returns.

After 1852 the difficulty was resolved by the ending of the preference given to British colonial sugars entering the United Kingdom. British customs duties no longer distinguished between "colonial" and "foreign," and British abstracts of Jamaica Blue Book figures were used to show imports of Jamaica sugar into Britain. At the same time it is possible that the Jamaica figures became more accurate, for in that year an export duty was levied on sugar sent out of the Island.

The change in the sugar duties also affected the records of sugar prices. The figures quoted are, until 1853, average prices in London of British West Indian muscovado (raw) sugar. After that year they are average prices in London of raw cane-sugar, not specifically British West Indian.

Exact sources of price and import figures are quoted at the end of the table.

Year	Quantity Exported (cwts.)	Average Price per cwt. in London (excluding duty)	Quantity Exported (cwts.)	Average Price per cwt. in London (excluding duty)	Year
			B. B. 723,470		
1831	1,429,093	23/8	T. R. 633,471	25/4	1849
			B. B. 592,487		
1832	1,431,689	27/8	T. R. 574,796	26/1	50
			B. B. 485,744		
1833	1,256,991	29/8	T. R. 627,768	25/6	51
			B. B. 537,072		
1834	1,256,253	29/5	T. R. 511,247	22/5	52
			B. B. 420,908		
1835	1,148,760	33/5	T. R. 441,197	24/6	53
1836	1,054,042	40/10	440,911	21/1	54
1837	904,299	34/7	514,651	26/4	1855
1838	1,053,181	33/8	457,958	29/5	56
1839	765,078	39/2	549,662	35/2	57
1840	517,217	49/1	626,580	27/4	58
	B. B. 636,197				
1841	T. R. 527,810	39/8	541,957	25/11	59
	B. B. 805,967				
1842	T. R. 779,149	36/11	599,739	26/10	1860
	B. B. 565,168				
1843	T. R. 659,575	33/9	654,848	23/5	61
	B. B. 527,354				
1844	T. R. 529,934	33/8	615,083	22/1	62
	B. B. 704,244				
1845	T. R. 742,855	32/11	560,482	21/6	63
	B. B. 571,746				
1846	T. R. 572,875	34/5	522,499	26/9	64
	B. B. 881,148				
1847	T. R. 751,408	28/3	483,681	22/1	65
	B. B. 570,635				
1848	T. R. 627,008	23/8	600,837	20/3	1866

Sources: Exports: *1831–39,* "Return to Two Orders of the Hon. The House of Commons, dated 25th Feb. 1850." *1840–52,* "Returns of Trade to the U.K. from British Possessions, 1831–1853. Ordered by the House of Commons. 1854." *1841–66,* Jamaica Blue Books. Prices: as above (excepting Blue Books). Also "Returns as to the Sugar Trade. Ordered by the House of Commons to be printed. 1887."

Appendix 3. Immigration Statistics, 1834–1865

WE ARE concerned here with imported, as distinct from voluntary unrecruited immigrants. Even so, there is no record of the number of various skilled workers who were occasionally brought into the Island on the bounty system by individual employers after January 1842. The total number of these, however, was relatively small, and the following figures give a satisfactory over-all picture.

A. Bountied Imports, 1834–42, Excluding People from Africa or Liberated from Slave Ships

From Gt. Britain	2,685
" Germany	1,038
" Bahamas	408
" United States	235
" Canada	135
TOTAL all sources	4,501

Source: C.O. 137/273, Elgin to Stanley, No. 108, 15 April 1843, with enclosures.

B. Number of Liberated Slaves and Other Africans

1834–39	1,388
1840–44	2,533
1845–49	3,936
1850–54	1,324
1855–59	362
1860–64	1,837
1865–	nil
TOTAL 1834–67	11,380

Source: G. W. Roberts, "Immigration of Africans into the British Caribbean," *Population Studies*, 7, No. 3, 1954.

C. Number of Indian Immigrants

1834–42	nil
1843–45	261
1846	1,851
1847	2,438
1848–59	nil
1860	598
1861	1,523
1862	1,982
1863	542
1864–65	nil
TOTAL 1834–65	9,195

Sources: 1843–1847, I. M. Cumpston, *Indians Overseas in British Territories, 1834–1854,* Oxford Univ. Press, 1953; 1860–63, F. H. Hitching, *The Colonial Land and Emigration Commission,* Univ. of Pennsylvania Press, 1931.

D. Other Immigrants (*These all entered in 1854*)

Chinese from Hong Kong	267 (excluding 43 who died at sea)
Chinese from Panama	197
Portuguese from Madeira	167
TOTAL all sources	631

Sources: C.O. 137/324, Barkly to Grey, Nos. 91 and 111, 10 Aug. and 8 Nov. 1854; Land and Emigration Commissioners, *15th General Report,* London, H.M.S.O., 1855.

E. Summary [1]

Period	Total No. Entered	Races
1834–49	16,908	Europeans, Africans, Indians
1850–59	2,317	Africans, Chinese, Portuguese
1860–65	6,482	Indians, Africans
TOTAL 1834–65	25,707	

1. Excluding bountied imports from Europe after 1842.

F. Numbers of Indians and Africans Returning Home
When Indentures Expired

	Total Entries	Departures
Africans	11,380 [1]	122 [2]
Indians	9,195	1,726

1. Not all Africans were indentured. Early imports until 1843 had been on a bounty system.
2. I am grateful to G. W. Roberts for a note enabling me to calculate this figure.

Sources: I. M. Cumpston and G. W. Roberts.

G. Foreign-born Residents in Jamaica, 1844 and 1861

	African [1]	East Indian	Chinese	British and Other British Colonial	European and European Colonial	American	Others	Total
1844	33,519	1	—	7,960	2,314	480	237	44,511
1861	10,514	2,262	239	3,563	1,047	335	233	18,193

1. The inclusion of Africans imported during slavery accounts for the large number in 1844.

Sources: Jamaica Censuses, 1844 and 1861. The figures are not entirely dependable because the Census returns were probably rather inaccurate.

H. Immigrant Labour in the Various Parishes, 1862–65

Parishes	1862	1863			1864			1865		
	Total	Africans	Indians	Total	Africans	Indians	Total	Africans	Indians	Total
Hanover	101	19	153	172	—	146	146	—	146	146
Westmoreland	1,011	304	1,021	1,325	296	921	1,217	273	633	906
St. Elizabeth	124	—	113	113	—	126	126	—	26	26
St. James	176	—	276	276	19	240	259	—	240	240
Trelawny	427	57	522	579	56	504	560	—	476	476
St. Ann	64	16	61	77	15	61	76	15	68	83
Manchester	156	5	159	164	5	123	128	5	123	128
Clarendon	470	13	488	501	13	377	390	—	334	334
Vere	320	38	291	329	35	292	327	25	298	323
St. Dorothy	120	74	56	130	76	92	168	30	84	114
St. John	75	12	65	77	11	60	71	—	59	59
St. Catherine	103	102	—	102	185	—	185	52	28	80
St. Thomas-Vale	165	—	221	221	—	214	214	—	220	220
St. Mary	376	43	295	338	32	253	285	32	216	248
Metcalfe	366	130	204	334	11	243	254	11	249	260
St. George	271	119	102	221	55	97	152	55	87	142
Portland	56	13	40	53	—	46	46	—	98	98
St. Thomas-East	376	434	—	434	411	—	411	232	—	232
St. David	28	96	—	96	86	—	86	68	—	68
Port Royal	32	65	—	65	66	—	66	32	—	32
St. Andrew	67	126	—	126	105	7	112	46	2	48
Kingston	—	—	—	—	—	—	—	—	—	—
TOTALS	4,884	1,656	4,067	5,723	1,477	3,802	5,279	876	3,387	4,263

Source: Jamaica Blue Books.

Appendix 4. Island Revenues, Expenditures, and Revenue Sources, 1840–1865

In his report on the Blue Book for 1864, Governor Eyre (C.O. 137/393, "separate" dispatch to Cardwell, 25 Sept. 1865) commented on the unreliability of the financial returns of the receiver general. His comments are worth quoting in full, for they may save future students much perplexity:

> The form in which these Returns have for years past appeared in the Blue Books does not afford a clear statement of the actual transactions of the year, or enable any one to classify all the receipts or payments under distinct headings.
>
> This arises from the peculiar manner in which the Treasury Books have been kept during the incumbency of the late Receiver General, and which succeeding Governors have found it impossible to alter during his lifetime.
>
> The Returns do not even show the whole Revenue and Expenditure, as much of that connected with the Roads, with the Parishes and with Immigration is omitted, and sums devoted to these objects do not appear.
>
> Loans, interest, redemption of loans, transfers of general revenue to particular accounts or from one account to another are all jumbled up together with ordinary receipts or payments and add to the confusion and many sums are thus put down under some general heading which comprehends items that ought to be separate and distinct.

Eyre went on to give examples, such as the omission of revenues from "additional import duties" (£10,905) because they had been specifically appropriated to road construction or maintenance. In the same way, about £7,370 of export duties were not shown, because they were appropriated to immigra-

275

tion. Other revenues and expenditures had also been entirely
omitted from the accounts, which were so incompetently presented that they "tend rather to mystify than elucidate the
transactions of the Treasury."

In 1864 the receiver general, Alexander Barclay, had resigned. He was then over 90 years old. The office was temporarily filled by Edward Jordon who immediately began to
introduce much-needed reforms (see C.O. 137/387, Eyre to
Cardwell, confidential, 7 Jan. 1865, in which he encloses a
letter from Mr. Westmorland, a member of the Executive
Committee, advocating Jordon's suitability for the office).
Eyre, too, had spent much time revising and commenting on
the returns for that year, and the change is obviously illustrated in the table which follows.

Jamaica Government

Year	Revenue	Expenditure	Surplus	Deficit
1840	160,836	224,647	—	63,811
1841	271,206	268,535	2,671	—
1842	321,946	303,196	18,750	—
1843	387,506	325,396	62,110	—
1844	290,251	294,060	—	3,809
1845	279,553	276,662	2,891	—
1846	260,545	277,215	—	16,670
1847	247,393	295,414	—	48,021
1848	189,997	233,192	—	43,195
1849	154,952	157,190	—	2,238
1850	173,076	225,983	—	52,907
1851	193,228	232,483	—	39,255
1852	212,491	202,543	9,948	—
1853	145,482	144,112	1,370	—
1854	115,805	211,440	—	95,634
1855	319,212	302,678	16,534	—
1856	221,768	213,613	8,155	—
1857	210,727	207,299	3,448	—
1858	216,483	191,321	25,162	—
1859	279,935	262,142	17,793	—
1860	262,339	255,239	7,100	—

Year	Revenue	Expenditure	Surplus	Deficit
1861	275,027	274,565	462	—
1862	291,088	292,402	—	1,314
1863	293,354	302,286	—	8,932
1864	454,902	401,546	53,356	—
1865	464,749	422,616	42,133	—

In view of Eyre's criticisms, which are well supported by the state of the accounts recorded in the Blue Books, there would be no point in attempting any detailed presentation of annual financial statements. The following summary of total annual revenues and expenditures is given because it illustrates, very clearly, the extent to which the financial situation was dependent on the welfare of the sugar industry. The years of deficit are all years of crisis in sugar production and marketing. It may be that Barclay, who was an estate owner and until the early 1860's custos of St. Thomas in the East, to some extent manipulated the correlation, but not enough is known about him to permit such an accusation here. The figures quoted have been taken from the Blue Books.

It was pointed out in Chapter 5 that the 1850's brought a change in fiscal and financial policies in the Island. Taxes on hereditaments were abandoned, and duties on imports were increased. In 1853 export duties on Island produce, which had not been levied since 1846, were reintroduced at higher rates.[1] In 1856 the Island Government assumed control over the finances of the parochial vestries. Parochial revenues were merged with Island revenues, and parochial estimates for

1. In 1847, after the Sugar Duties Act, there had been changes in fiscal policy. Import and tonnage duties had been reduced, and the governor, in a belated report on the Blue Book of 1847 (C.O. 137/302, Sir C. Grey to Earl Grey, No. 32, 10 March 1849) listed the following as the sources of revenue: land tax and quit rent; import duties (reduced); tonnage duties (2/6 per ton on all vessels with certain exemptions for British and other ships in certain circumstances. Also other levies of several pence per ton earmarked for various uses—fortifications, lighthouse, hospitals, etc.); rum duty (1/6 gallon on local sales); stamp duties; taxes on stock, trades, and carriages. There were no export-duty revenues.

Certain Parochial and Island Taxes in St. Mary in 1842

Source	PAROCHIAL		ISLAND	
	Rate	Revenue (£)	Rate	Revenue (£)
Hereditaments (payable on 6% of assessed value)	5/6 in £	17,074.16.8	6d. in £	1,522.5.2
Horses (1,274)	7/6 each	477.15.0	2/6 each	159.5.0
Breeding mares (1,681)	1/6 each	126.1.6	6d. each	42.0.6
Horned stock (11,896)	9d. each	446.2.0	3d. each	148.14.0
Asses (none)	?	—	2½d.?	—
Wheels (except on estate vehicles)	24s. each	19.4.0	12s. each	9.12.0
Trades tax		227.8.0	?	56.12.0
Transient traders	(none) ?	—	—	—
Rum licenses, 28	£12 each	336.0.0	—	—
Sugar and coffee licenses			—	—
Gun licenses, 19	4s. and 6s. each	1.4.0	—	—
Hawkers' licenses, 49	10s. each	9.10.0	—	—
Pounds for strays	£3 each	147.0.0	—	—
Land tax and quit rent	—	112.16.4	3d. & 1d. per acre	857.7.0

Source: C.O. 137/264, Fyfe's Report, Oct. 1842.

various expenditures were subject to approval by the governor in Executive Committee. In the following pages of this Appendix available information has been tabled to give a comparison between fiscal arrangements at the beginning and at the end of our period. With regard to the first table showing "Direct Parochial and Island Taxes in St. Mary in 1842" it must be remembered that whereas the Island levies were the same in all parishes, parochial rates varied from one parish to another. After 1856, however, all taxes were equally imposed throughout the Island.

Certain Island Taxes in 1863

Source	Rate	Source	Rate
Houses of ann. value		Horned stock, each	1/–
£12	1/6 in £		
Land tax, per acre		Breeding stock, each	6d.
or per foot	1d.		
"Ditto for livery"	10/–	Working cattle, each	6d.
Horses, each	11/–	Estates' horses or	
		mules, each	6d.
"Ditto for livery"	7/–	Sheep, each	2d.
Asses, each	3/6d.	Boats plying for	
		hire, each	20/–
Stallions and mares,		Carts	9/– per
each	7/–		wheel
Spring carriages	15/– per	Hackney carriages	20/– per
	wheel		wheel

Source: Jamaica Blue Books, 1861–63.

In addition to the above, there were, throughout the period, other revenues derived from tonnage duties on vessels, stamp duties, fees for various services rendered by public officials, postage stamps, market dues, poundages, and licenses for trade and other purposes. Details of these are not available for the early 1840's,[1] but in the Blue Book for 1861 the current rates are listed as follows:

1. But some of these would have varied according to different parochial assessments.

"Tonnage" and other Fees, etc. in 1861

1. Customs tonnage.   2/– per ton on all vessels, except droggers (vessels employed in transport of estate produce from local wharves to shipping points) and vessels from ports within the Tropic of Cancer. 2/– per ton *once a year* on those excepted above.

2. Transient poor or
   Hospital tax: 2*d*. per ton on all vessels trading between the Tropics. 4*d*. per ton on all vessels trading north of Cancer. 1/4 per ton *once a year* on sugar droggers and other coasting vessels.

3. Health officers fees: on every schooner or sloop, 6/–; on every brig or brigantine, 9/–; on every barque or ship, 12/–.

4. Rum duties: On all rum and other spirits distilled in the Island and sold for consumption, 2/6 per gallon.

5. Stamp duties: Various.

6. Fees: Various.

7. Postage stamps: According to distance.

8. Miscellaneous: Sale of spirits licenses, Market dues, and Poundages.

9. Licenses: Metal Dealers', £12 a year; Fire arms, 10/– a year; stills, making up to 2,500 gallons a year, £3, and for every additional 100 gallons, 2/– extra.

Finally, we can compare import and export duty schedules in the early 1840's and early 1860's. The following sources have been used: *1842*, import and export duties, C.O. 137/260, in which the Jamaica Import Duty Act of 1840 (December) is quoted, and C.O. 137/261, Metcalfe to Stanley, No. 72, 9 Feb. 1842, in which the governor states amendments to the 1841 schedules which were introduced in two new acts of the session 1841/2. The import duties for *1857* and *1863* are from "Statistical Tables Relating to the Colonial and Other Possessions of the United Kingdom," Pts. III and IV. The list for 1857 is not as full as those for other years and includes only so-called "principal articles." For all three years, 1842, 1857, and 1863 the lists given contain selected items. The export duties (on Jamaica produce) in *1861* are from the Blue Book of that year and, apparently, remained unchanged for the remaining years up to 1865.

Duties on Selected Imports 1842, 1857, 1863

Imports	Duty in 1842	Duty in 1857	Duty in 1863
Beef, salted	2/ per 200 lbs.	?	14/ per 200 lbs.
Butter	2/6 per firkin	9/– per cwt.	9/– per cwt.
Candles, tallow	1/– per 56 lbs.	2/6 per 56 lbs.	2/6 per 56 lbs.
Cheese	3/– per cwt.	?	10/– per cwt.
Cornmeal	6d. per barrel	1/– per barrel	1/– per barrel
Flour, wheaten [1]	1/– per barrel	6/– per barrel	8/– per barrel
Coal	6d. per ton	?	nil
Fish, dried	9d. per quintal	2/– per cwt.	3/6 per cwt.
Herrings	3d. per box	2/– per barrel	2/– per barrel
Mackerel, pickled	1/6 per barrel	4/– per cwt.	4/– per barrel
Hams and Bacon	3/– per cwt.	?	10/– per cwt.
Machinery	?	?	4% ad val.
Pork, salted [2]	2/– per barrel	10/– per barrel	14/– per barrel
Rice	1/– per cwt.	?	3/– per cwt.
Soap [3]	9d. per box	?	3/– per box
Staves (wood) [4]	6/– per 1,000	?	4/– per 1,000
Shingles (cedar) [5]	1/– per 1,000	?	3/– per 1,000
Lumber (white pine) [6]	4/– per 1,000 ft.	?	8/– p. 1,000 ft.
Goods, unenumerated [7]	3% to 5% ad val.	12.5% ad val.	12½% ad val.

1. The barrel of flour, and probably of cornmeal also, was 196 lbs. in weight.
2. The barrel of pork, salted, was 200 lbs.
3. The box of soap was 56 lbs.
4. In 1842, specified as "oak."
5. In 1842, cedar not specified.
6. In 1842, white pine not specified.
7. In 1857 and 1863 certain British manufactures were charged at 4% or 10% ad val., but the majority of items thus assessed (including textiles and clothing) were charged at 12½% ad val.

Duties on Exports Jamaica Produce, 1842 and 1861

Exports	Duty in 1842	Duty in 1861
Sugar	1*d*. per cwt.	3/– per hogshead [1]
Rum	¼*d*. per gallon	2/6 per puncheon [2]
Coffee	3*d*. per cwt.	4/– per tierce [3]
Ginger	3*d*. per cwt.	1/– per cwt.
Dyewoods [4]	3*d*. per ton	1/– per ton
Mahogany	—	5/– per 1,000 ft.
Arrowroot	—	1/– per cwt.
Pimento	—	6*d*. per 120 lbs.
Coconuts	—	1/– per 1,000
Beeswax	—	2/ per cwt.
Honey	—	1/– per cwt.

1. I.e. about 18 cwt., making about 2*d*. per cwt.

2. According to a Jamaica act of 1852 (C.O. 137/313, Sir C. Grey to Earl Grey, No. 41, 12 May 1852), 2 hogsheads of rum were, for purposes of duty, to be rated as equal to 1 puncheon. This is the only evidence found of the size of the puncheon during our period. Present-day measures (wine and spirit) give 2 hogsheads as equalling 1 pipe, or 126 gallons. If we apply this to the 1852 regulations, the duty on rum in 1861 was about ¼*d*. per gallon.

3. In 1852 3 tierces of sugar were given as equal to 2 hogsheads, or about 36 cwt. If the same applied to the coffee tierce in 1861, the duty would have been about 5½*d*. per cwt.

4. In 1842 hardwoods were 1/– a ton. This rate probably included mahogany. In 1861 all woods except mahogany were charged at 1/– a ton.

Appendix 5. Imports of Selected Items, 1841–1865

ANY ATTEMPT to produce figures of imports [1] in a manageable table would be made almost impossible by the form in which the data is presented in the Blue Books. These volumes, which until 1863 are in manuscript, list imports under three headings: goods delivered from the ship for the Island trade, goods delivered from the ship to the warehouses, and goods delivered from the warehouses for the Island trade. But the warehouses also supplied goods for the re-export trade. A series of calculations involving all the figures of imports and figures of withdrawals from the warehouses for both re-export and home consumption might therefore provide fairly useful (depending on the accuracy of the original data) figures of the quantities of various imports which were annually available for the Island internal trade.

The following table, which consists only of those quantities listed in the Blue Books as delivered from the ship for the Island trade (or for home consumption), is intended to serve a much more limited purpose, namely to give a rough indication of the volume of the trade in certain imports which were in general demand.

It will be noticed that there are differences between the figures given below for 1851 and those given by R. M. Martin and quoted in Table 1, above, p. 12. The reason is that Martin's figures are of total imports. They were used because they included data for the pre-1840 years and thus allowed some comparison between conditions before and after full emancipation. The Blue Books for years before 1840 often lack information.

1. That is, of imports entering the Island trade in each year. Figures of total imports, including quantities for re-export, are to be found (for 1850 and subsequently) in "Statistical Tables relating to the Colonial and other Possessions of the U.K."

Imports of Selected Items in Alternate Years, 1841–65

Years	Salted Beef (cwts.)	Salted Pork (cwts.)	Fish Dried (cwts.)	Flour Wheat (barrels)	Corn (bushels)	Cornmeal (barrels)	Rice (lbs.)	Soap (cwts.)
1841	1,689	29,064	?	?	94,497	27,826	4,337,888	154
1843	2,668	?	150,139	?	184,629	18,723	4,329,360	505
1845	3,694	14,157	120,186	32,004	170,863	13,668	3,178,624	1,602
1847	2,917	7,565	103,946	8,446	131,422	15,915	2,452,350	1,244
1849	1,401	13,227	95,449	35,973	82,574	19,672	1,148,448	3,178
1851	1,498	6,825	105,707	28,395	57,144	7,091	1,162,448	1,508
1853	4,965	26,788	100,183	79,719	79,622	18,851	2,042,544	756
1855	3,436	5,600	89,789	21,512	29,371	7,067	206,080	890
1857	3,541	7,838	90,043	45,348	24,448	17,388	9,468,704	20,153
1859	3,853	17,508	80,015	78,636	28,842	15,317	4,309,648	13,257
1861	3,797	20,008	98,766	92,253	25,989	9,365	4,339,440	18,474
1863	4,582	29,000	74,208	90,228	20,709	18,480	5,276,992	31,305
1865	3,544	14,807	61,878	90,546	27,776	18,202	3,560,032	?

Index